FARMERS' ALMANAC

Calculated for the United States
for the year of our Lord

🕰 2021 🕰

Being the first after bissextile, or leap year, and until the
FOURTH OF JULY
The 245ᵗʰ Year of the Independence of the
UNITED STATES

Containing early America at its best, delightfully threaded through with
a measure of good humor, amusing anecdotes, wise-old weather predictions,
helpful hints, and good reading for every member of the
family done on a high moral plane.

EDITED BY PETER GEIGER, PHILOM.
MANAGING EDITOR, SONDRA DUNCAN, PHILOM.

COPYRIGHT © 2020 BY ALMANAC PUBLISHING COMPANY

ISSN: 0737-6731

FARMERS' ALMANAC P.O. Box 1609, Lewiston, Maine 04241
FarmersAlmanac.com

FARMERS' ALMANAC STORE

A Few of our Favorite Things

Maine-Made Soaps

Mesh Shopping Bag

Bamboo Travel Mug

Bee Kind Hat

2021 *Farmers' Almanac*

Fly Fishing Hat

CONTENTS

FarmersAlmanac.com

ABOUT US
From The Editors 8

ASTRONOMY
What is a Supermoon? 108
Full Moon Names & Dates 109
Annual Meteor Showers 110
2021 Visible Planets Guide 111
2021 Eclipses 112
Mercury Retrograde 115
Astrology & Astronomy Explained....116
Explanation of Calendar Pages.......126
Monthly Calendar/Astronomical Pages
   Sept. 2020–Dec. 2021....... 130-160

BEST DAYS & PLANNING CALENDARS
Fall Foliage Dates 39
Best Days to Set Eggs 80
Animal Gestation Table..................... 80
Moon's Astrological Place 117
2021 Best Days Calendar..................118
2021 Best Days to Fish.......................122
Average Frost Dates...........................162
Gardening According to the Moon
   Quick View....................................... 166
2021 Gardening According to the
   Moon 12-Month Calendar........... 168

FOOD & RECIPES
Homemade Pet Treats 22
Winning Banana Recipes................. 40
New Recipe Contest Details............. 42
Yams or Sweet Potatoes?...................44
Baking Substitutes..............................179

HEALTHY LIVING
Build Your Immunity Naturally......... 28
Make Your Own Healing Herbal Bath 30

HOME & GARDEN
Helpful Hints & Hacks...............12, 14, 16
10 Easy Money-Saving Hacks 20
Seed Starting Dates............................ 24
Grow Your Own Sponges................... 26
Dishwasher Detergent Substitutes..... 38
Save Money Fill Your Pantry With
   These Items.................................... 38
Which Holiday Cactus Do You Have?..... 56
Mouse in Your Car?.............................. 72
Top 10 Deer-Resistant Plants........... 74
Animals With Accidental Green
   Thumbs.. 78
4 Infuriating & Frightening
   Invasive Species in the Country... 98
Average Frost Dates............................162

TRIVIA & MORE
Cardinal Legends & Lore...................36
5 Weather-Food Myths You Should
   & Shouldn't Believe..........................48

(continued)

Clearing the Air on Weather vs. Climate 50

What in the World is Workamping? 88

(YES, you could get rid of your CPAP!)

SLEEP APNEA • DIGESTIVE AILMENTS • SINUSITIS • INJURIES • RASHES & ECZEMA

You can address all of these ailments naturally – WITHOUT DRUGS!

Sleep Apnea Relief
Ensure deep, steady breathing throughout the night *WITHOUT CPAP*. A natural herbal solution.

Leg Relaxer
Relax cramped muscles and calm irritated nerves. Soothes restless legs so you can sleep peacefully.

Sinus Infection
Antimicrobial power in either a convenient nasal spray or neti-pot rinse. Don't bathe the germs, kill them.

Food Poisoning
Food Poisoning Relief (AKA "The Antidote") *effectively terminates food poisoning* and relieves the condition within an hour.

Respiratory Relief
A proven natural solution for relief from bronchitis and pneumonia and for acute or recurring respiratory distress.

Injury Repair
Bruise, Strain & Tear Repair heals damaged tendons and ligaments naturally. Don't mask the pain, heal the damage.

NATURE'S RITE™

Natural products that *work!*

For more products & more savings, visit MyNaturesRite.com or call 800-991-7088

Use Coupon Code FARM-20 for 20% OFF Entire Order!

SATISFACTION GUARANTEED
100% Money Back Guarantee

Dear Friends,
I developed these natural healthcare products to empower you in your quest for natural healing. They represent the best solutions that I have found through years of laboratory, clinical and experiential research and development.
Best of Health,

**Steven Frank, Founder,
Innovative Herbalist
Nature's Rite**

CONTENTS

  FarmersAlmanac.com

Fascinating Facts You May Not Know About the North & South Poles...54

If-Then Logic 58

Philosofacts....................................... 10, 65

Reinventing Christmas......................104

Native American Legends & Lore of Stars 106

Riddles & Brainteasers 184

WEATHER

20 Signs of a Tough Winter...............46

Clearing the Air on Weather vs. Climate... 50

How Does the *Farmers' Almanac* Make its Predictions?..................... 60

Winter & Summer Weather Outlook Map.. 61

2021 Weather Outlook.......................... 62

A Look Back at Winter 2019-2020 ...68

Atmospheric Pheomena That Affect Weather? 70

Can Birds Predict the Weather?..... 96

Hurricane Tips & Names 128

Weather Zone Map...........................129

Monthly Weather Forecasts Sept. 2020–Dec. 2021 131-161

Emergency Supplies Checklist........177

FEATURED ARTICLES

5 Easy Ways to Choose Eco-Friendly Alternatives 18

Clearing the Air on Weather Vs. Climate... 50

What in the World is *Workamping*? 88

Where are all the Birds?..................... 92

Could Chickens be the Answer?.....124

Finding the way Home: Animals' Amazing Sense of Direction 174

MORE ALMANAC

Must-Have Online Store Items............2

Go Digital! E-Almanacs 21, 66

Customize Your Own Almanacs 44, 86, 176

FarmersAlmanac.com......................... 73

Online Membership Offer................172

Got Leaves? Branches? Grass Clippings? Turn Them Into Your Best Garden Yet! 84

Where are all the Birds? 92

Life Made Easier

Dear Friends,

As we put the finishing touches on the 2021 *Farmers' Almanac* (spring 2020), the world is in a very different place. The COVID-19 pandemic has and will continue to have far-reaching effects on life, some of which may never go back to normal, others constituting a new normal. Yet, just as nature has taught us, we all possess a resilience and we will bounce back, adjust, and adapt.

Our job as editors of the *Farmers' Almanac* is and always has been to provide you with information to help you thrive, no matter the obstacle. Think about how many challenges our founding editors and readers endured without the modern conveniences and medical advancements we live with today. Times have certainly changed, but our connection to nature— no matter how far or close the land is to you— continues to grow stronger.

We've been heartened to see many of our readers try new ways of doing things as they adjust to their "new normal." Some are raising backyard chickens for eggs; others are growing their own food for the first time or reusing and repurposing common items; and then there are those who are simply connecting with nature more and more.

In this edition, you will find our famous—or sometimes infamous— long-range weather forecasts for helping you plan your year ahead, as well as our Fishing Calendars, Best Days task lists, and Moon and Star Gaz- ing charts. Growing your own food, whether on a balcony or backyard garden, is a great way to reconnect with nature. This year, on page 84, we included helpful information on how you can turn backyard brush, grass clippings, or other landscape debris into a raised garden bed (called Hugelkultur). We also featured tips on when it's best to start seeds, and our very popular Gardening by the Moon Calendars that suggest, where climate permits, the "best" time to do various gardening chores.

Animals, both wild and domesticated, also teach us how to persevere. Think about how amazing it is that a monarch butterfly can make a 3,000-mile trip from Canada to Mexico each year; or how earthworms journey through soil and help your garden grow more prolifically; or how the sight of cardinals and other birds can brighten your day. You'll find these amazing animal stories, as well as homemade recipes for pet treats, in this edition.

We hope that the tips and articles in this year's *Farmers' Almanac* help make your life a bit easier and happier. Be well, dear friends, and take time to observe the miracle of nature, no matter how busy life becomes.

Stay well!

Peter Geiger
Philom., Editor

Sandi Duncan
Philom., Managing Editor

Train at home to

Work at Home

Be a Medical Billing Specialist

WORK AT HOME!

✓ Be home for your family
✓ Be your own boss
✓ Choose your own hours

SAVE MONEY!

✓ No day care, commute, or office wardrobe/lunches
✓ Possible tax breaks
✓ Tuition discount for eligible military and their spouses
✓ Military education benefits & MyCAA approved

Earn up to $37,800 a year and more!*

Now you can train at home to work at home or in a doctor's office, hospital or clinic making great money...up to $37,800 a year and more as your experience and skills increase! It's no secret, healthcare providers need Medical Billing Specialists. In fact, the U.S. Department of Labor projects 10% growth, 2018 to 2028, for specialists doing medical billing.

10 Years	**10%**
5 Years	**Increase In Demand!****

Experts train you step by step...be ready to work in as little as four months!

With our Medical Billing program, you learn step by step with easy-to-understand instruction, plenty of examples, plus Toll-Free Hotline & E-mail Support. Graduate in as little as four months and be ready to step into this high-income career!

Get FREE Facts. Contact us today!

U.S. Career Institute®
2001 Lowe St., Dept. FAAB2A90
Fort Collins, CO 80525

1-800-388-8765
Dept. FAAB2A90
www.uscieducation.com/FAA90

SENT FREE!

YES! Rush me my free Medical Billing information package.

Name _____ Age ____

Address _____ Apt ____

City _____ State____ Zip_____

E-mail _____ Phone _____

CL396

Accredited • Affordable • Approved
Celebrating over 35 years of education excellence!

*With experience, https://www.bls.gov/oes/current/oes433021.htm, 6/4/19
** https://www.bls.gov/ooh/office-and-administrative-support/financial-clerks.htm#tab-6, 10/3/19

DEAC
DISTANCE EDUCATION ACCREDITING COMMISSION

BBB
ACCREDITED BUSINESS
A+ Rating

ONE *kind* WORD *can* **warm** **3** WINTER *months*

thought of the year

KINDNESS ❤ IS ❤ WISDOM

When you plant a GARDEN you plant HAPPINESS

A **real friend** never gets in your way, unless you happened to be on the way down.

You can't buy **HAPPINESS** but you can buy **ICE CREAM** and that's sort of the same thing.

DON'T JUDGE EVERYTHING BY APPEARANCE.

THE EARLY BIRD MAY HAVE BEEN UP ALL NIGHT.

NATURE IS A miracle We COUNT ON

A *good* supervisor is one who can step on your toes and not mess up your *shine*.

Going Bananas?

Too many bananas? Peel them and then freeze for use in smoothies. Just toss them in the blender. No need for ice cubes.

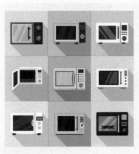

Keep it Moist

When reheating pizza or other baked goodies in a microwave, place a small cup of water in with the food. It will help keep the food moist.

Baguette Refresher

Sprinkle the crust with water, wrap it in aluminum foil, and bake in the toaster oven for 5 minutes. It comes out as fresh as the day it was baked.

Broke a Glass?

Grab a slice of bread. Works well to pick up glass shards that a broom or vacuum can't get.

Frozen Lemons

Slice a lemon and freeze the slices for use in your water. First, pat them with a paper towel and place in a single layer on a baking sheet lined with parchment paper. Once frozen, bag them up. A great tip for those who have lemon trees and don't want them to go to waste!

Header illustration by Martina Fugazzotto

Homemade
Tub/Shower Cleaner

Heat 1 cup of dish soap
(the blue Dawn soap works best) in the
microwave for approximately 1 minute.

• • • • • •

Mix in an equal part of white vinegar to the soap.

• • • • • •

Place mixture in spray bottle
and then spray your tub walls and tub.

• • • • • •

Leave for several hours.

• • • • • •

Then, depending on how severe your soap
scum is, either wipe with a towel or use a brush
(tougher soap scum will require the latter).

• • • • • •

Either way, the soap scum comes
off without much elbow grease.

Helpful Hints

Recipe Hanger

Pant hangers make
an effective recipe
holder. Hang from
a cabinet door and
use the clips to hold
the recipe or pages
open (works well on
smaller cookbooks).

Orange Fire Starters

Save and dry orange
peels. They work
well as fire starters.

Fruit & Vegetable
CLEANER

**Hydrogen peroxide is
a great way to remove
dirt, pesticide residue,
and harmful surface
bacteria from your
fruits and vegetables.**

Add 1/4 cup
of peroxide
to a sink or
washtub full
of cold water.

Add the
fruits and
vegetables, and
let them soak
for a minute.

Rinse
thoroughly
with water.

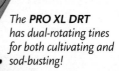

Helpful Hints

Snap a Card

Take a picture of a business card when someone gives you one. This way, you have it on your phone, even if you lose the actual card.

Travel Tip

Place a binder clip on the head of razors to protect them and you when traveling.

— Garden Secret —

Heading out to garden? Scrape your fingernails along a bar of soap to create a barrier that keeps dirt from getting deep under your nails. Once you're done working with the dirt, grab a nail brush and scrape out the barrier.

Shoelace SECRET

When shoelaces won't stay tied, wet the shoelace and then tie it. It will stay tied.

GET MORE HELPFUL HINTS

FarmersAlmanac.com

Sign up for our weekly newsletter and follow us on Pinterest!

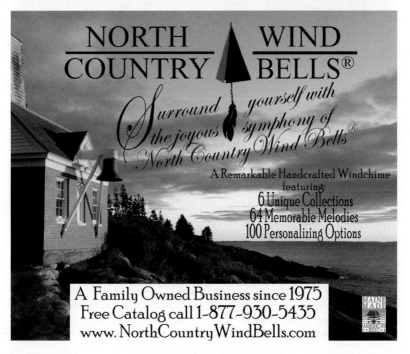

By Jim Kneiszel

5 Easy Ways to Choose Eco-Friendly Alternatives for Everyday Products

Do you think it's challenging, expensive, or time-consuming to do the right thing for the environment? Guess again! Here are five simple swaps you can make to show you care about sustainability without breaking the bank:

BEESWAX
Food Wrap

More than 300 million tons of plastic are consumed globally every year, including a trillion single-use plastic bags. And it takes 10-20 years for a plastic bag to decompose. One way to put a dent in those numbers is to switch from plastic wrap to sustainable beeswax wrap for your household needs. A now-popular eco-friendly product, wraps made of beeswax and cotton do a great job of protecting your leftovers. While more expensive than plastic wrap—a four-pack of beeswax wrap costs about $12 on Amazon.com—the wrappers can be washed in cold water and reused for about a year before requiring replacement. And if you don't want to buy the manufactured wraps, the internet is flooded with DIY plans for making your own using cloth and beeswax beads.

BAMBOO *Toilet Paper*

It's well known that bamboo is a common replacement for many wood products, from flooring to kitchen utensils. But folks concerned about the environment can bring the benefits of bamboo even closer to home. How about trying bamboo toilet paper? Traditional toilet paper from the major manufacturers uses mainly virgin timber—in fact, an estimated 15 million trees are cut down for bathroom tissue every year, though several companies have moved to some recycled paper products.

Unlike traditional timber, however, bamboo is the fastest-growing plant on the planet (it can produce an amazing 40 inches of new growth per day), and the plant regenerates without replanting. Internet-based tissue companies touting an environmental commitment are popularizing the use of bamboo and pushing profits from sales back into environmental awareness efforts. Bamboo toilet paper does require a commitment on the part of the buyer as it is still more expensive, about $30 for 24 rolls compared to the typical $20 or less for the same number of rolls of traditional toilet paper.

PLANT-BASED *Party & Picnic Supplies*

Disposable plates, containers, and utensils are so convenient for parties, picnics, and even everyday use. But the joy derived from the convenience of traditional Styrofoam, paper, and plastic products is usually accompanied by a little guilt over contributing to the growing problem of landfills teeming with waste that won't break down for years or decades. But there is a solution to this disposal dilemma: plant-based and compostable cutlery and containers.

Plates, bowls, and containers for leftovers are being made from sugarcane. Sellers of these new products, usually found online, say they are more functional than the petroleum-based versions we see everywhere.

The sugarcane products are grease- and cut-resistant, sturdy enough to contain soups and noodles, and 100% compostable at commercial composting facilities.

Compostable cutlery is made from potato and corn starches and vegetable oils, as indicated in the names of leading brands, including Spudware and Taterware. These compostable products are high-heat tolerant, can be reused many times, and ultimately recycled into soil.

Wheat & Corn-Based GOLF TEES

While the golf industry hasn't been able to produce a suitable ball made from recycled or green materials, the same is not true for the golf tee. It is estimated that US golfers go through 2 billion tees per year as they knock balls around the course. That's a lot of trees to cut down for wooden tees. Thankfully, eco-friendly golf supply companies are now making the tees out of wheat straw and corn, natural materials that break down quickly when scattered around the fairways.

SOY INSULATION *& Household Finishes*

Many products, including paints, strippers, spray foam insulation, and adhesive for plywood and particle board used in home construction and home improvement, were made from volatile products that threatened consumers' health or polluted the environment. That is quickly changing, however, and soybeans are one of the natural products that are making our homes safer and more sustainable. Two products in particular, stains and insulation, have been dramatically improved through the use of soy. Soy-based stains preserve and beautify wood decks, replacing oil-based products thought to have a negative environmental impact. And soy is now offered as an eco-friendly alternative ingredient in spray foam insulation products that lower heating costs and make homes more comfortable.

№ 1

Don't fret over a lost leather glove. Turn the remaining one into a small tool carrier. Cut off the fingers at mid-length. Make two vertical slits in the back and run a belt through them. Then, load up the fingers with lightweight tools.

№ 2

No napkin rings? Use metal cookie cutters as unique napkin holders for family dinners. If you want, spray paint them to match your décor or decorating theme.

№ 3

Remove mildew stains with a mixture of lemon juice and salt. Moisten stained spots with the mixture. Place the item in the sun for bleaching. Rinse and dry, then launder as usual.

№ 4

No drain cleaner? Pour 1 cup baking soda down the drain. Add 1 cup of white vinegar. Flush the drain with hot water when bubbling stops.

10 Easy Money-$aving Hacks

№ 5

Make colorful garden planters out of gently chipped mugs or cups.

№ 6

Don't spend money on paint remover, rug deodorizer, or stain remover. Take off old paint from metal screws and nails with nail polish remover. Sprinkle dried chamomile or lavender blossoms onto carpets before vacuuming for a fresh, clean scent. Use a damp rag dipped in baking soda to scrub unwelcome crayon marks.

№ 7

To prevent rust on steel wool scrubbing pads, place them in a plastic bag and store them in the freezer.

№ 8

Hang brooms and brushes to make them last longer. Once fibers and bristles are bent out of shape, these tools no longer function well.

№ 9

Remove burned food on pots and pans with a mixture of half water and half vinegar. Soak overnight. Burned food comes off easily with a light scouring.

№ 10

Out of dishwashing liquid? Use baking soda! Baking soda does a multitude of tasks, so of course it will clean dishes! Simply mix baking soda with a little bit of water in a bowl to form a paste. Dip your sponge in the paste and use it as "soap" to clean dishes, pots, and pans.

Dripping Springs Ollas
presents
Automatic Irrigation

Learn More

On-the-Go?

The *Farmers' Almanac* digital editions easily go with you!

 FarmersAlmanac.com/digital-editions

*Feel like baking?
Don't forget
your furry "kids"*

Homemade Pet Treats

Beef Barley Dog Biscuits

INGREDIENTS

1/2 cup extra-virgin olive oil
4 Tbsp parsley
2 cups beef broth
2 cups barley flour
3-4 cups rye flour

DIRECTIONS

Preheat oven to 350°F. In a large bowl, combine olive oil (extra-virgin olive oil is more expensive, but lower-grade olive oils are blended with other vegetable oils that may contain corn or soy) and parsley. Heat beef broth and add to the olive oil mixture. Stir in barley flour and let cool until lukewarm.

Gradually blend in rye flour, adding enough to form stiff dough. Transfer to a floured (rye flour) surface and knead until smooth (about 3-5 minutes). Shape dough into a ball and roll to 1/4" thick. Use a cookie cutter of your choice or cut into small squares. Transfer to ungreased baking sheets, spacing them about 1/4" apart. Gather up scraps, roll out again, and cut additional biscuits.

Bake for 30 minutes. Remove from oven and turn over. Bake for an additional 30 minutes, or until golden brown on both sides. After you finish baking all batches, turn off the oven, spread the biscuits in one baking pan and set them in the oven to cool for a few hours or overnight. The extra time in the oven as it cools off helps make the treats crunchier.

Easy Peanut Butter Dog Biscuits

INGREDIENTS

3/4 cup white whole-wheat flour
1/4 cup all-purpose flour
1/4 cup quick oats
1/4 cup cornmeal
1/2 cup water, more if needed
1/4 cup canola oil
1 egg
2 Tbsp natural peanut butter
3-4 cups rye flour

DIRECTIONS

Preheat oven to 350°F. Combine water, oil, eggs, and peanut butter. Mix these ingredients until well combined. In another bowl, combine the dry ingredients. Add the dry ingredients into the wet ingredients and mix until well combined.

Roll out dough on a lightly floured surface until the dough is about 1/8" thick. Cut into smaller pieces by either using cookie cutters or just cutting into squares. Place cut slices onto a baking sheet lined with parchment paper.

Bake for 10 minutes, remove from oven, turn treats over, and return to oven to bake for another 10 minutes. Turn the oven off, and leave treats in the oven for another 20 minutes. Remove from oven and allow to cool completely prior to serving to your dogs.

• Homemade Cat Treats •
Easy as 1, 2, 3 Tuna Treats

INGREDIENTS

1 cup whole-wheat flour
1 6-ounce can tuna in oil (do not drain)
1 Tbsp oil
1 egg
3-4 cups rye flour

DIRECTIONS

Preheat oven to 350°F. Mix all ingredients in a mixing bowl, adding a little water if dough is too stiff. On a lightly floured surface, roll the dough to 1/4" thickness.

Use your favorite cookie cutter to cut into shapes or simply cut small squares out (keeping in mind the size of your shapes).

Place on ungreased baking sheet and bake for 20 minutes or until firm.

Store in an airtight container.

Visit us at FarmersAlmanac.com for more articles & tips for happy pets

Gum in your pet's hair?
Saturate the gum with olive oil. Rub with your fingers to soften and comb it out. To remove olive oil, shampoo the dog as you normally would.

To remove cat and dog hair from clothes and furniture, rub them with damp rubber gloves or try using a dryer sheet to remove the fur.

Fight pet odors naturally. Deodorize your pet's bedding between washings by sprinkling it generously with baking soda. Let it sit for 15 minutes, then vacuum it up. Pet odors are gone, without harsh chemicals!

DIY flea collar: Make your flea collar with essential oils. However, always do your homework before choosing an oil for your pet. Cedar oil and lavender oil are two pet-friendly options. To use: add 5 drops of oil to a tablespoon of water, then dab the solution on a collar or bandana that your pet can wear. ONLY for external use.

SEED-STARTING DATES

Some you'll want to start indoors; others can be directly sown outside.

Here are our recommendations:

Beans: outside 2 weeks after LF

Beets: outside 2-4 weeks before LF

Broccoli: inside 4-6 weeks before LF

Cabbage: inside 6-8 weeks before LF

Carrots: outside 2-4 weeks before LF

Celery: inside 10-12 weeks before LF

Corn: outside 2 weeks after LF

Cucumbers: outside 3 weeks after LF

Kale: inside 4-6 weeks before LF

Leeks: inside 10-12 weeks before LF

Lettuce: inside 4-6 weeks before LF

Onions: inside 10-12 weeks before LF

Peas: outside 4-6 weeks before LF

Peppers: inside 8-10 weeks before LF

Pumpkins: outside 2-4 weeks after LF

Radishes: outside 4-6 weeks before LF

Spinach: outside 4-6 weeks before LF

Squash: outside 3 weeks after LF

Tomatoes: inside 6-8 weeks before LF

(LF = last frost)

17 Fabulous Flowers for Fall

ANISE HYSSOP

AMARANTH

ASTERS

CELOSIA

CHRYSANTHEMUMS

COSMOS

DAHLIA

DIANTHUS

FLOWERING KALE

PANSY

RUDBECKIA

SALVIA

SEDUM

SUNFLOWERS

SWEET ALYSSUM

VERBENA

VIOLAS

Grow Your Own . . . SPONGE?!?! Here's How!

By Jean Grigsby

Growing luffa plants is an enjoyable and educational gardening and crafting project. What could be more, ahem, absorbing than to grow a vegetable and then transform it into a sponge?

Luffas are the source of loofah (or loofa) sponges used for bathing and cleaning. Loofahs are made by drying the fibrous interior of the fruit of the luffa plant.

It's a Gourd First

Luffas are part of the gourd family *Cucurbitaceae* that also includes gherkins, pumpkins, and watermelons (who knew that watermelons were gourds?). The most common species used for loofahs is *luffa aegyptiaca*, which is also known as dish cloth gourd, Egyptian luffa, smooth luffa, and vegetable sponge. This luffa has yellow flowers, vines that can grow up to 25 feet, and gourds that look like zucchini.

Luffa seeds are readily available from many suppliers. Select your seeds carefully to ensure you get the right seeds and proper instructions for your har-diness zone (luffas need 140+ days of warm, frost-free days in order ripen). In general, the seeds can be sown directly into the warm ground in zone 6 and higher. In zone 5 and lower, seeds must be started indoors to ensure sufficient growing time.

Luffas need plenty of sun, lots of water, and well-drained soil, so plant them accordingly. Use a fence or sturdy trellis to support the vines, so the gourds won't rot on the ground or grow crookedly–especially if you want long, straight loofahs.

Harvesting Your "Sponge"

The gourds are ready to be harvested once they're about two feet long. They'll turn yellow-brown, feel lightweight, and their skins will be brittle and pulling away from the fibrous interior.

The gourds are ready to be harvested once they're about two feet long. They'll turn yellow-brown, feel lightweight, and their skins will be brittle and pulling away from the fibrous interior.

After harvesting, scrape away the skin. Use the long threads that run the length of the gourd to help "unzip" the skin. What's left is your almost-loofah, which will have lots of seeds and extra plant material that you can get rid of by rinsing in a bucket and changing out the water several times. Resist the temptation to use a sink, because you may clog your drain. You may need to beat your almost-loofah against the side of the bucket to remove any especially stubborn seeds. The kids can soak up the fun by doing the dunking and beating! Just be sure to save the seeds for next year's crop.

As a final step, hang your almost-loofahs on a line to dry in the sun, which will help to bleach them. This is a great opportunity for kids to witness the magic of nature as your almost-loofahs dry and transform into genuine loofahs.

Keep the loofahs whole or slice them lengthwise for use as dish scrubbers. If you're a soap maker, try slicing the loofahs widthwise (like slice and bake cookies) and fill them with soap to make pretty, sudsy exfoliators. Experience even more enjoyment by letting your kids get creative with their ideas for using loofahs. You won't be able to scrub the smiles off their faces.

Boost your Immunity Naturally

— Elderberry Syrup —
A MAGIC IMMUNITY ELIXIR?

For centuries, traditional European folk medicine has touted the benefits of elderberry extract and elderberry syrup for immune support, and now modern science is finally catching up.

Studies have found that a commercial preparation of elderberry extract called Sambucol is more effective than other over-the-counter remedies at shortening the duration and severity of the flu.

This comes as no surprise to the many people who swear by elderberry syrup, which is said to boost the immune system, prevent the flu or colds, alleviate excessive mucus and soothe sore throats.

• •

DIY ELDERBERRY SYRUP

ingredients:

1 cup black elderberries + 3 cups water + 1 cup raw honey

directions:

Place berries and water in a saucepan. Bring to a boil, reduce heat, and simmer for 30 minutes. Crush the berries and strain the skins. Allow to cool before stirring in honey.

For best results, take one tablespoon daily when you're well. You can take it on its own, or add it to fruit smoothies, yogurt, ice cream, or maple syrup. If you do come down with a cold or the flu, take a teaspoon every few hours until you recover.

Elderberry syrup is as good for kids as it is for adults, but it's important to remember never to give products containing raw honey to children under the age of 2.

Think Zinc

Zinc is an essential mineral that promotes healthy immune function and healing. Zinc lozenges are effective in relieving common cold symptoms and reducing its duration. Take a dose once or twice daily at first sign of a cold, for up to two weeks, or per the advice of your holistic physician. Zinc's antioxidant properties are similar to that of vitamin C. You can also consume natural food sources of zinc such as egg yolks, seafood, sardines, pecans, pumpkin seeds, and sunflower seeds. Herb sources of zinc include alfalfa, chickweed, dandelion, chamomile, cayenne, parsley, and rose hips.

ADD GARLIC

Garlic fights infection, boosts immune response, and wards off the common cold and flu. Add fresh garlic to your dishes or take garlic supplements for its health-enhancing benefits.

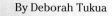

By Deborah Tukua

Make Your Own Healing Herbal Bath

Soaking in a fragrant herbal bath is relaxing, refreshing, and restorative. The therapeutic properties of the essentials oils in herbs are released when infused in hot water. *The Holistic Herbal* author David Hoffman states, "The best and most pleasant way of absorbing herbal compounds through the skin is by bathing in a full-body bath with a pint of infusion added to the water. Any herb that can be taken internally can also be used in a bath."

Roman, Greek, Ottoman (Turkish), Japanese, British, and other major empires throughout recorded history indulged in lavish bathing rituals. And every culture has used local healing plants as medicine. As we begin to understand how important it is to use more natural, healthy ingredients, many have set out to create custom therapeutic baths at home, where they control the exact ingredients going into their bathing solution.

Many of the herbs in this article offer medicinal, antibacterial, antispasmodic, antiseptic, and anti-inflammatory properties. These properties nourish, soothe, and heal the skin, relieve tired or aching muscles, calm and clear the mind, and invigorate the body.

Here's a list of herbs that work well in baths and their therapeutic benefits:

BASIL: Eases stress, relieves muscle spasms, and improves skin hydration

CALENDULA: Promotes healing of skin abrasions, eczema, sunburn, diaper rash

CHAMOMILE: Relieves stress and anxiety, eases muscle soreness, soothes skin

COMFREY: Heals skin abrasions, rashes, sunburn, insect bites and stings

ELDERFLOWER: Firms and smooths skin, promotes blood circulation

EUCALYPTUS: Clears nasal passages, relieves joint pain and sore muscles

HOPS: Relaxing, eases tension and anxiety

HYSSOP: Relaxing, eases post-sport/ exercise stiffness

LAVENDER: Relaxing, stress-reducing, uplifting, eases headaches

LEMON BALM: Refreshing, heals minor wounds & skin disorders, soothes tired muscles

PEPPERMINT: Refreshing, relaxes muscles and cramps, pain reducer, relieves itching, cold and flu treatment

ROSEMARY: Stimulating, eases muscle pain and tension, mild astringent

SAGE: Stimulating, cleansing astringent, antiseptic

THYME: Cleansing, heals skin abrasions

YARROW: Fever reducer, cold & flu treatment, heals skin abrasions and reduces swelling, relieves cramps

(continued)

How to Use Herbs in the Bath

Select a single herb or a combination of therapeutic herbs for your bath to yield the benefits you desire. Using three or more herbs together gives a more interesting and pleasant fragrance. You can add rose petals to your choice of herbs to further improve the scent.

To avoid clogging the drain, and making a mess in the tub, never add loose herbs directly to the bath water. Place desired herbs in a bath bag or make an herbal infusion.

The bath water should be hot enough to release the herbal essences but not hot enough to burn your skin.

If desired, place a small pillow behind your head. Lie back and relax in the tub for 15 to 20 minutes.

Herbal Bath Infusion

To make a concentrated bath infusion, put 2 ounces of dried or 4 ounces of fresh herbs into a quart-sized jar. Pour 1 pint of boiling water into the glass jar. Affix the lid and set aside. Leave the concoction undisturbed for a minimum of 30 minutes while it infuses.

While filling your tub with very warm water, strain the infusion through a sieve. Pour the infusion into the tub, sit back, relax, and enjoy! (Discard herbs after using.)

SEW YOUR OWN BATH BAG

Reusable bath bags or sachets can be purchased at local shops and online. You can also place the herb mixture into an old, clean stocking or cotton cloth. To make your own bath bags, take two pieces of muslin or cotton fabric scraps, approximately 4" x 3", and stitch together on 3 sides. Add 2 tablespoons dried herbs to the bag and tie the loose end securely with ribbon or twine. Hang the filled bag of herbs under hot running water while drawing your bath. After taking a bath, discard used herbs. Rinse out the bag and allow it to dry completely before refilling.

Make Your Own Therapeutic Bath Blends

While we don't offer specific amounts of herbs to use when crafting your bath mix (most use equal parts of each), in general use a total of 3-4 ounces of herb mixture per tub.

Relaxing Bedtime Bath

Fill a bath bag or make an infusion with equal parts of these soothing herbs: lavender, hops, chamomile, and lemon balm.

Place the herbal bag under running water while filling your bathtub. Or add an infusion to your bath water.

Lie back and unwind.

Aching Joints & Sore Muscles

Fill a bath bag or make an infusion with equal parts of rosemary, peppermint, and lavender or chamomile.

Place the herbal bag under running water while filling the bathtub. Or add an infusion to your bath water.

Soak in the tub for at least 15 minutes.

Cold & Flu Bath Treatment*

Fill a bath bag or make an infusion with a combination of peppermint, elderflowers, and yarrow or hyssop.

Place the herbal bag under running water while filling your bathtub. Or add an infusion to your bath water.

Soak in the tub for at least 15 minutes for relief.

*Lavender, rosemary, and eucalyptus can be substituted for the herbs in this cold and flu treatment.

Foot Baths

Warm herbal foot baths are relaxing and soothing to tired, aching feet. So, kick off your shoes, sit back, and enjoy!

Foot Bath Herbal Benefits:

ARNICA: Heals sprains and bruises (use to treat unbroken skin only)

LAVENDER: Refreshing tonic, relieves aches

LOVAGE: Natural deodorant

MARJORAM: Heals wounds, soothes, relieves pain

PEPPERMINT: Refreshing tonic, combine with lovage

SAGE: Soothes, cleanses, and heals

THYME: Cleanses and heals

Add 1 ounce of dried herbs or 2 ounces of fresh herbs to a glass jar. Pour 12 ounces of boiling water in the jar and affix lid. Steep undisturbed for 30 minutes. Strain mixture. Stir in 1 tablespoon of sea salt for its healing and soothing properties.

To use, set a large bowl on the floor in front of a comfortable chair. Pour the infusion into the bowl and fill with hot water. Test temperature of water with fingers before using. Relax in the chair while soaking your feet for 10 to 15 minutes. Feel the stress and tension leave your body through your feet.

CARDINAL
Legends & Lore

Cardinals are beautiful birds, beloved by birders and non-birders alike. However, they are more than just familiar and easily identified guests at feeders and baths. Northern cardinals are associated with a great deal of folklore, legends, and spiritual beliefs in many different cultures.

It was spriritual beliefs, in fact, that gave northern cardinals their name. When European settlers arrived in North America, they noticed these birds' bright red hue and how closely it resembled the red vestments of Roman Catholic bishops—cardinals. The similarities continue as the bird's jaunty crest is similar in shape to the church officials' headgear, especially the tall, pointed mitre.

Coloration is not all that makes cardinals a key figure in different spiritual beliefs. It is common folklore that a visit from a cardinal represents a loved one visiting from heaven. While this belief cannot be traced to a single origin, birds have often symbolized heavenly visitors, messengers to the gods, or even the gods themselves in feathered form. This belief has been part of ancient Egyptian, Celtic, Maori, Irish, and Hindu spiritualism, as well as the lore and legends of many Native American tribes, including the Ojibwe, Lakota, Odawa, Sioux, Algonquin, and Menomini.

ROMANCE

The Choctaw tribe specifically references the "redbird" as a matchmaker between a maiden and a brave, responsible for bringing them together. This is why cardinals are often associated with romance, and it is believed that if you are single and see a cardinal, romance is in your near future. At the same time, if you are in a relationship and a cardinal crosses your path, it is said to be a reminder to honor your partner and remember the romance that brought you together.

A Message from Your Loved Ones?

Cardinals are beautiful birds, beloved by birders and non-birders alike. However, they are more than just familiar and easily identified guests at feeders and baths. Northern cardinals are associated with a great deal of folklore, legends, and spiritual beliefs in many different cultures.

By Melissa Mayntz

How to Attract Cardinals

It's easy to bring northern cardinals right to your yard when you meet their needs for food, water, and shelter!

CARDINALS' FAVORITE FOODS
- Sunflower seed
- Safflower seed
- Peanut hearts
- Berries
- Suet crumbles

Use broad, open feeders where these songbirds will feel most comfortable!

This connection between cardinals and romance is not unfounded. These birds are largely monogamous, and a male cardinal will bring food to his mate while she sits on the nest, offering it to her in a gentle, kiss-like gesture. Cardinals also remain together as dedicated pairs throughout the year, unlike many songbirds that split up after the mating season.

Cardinals are associated with more than just couples, however. After cardinal eggs hatch, both parent birds tend to the chicks, and even after the chicks have matured, they stay in family groups. Cardinal groups are sociable, though, and unrelated birds may join the group or move between groups, just as our own families grow and change and our own circles of friends adjust throughout the years.

This sociability also connects to the heavenly visits symbolized by the appearance of a cardinal. Because of these birds' bright plumage, they more easily catch our eyes, particularly on drab winter days when other colorful birds are absent. This is exactly when we are feeling more sociable, what, with holiday parties and all. It's also a time when we're more likely to be missing loved ones, but a cardinal can be a cheerful reminder of those who can't be with us during these special times.

Cardinals are cherished, not just for their bright colors and social personalities, but for the meaning they hold in our lives. From heavenly visitors to spiritual guides to cheery guests on winter days, cardinals are sure to always make us smile.

Melissa Mayntz is a freelance writer, avid birder and author of **Migration: Exploring the Remarkable Journeys of Birds** *(Quadrille Publishing, 2020). Find her at BeYourOwnBirder.com.*

WATER FOR CARDINALS
- Broad, open basins
- 1-2 inches deep
- Ground-level or pedestal baths
- Heated baths for winter water

Clean bird baths weekly to minimize diseases and keep water fresh!

CARDINAL SHELTERS
- Dense vines and shrubs
- Layered thicket-like areas
- Evergreen pine and spruce trees
- Tall brush pile

Minimize pruning so cardinals always have someplace safe to hide!

Dishwasher Detergent Substitutes

Run out? When you're in a pinch, these substitutes clean your dishes, but may not provide the ultimate level of clean you expect from your dishwasher on a daily basis.

Baking Soda

Baking soda (sodium bicarbonate) is a good cleaner and helps control odors. Fill the detergent cup with baking soda and run the cleaning cycle as usual.

Baking Soda + Dish Soap*

Add 1-2 drops of liquid dish soap to the detergent cup filling the remainder with baking soda. Run on normal cycle.

Borax

This natural mineral element, which is also known as sodium borate, is an ingredient in many commercial dishwasher detergents. Fill the detergent cup with the borax powder and wash accordingly.

BONUS! DIY Dishwasher Cleaner

Use unsweetened lemonade mix to clean your dishwasher. Fill the detergent cup with the mix and run the washer empty. The citric acid helps remove stains.

....

Never use dish soap by itself as it may cause an explosion of bubbles.

SAVE MONEY!

Keep Your Pantry Stocked With These Important Ingredients

Soup stocks and broth: Chicken, beef, and vegetable.

Vinegar: Red wine, rice wine, apple cider, balsamic.

Oils: Avoid over-processed canola and vegetable oils and invest in cold-pressed olive oil, virgin coconut oil, or avocado oil. They may cost a little more, but a little goes a long way.

Olives: They perk up any salad or pasta dish with loads of flavor while adding healthy fats.

Nuts: Raw, roasted, toasted or baked, to add crunch to salads, and make pestos.

Honey and molasses

Pantry-ready essential vegetables: Potatoes, onions and garlic—use a wooden crate or box to store them off the floor.

Peanut butter: Great ingredient and protein source not only for sandwiches, but many other recipes.

Pastas: They keep for a long time and can be made into a variety of hot and cold dishes.

Coffee and tea

Peak Foliage Dates for the contiguous U.S.

Location	Dates	Location	Dates
Alabama (Northern)	Oct 19–Nov 4	Missouri (Northern)	Oct 5–21
Arizona	Oct 5–21	Missouri (Southern)	Oct 12–28
Arkansas	Oct 19–Nov 4	Montana (Central)	Sep 28–Oct 9
Arkansas (Ozarks)	Oct 12–28	Montana (Western)	Oct 5–21
California (Northern)	Oct 15–31	Nebraska	Oct 5–21
Colorado	Oct 5–14	Nevada	Oct 12–28
Connecticut	Oct 12–28	New Hampshire (Inland)	Sep 28–Oct 9
Delaware	Oct 19–Nov 4	New Hampshire (Coastal)	Oct 5–21
Florida	Nov 2–11	New Jersey (Inland)	Oct 12–28
Georgia (Northern)	Oct 19–Nov 4	New Jersey (Coastal)	Oct 19–Nov 4
Idaho	Oct 5–21	New Mexico	Sep 28–Oct 9
Illinois (Northern)	Oct 5–21	New York*	Sep 28–Oct 28
Illinois (Southern)	Oct 12–28	North Carolina (Inland)	Oct 12–28
Indiana (Northern)	Oct 5–21	North Carolina (Coastal)	Oct 19–Nov 4
Indiana (Southern)	Oct 12–28	North Dakota	Oct 5–21
Iowa	Oct 5–21	Ohio	Oct 5–21
Kansas (Northern)	Oct 5–21	Oklahoma	Oct 26–Nov 4
Kansas (Southern)	Oct 12–28	Oregon	Oct 12–28
Kentucky (Eastern)	Oct 5–21	Pennsylvania	Oct 5–21
Kentucky (Western)	Oct 12–28	Rhode Island	Oct 12–28
Louisiana	Nov 2–11	South Carolina	Oct 19–Nov 4
Maine (Inland)	Oct 1–17	South Dakota	Oct 5–21
Maine (Coastal)	Oct 5–21	Tennessee	Oct 12–28
Maryland (Inland)	Oct 12–28	Texas	Nov 2–11
Maryland (Coastal)	Oct 19–Nov 4	Utah	Oct 5–21
Massachusetts (Inland)	Oct 5–21	Vermont (Northern)	Sep 24–Oct 10
Massachusetts (Coastal)	Oct 12–28	Vermont (Southern)	Oct 5–14
Michigan (Northern)	Oct 1–17	Virginia (Inland)	Oct 12–28
Michigan (Southern)	Oct 5–21	Virginia (Coastal)	Oct 19–Nov 4
Minnesota (Northern)	Oct 1–17	Washington	Oct 12–28
Minnesota (Southern)	Oct 5–21	West Virginia	Oct 5–21
Mississippi (Northern)	Oct 19–Nov 4	Wisconsin	Oct 5–14
		Wyoming	Oct 5–14

*Depending on elevation and distance from the coast. All peak times are usually earlier at higher elevations.

Winning Banana Recipes

DIRECTIONS

Heat oven to 350°F. Coat bottom and insides of a 10" springform pan with cooking spray. In a large bowl, stir together vanilla wafer crumbs and butter until well combined; pat crumbs into bottom of pan to form a crust. Bake 8-10 minutes or until light golden brown and set.

In a large mixing bowl, use a mixer on medium speed to beat cream cheese until creamy, about 1-2 minutes. Beat in sweetened condensed milk, cream of coconut, and banana until well combined, about 1 minute. Beat in eggs until well incorporated, about 2 minutes. Pour batter onto crust; bake 50 minutes.

Remove pan from oven and sprinkle macadamia nuts and coconut on top; evenly drizzle with warm dulce de leche. Return pan to oven and bake an additional 10 minutes, or until cheesecake is well-risen and barely wobbles. Cool cheesecake on a wire rack for 1 hour, before lightly covering and chilling 4 hours or until ready to serve.

Makes 10 servings

1st Place—$250 WINNER

Banana-Macadamia Nut Tres Leches Cheesecake

Emily Hobbs—Springfield, MO

INGREDIENTS

1-1/2 cups ground vanilla wafer cookies
1/4 cup unsalted butter, melted
3 (8 oz.) packages cream cheese, softened
1 can sweetened condensed milk
3/4 cup cream of coconut
3/4 cup mashed ripe bananas
4 large eggs
1/3 cup finely chopped macadamia nuts, toasted
1/3 cup sweetened flaked coconut, toasted
3/4 cup dulce de leche, warmed

2nd Place—$150 WINNER
Banana Foster Dessert Burritos
Gilda Lester—Millsboro, DE

INGREDIENTS

4 bananas, peeled

3 tbsp fresh lemon juice

3/4 cup light brown sugar, packed

1/2 tsp cinnamon

3 tbsp butter, room temperature

3/4 cup dark semi-sweet chocolate chips, finely chopped

8-6" flour tortillas

1 cup (approx.) canola oil

Powdered sugar

Vanilla ice cream (optional)

Mint sprig for garnish

Kitchen twine

DIRECTIONS

Split each banana in half lengthwise; then cut each half in half (you will have 16 banana pieces). Sprinkle banana pieces with lemon juice.

In a medium bowl, mix brown sugar and cinnamon. Add butter and work with fingertips until mixture is crumbly. Mix in chopped chocolate. Spread 1 heaping tablespoon of brown sugar mixture in the center of each tortilla. Top with two banana pieces, and sprinkle remaining brown sugar mixture on top.

Fold one end of each tortilla over bananas; then tuck in sides and roll up to completely enclose bananas. Tie each around center with kitchen twine.

Heat oil in a 10" skillet to 350ºF. Add 4 burritos and fry 3-4 minutes per side or until crisp and golden. Remove, and place on a paper towel to absorb excess oil. Repeat with remaining burritos.

To serve: Remove twine. Cut each burrito diagonally. Place 2 burritos on a plate and sprinkle with powdered sugar. Repeat with remaining burritos. Serve with a scoop of vanilla ice cream. Garnish with mint.
Makes 4 servings

Turn to page 42 for this year's recipe contest ingredient!

3rd Place—$100 WINNER
Maaaa-Nana Mini Tarts
Satwinder Chahal
Surrey, British Columbia, CA

INGREDIENTS
2 ripe bananas

1.75 oz. (50 g) goat cheese

4 slices prosciutto

18 frozen mini tart shells

1/2 tsp allspice

DIRECTIONS

Preheat oven 375ºF. Allow mini tart shells to thaw out while oven heats up.

In a microwaveable bowl, place banana, goat cheese, and allspice. Microwave for 25 seconds. Mix all ingredients in bowl with fork until a smooth consistency. Place aside.

Line a baking sheet with parchment paper and place prosciutto directly on it. Place mini tart shells on a separate baking sheet. Bake prosciutto and mini tart shells for 10 minutes in the middle of oven.

Allow prosciutto to cool while you fill cooked tart shells to the top with banana goat cheese mixture.

Roughly chop the prosciutto into small bits. Liberally distribute over the top of the filled tarts.

Broil the assembled tarts on high for 1 minute. Turn off oven and leave tarts in oven for another minute. Cool and serve.
Makes 18 mini tarts

Eat More Sweet Potatoes!

–Here's Why–

In pies or cut into fries, candied, baked, boiled, or mashed, sweet potatoes are a treat for the taste buds. But did you know they're also one of the most nutritious foods you can eat?

In 1992, nutritionists at the Center for Science in the Public Interest compared dozens of common vegetables and ranked the sweet potato highest in nutritional value.

Points were awarded for dietary fiber content, complex carbohydrates, protein, and high concentrations of vitamins and minerals. Points were deducted for fat content—particularly dangerous saturated fat—sodium, cholesterol, refined sugars, and caffeine.

With a whopping 184-point score, the sweet potato outranked the second most nutritious vegetable—the common potato—by more than 100 points!

Vitamin Power

Sweet potatoes contain two times the recommended daily allowance of vitamin A, almost half of the daily recommendation for vitamin C, and four times the recommended daily allowance for beta-carotene. They are also rich in potassium and when eaten with the skin, provide more fiber than an entire bowl of oatmeal.

Energy Source

Sweet potatoes also offer natural sugars and complex carbohydrates, which means they provide high amounts of energy over an extended period of time.

Because sweet potato digests slowly, it causes your blood sugar to rise gradually, making you feel satisfied and energetic for longer.

That is in contrast to foods containing simple carbohydrates or refined sugar, which cause your blood sugar to quickly skyrocket and fall just as quickly, leaving you feeling tired and fatigued.

Sweet potatoes also offer the lowest glycemic index rating of any root vegetable, which means that, despite their sweet flavor, they are good for diabetics and others who need to limit their sugar intake.

YOU COULD WIN! *Looking for Sweet Potato Recipes*

This year our recipe contest is asking for recipes that include sweet potatoes in their ingredient list. Do you have a favorite that includes at least one sweet potato? Be sure to send it to us!

CASH PRIZES: The top 3 winning recipes will earn cash prizes—$250, $200, and $150. Plus, the lucky winners will get their recipes published in the 2022 *Farmers' Almanac* print and online editions. No professional cooks, please. Recipes must be submitted by 2/14/21. All recipes become property of Almanac Publishing Company.

TO SUBMIT: Enter online at FarmersAlmanac.com/recipe-contest or mail to:

Farmers' Almanac Recipe Contest, 70 Mt. Hope Ave., Lewiston, ME 04240 USA.

Check out page 40 for last year's winning banana recipes.

YAM or SWEET POTATO?

How Do You Know Which Is Which?

In spite of all of the confusion, it's quite easy to tell yams from sweet potatoes:

YAMS have dark, bark-like skins, with a white flesh. Some have purple or red flesh. Yams are drier and starchier than sweet potatoes, and are even made into flour.

SWEET POTATOES have gold or copper/bronze skins and moister orange flesh.

Yams are high in fiber, potassium, and vitamin C. Pound for pound, a sweet potato has fewer calories, fat, carbs, potassium, vitamin C, and fiber than a true yam. Sweet potatoes have more sugar and calcium, and more vitamin A than a yam (courtesy of its bright orange color).

If you want to try cooking some real yams, look to African or Caribbean recipes, and if you want to be sure you're getting authentic yams, go to a grocery store that specializes in foods from those regions.

"To you, it's the **perfect lift chair.** To me, it's the **best sleep chair** I've ever had."

— J. Fitzgerald, VA

Three Chairs in One
Sleep/Recline/Lift

You can't always lie down in bed and sleep. Heartburn, cardiac problems, hip or back aches – and dozens of other ailments and worries. Those are the nights you'd give anything for a comfortable chair to sleep in: one that reclines to exactly the right degree, raises your feet and legs just where you want them, supports your head and shoulders properly, and <u>operates at the touch of a button</u>.

Our **Perfect Sleep Chair®** does all that and more. More than a chair or recliner, it's designed to provide total comfort. **Choose your preferred heat and massage settings, for hours of soothing relaxation.** Reading or watching TV? Our chair's recline technology allows you to pause the chair in an infinite number of settings. And best of all, it features a powerful lift mechanism that tilts the entire chair forward, making it easy to stand. You'll love the other benefits, too. It helps with correct spinal alignment and promotes back pressure relief, to prevent back and muscle pain. The overstuffed, oversized biscuit style back and unique seat design will cradle you in comfort. Generously filled, wide armrests provide enhanced arm support when sitting or reclining. **It even has a battery backup in case of a power outage.**

White glove delivery included in shipping charge. Professionals will deliver the chair to the exact spot in your home where you want it, unpack it, inspect it, test it, position it, and even carry the packaging away! You get your choice of stain and water repellent custom-manufactured Duralux with the classic leather look or plush microfiber in a variety of colors to fit any decor. **Call now!**

The Perfect Sleep Chair®
1-888-730-4236
Please mention code 112419.

20 Signs of a Tough Winter

Before there were weather apps for your smartphone, Doppler radar, or the National Weather Service, people looked to the signs of nature to prepare for what's to come. Here are what many people believe and folklore suggests are signs of a hard winter to come:

Thicker-than-normal onions or corn husks.

Hornets' nests that are higher up than usual.

The early arrival of the snowy owl.

The early departure of geese and ducks.

Frequent halos or rings around the Sun or Moon (predict numerous snowfalls).

Woodpeckers sharing a tree.

Heavy & numerous fogs during the month of August.

The early migration of the monarch butterfly.

Unusual abundance of acorns.

Early arrival of crickets on the hearth.

Pigs gathering sticks.

Spiders spinning larger-than-usual webs & entering the house in great numbers

Ants marching in a line rather than meandering.

Early seclusion of bees within the hive.

Muskrats burrowing holes high on the riverbank.

Mice chewing furiously to get into your home.

Thick hair on the nape of a cow's neck.

If a woolly worm caterpillar's orange band is narrow, the winter will be snowy.

Squirrels gathering nuts.

Raccoons with thick tails and bright bands.

Fact or Fiction?

5 Weather-Food Myths You Should & Shouldn't Believe

From the clothes we wear, to the events we attend, we plan nearly every minute of our lives according to the weather. But what about allowing weather to dictate your dining habits? Well, here are five sayings that pair weather with food. (And yes, some of them should be taken with a grain of salt!)

By Tiffany Means

1 A coffee or hot toddy is the best winter warm-up drink.

Hot coffee. Mulled wine. Hot buttered rum. Nothing knocks off winter's chill like a hot beverage! But while hot liquids give you the sensation of being warm, there's a catch: those containing caffeine and alcohol can remove fluids from the body by making you urinate more often. And the more fluids our bodies lose, the greater the risk of dehydration. If you plan to sip that hot toddy and then head outdoors into the dry moisture-zapping cold air, be sure to chase it with a glistening glass of H2O. **MYTH**

MYTH

2 If stranded without water in winter, eat snow.

Sure, snow is an excellent source of water (and it's fun to catch on your tongue), but eating it the wrong way in an emergency situation can actually be life threatening. Eating snow lowers your body temperature (since your body must expend heat energy to melt snow into liquid water after you ingest it). This means it can hasten the onset of hypothermia—a drop in body temperature below 95ºF. To avoid this danger, melt fresh snow over a fire, a candle flame, or in sunlight first, and then drink up. (And yes, the same goes for eating icicles.)

3 Eating hot foods in hot weather helps keep you cool.

As counterintuitive as it sounds, foods that are hot—in temperature and spice—may be better at cooling you off than ice cream! Cold foods, which are a much colder temperature than our bodies, only temporarily cool us down. However, hot and spicy foods provide a longer-lasting chill because they make us sweat. When we eat hot foods, our brains respond to the "fiery" pain in our mouths and the "fiery" hot flashes we feel by triggering sweat and tears. So, when consuming hot soups and hot peppers in summer, this means we perspire even more heavily; and the more sweat there is to evaporate from the surface of our skin, the cooler we feel.

FACT

4 In summer, don't swim until an hour after eating.

Remember being told not to swim on a full stomach as a kid? That advice wasn't meant to test your patience; it was meant to teach water safety.

After eating, our bodies divert extra blood flow toward our guts to aid in digestion. This redistribution leaves poorer circulation in other parts of the body, including the arms, legs, hands, and feet. Poor circulation can trigger that "pins and needles" sensation as well as muscle cramping. And if your arm or leg muscles cramp while swimming, it could make floating and maneuvering in the water more of a chore. If you do cannonball into the pool immediately after lunch, you won't sink to the bottom and drown. But waiting at least 30 minutes could save you from an uncomfortable swim.

5 Colder climates make us crave more carbs.

Whether it's because our bodies need more energy to battle the bitter cold or because we're simply around more food during the festive winter months, carbohydrates are eaten more frequently during the cold season. Since carbs are harder to digest, our bodies must work harder to process them, which in turn makes us feel warmer.

There's also another reason for craving carbs when the weather turns cold: carbs can boost serotonin—the "happy" hormone that we tend to have less of in winter, thanks to weaker sunlight.

So, the next time you crave macaroni and cheese when the mercury dips, don't feel guilty...fuel up!

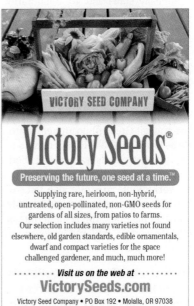

Clearing the Air on
WEATHER vs. CLIMATE

By Tiffany Means

Weather and climate. Most folks have heard these words countless times before, yet still can't quite put their finger on how the two differ or why this difference matters.

Weather is how the atmosphere is behaving now

While both weather and climate describe the atmosphere's conditions (like how hot or cold, wet or dry, sunny or cloudy it is), weather tells us how the atmosphere is behaving at this very minute and how it will behave in the near future—in the upcoming hours, days, and weeks. The weather is always in a state of flux because warm fronts, cold fronts, high pressure, and low pressure continually come and go, temporarily altering the atmosphere as they do.

Weather predates climate

Another way weather differs from climate? It is the older of the two sciences. One of the earliest-known texts about the atmosphere—a book titled *Meteorologica*, which was written by the ancient Greek philosopher Aristotle as long ago as 340 BC—attempts to explain how clouds, rain, snow, wind, and a host of other types of weather work. While Aristotle also talks of torrid, temperate, and frigid climate zones in his book, the ins and outs of climate weren't explored in depth until the 1800s.

With age, weather becomes climate

Weather observations are taken multiple times a day (usually every hour) in order to keep up with any changes as they occur. When a particular day ends, its temperatures, humidity, cloudiness, etc. become an afterthought as our attention moves to the next day's weather, but these outdated observations are never truly forgotten. Over long periods of time, patterns begin to appear in collections of individual weather observations. And recognizing patterns in past weather can offer clues about what conditions to expect on similar dates, and at similar times of the year, down the road. These average weather patterns are what we call climate.

Climate is how the atmosphere tends to behave on average

In recent decades, the word "climate" has become synonymous with "climate change"—the variation of regional climate over time. But climate, plain old climate, describes what the average weather is like over long stretches of time, such as months, years, and decades.

Every place on earth has a climate type—a label that expresses the average conditions typically experienced throughout the year. For example, if a region sees high temperatures year-round, it might have a tropical climate. Or if it rarely sees rainfall, it might have a desert climate.

Our planet also has a "global climate," which describes the temperatures, precipitation, etc. we experience, on average, worldwide.

Natural Climate Influencers

Since climate is associated with longer periods of time, climate conditions tend to remain fairly steady from one year to the next. A few factors that determine climate include:

LAND FEATURES: Proximity to oceans and large bodies of water generally result in milder climates. In contrast, landlocked areas are typically associated with extreme (hotter, colder, drier) regional climates.

VEGETATION: Plants and trees cool the Earth's surface through transpiration—the "breathing out" or evaporating of excess water from plant leaves. Because it takes heat energy to evaporate liquid water into water vapor, transpiration pulls heat from the surrounding air, causing the air to cool. So, if you live in an area with lots of vegetation, the heat is normally not as extreme, especially during the summer.

ELEVATION: The farther up you go in the atmosphere, the more air pressure and air temperature drop; so, the higher the elevation, the cooler a location's climate will be.

VOLCANOES: When volcanoes erupt, they spew a mix of rock, dust, ash, and gas miles high into the air. Depending on how violent the eruption is, this volcanic ash can hang in the air and spread great distances, shading Earth's surface from the Sun's incoming energy and cooling Earth's climate for months to years.

SOLAR OUTPUT: Every 11 years or so, the Sun—Earth's number one energy source—goes through periods when its surface is more or less active. During years when the Sun's surface activity peaks (solar maximums), our global climate warms slightly, while in less active years (solar minimums), the climate cools.

EARTH'S ORBIT: How the Earth journeys around the Sun also affects climate. If Earth follows an elliptical-shaped path around the Sun, global climate will be warmer than when Earth's path is more circular, as it currently is. The Earth's orbit changes from circular to oval about every 10,000 years.

All of these are natural (Mother Nature-caused) contributors that influence the climate, but there are unnatural (human-caused) influences, too.

(continued)

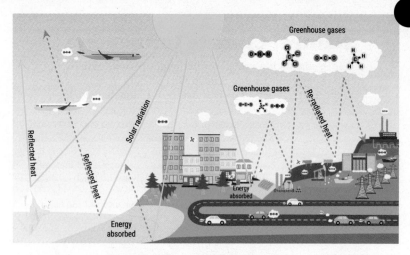

Human-Made Climate Changers

CONSTRUCTION: Bare ground and land that is covered by concrete and asphalt soak up more sunlight than natural surfaces and can store this heat for hours longer. This build-up of heat can make air temperatures several degrees warmer in cities than in surrounding areas, which in turn can warm the climate.

GREENHOUSE GASES: Greenhouse gases (like water vapor and carbon dioxide) are excellent at trapping heat in the atmosphere. Without naturally occurring greenhouse gases, the temperature on Earth would be uncomfortably cool, but when excess gases are released through the burning of oil, coal, gas, and other fuels, the climate warms significantly.

Why do Weather & Climate Matter?

It's easy for most folks to see why weather matters: it has an immediate effect on daily activities. And since we're often more interested in what will happen today than what's in store for next month or next year, climate can seem somewhat useless. But think about it: have you ever wondered what clothing to pack for next month's vacation? Wondered if a certain plant would thrive in your garden? Or been curious about your city's chances for a white Christmas? If so, then climate means just as much to you as weather… you simply might not have realized it until now.

 Visit us at FarmersAlmanac.com for regional weather forecasts

STOP PAIN FAST!

Smooth Gator's 60 Second Pain Relief is a topical pain relief cream made with all natural ingredients like ALOE, EUCALYPTUS, LAVENDER, TEA TREE, PEPPERMINT and WINTERGREEN.

This safe, no bad smell, non-greasy formula allows for more flexibility and movement while stopping your pain fast.

> Smooth Gator's 60 Second Pain Relief is the #1 product selected by our customers throughout North America.

Use for arthritis, sprains, strains, aches of the back, neck, knees, shoulders, elbows and much more!

It's easy, just apply a quarter-size amount of 60 Second Pain Relief on area affected by pain; don't rub in, just rub on, and it will absorb on its own. Wait one to two minutes, and your pain goes away.

44^{95}
for 8 oz.

Call Smooth Gator today at **727-278-3137** for your pain relief needs or visit **smoothgator.com**

FREE NATURAL LIP BALM
WITH EVERY ORDER!

Smooth Gator | 727-278-3137 | smoothgator.com

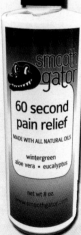

FASCINATING FACTS YOU MAY NOT KNOW ABOUT
THE NORTH & SOUTH POLES

NORTH POLE & ARCTIC REGION

1. There are two North Poles—Magnetic & True: True North is the actual North Pole. However, because the North Pole is actually floating on a sheet of ice, there can never be a physical "pole" to show its location. And, because the Earth's axis wobbles slightly, the exact location of True North changes according to the Earth's wobble.

Magnetic North: The compass needle points to the Magnetic North Pole. This is caused by the fluctuating molten iron within the Earth's core, which creates a magnetic field around the planet. The Magnetic North Pole is continually moving. At present, it is drifting toward Siberia.

2. No one owns the North Pole: Because the North Pole sits in the Arctic Ocean, which is about 13,400 feet deep, it is considered to be in international waters, which means no country can claim ownership.

3. It's NOT the coldest pole on Earth: The South Pole earns that title. According to NASA, the average summer temperature at the South Pole is -18°F, and in the winter, it's -76°F. The North Pole, by contrast, averages a summer temperature of 32°F and -40°F in the winter.

4. Things do live near the North Pole: Polar bears, orcas, humpbacks, arctic foxes, and reindeer are just a few. Several birds, including the arctic tern, visit the North Pole. Several species of fish, with the arctic cod being the most abundant, also call the North Pole home.

5. Shrinking: Due to climate change, ice sheets in the Arctic are quickly shrinking. Because ice reflects the Sun's heat while water absorbs the heat, the shrinkage will continue at a more rapid pace. For this reason, the Arctic region has become a major shipping thoroughfare as large ice-breaker ships carve a water route through the ice for cargo ships. With blocks of Arctic ice continuing to diminish, this task of ice breaking gets easier every year.

SOUTH POLE & ANTARCTIC REGION

1. Antarctica: The South Pole is located on the continent of Antarctica. The land at the South Pole is actually only about 100 meters (328 feet) above sea level, but the ice sheet over the land can reach a height of about 2700 meters (9000 feet).

2. No one owns the South Pole or Antarctica: Although many countries have laid claim to different parts of the continent, no one country controls the entire continent. Argentina, Australia, Belgium, Chile, the French Republic, Japan, New Zealand, Norway, the Union of South Africa, Russia, England and Northern Ireland, and the United States all may have or had settlements on Antarctica at one point in time.

3. Life in Antarctica: Antarctic life includes whales, seals, and many types of birds, including penguins. Antarctica is the only continent without ants, reptiles, and snakes. No polar bears live in the Antarctic.

Even though sled dogs are part of many ice cultures, they have been banned from Antarctica because it is feared they may spread some canine diseases to seals and other local animals.

4. Need a drink? 90 percent of the world's ice can be found in Antarctica, as well as 70 percent of the world's fresh water. If all of the ice in Antarctica melted, the sea level could rise 200 feet.

5. Shrinking: As is the case with the North Pole and due to climate change, ice in the Antarctic is shrinking. In fact, Antarctica has lost 3 trillion tons of ice in the last 25 years—most of it in the last 5 years.

Stand Up Straight and Feel Better

Discover the Perfect Walker, the better way to walk safely and more naturally

Traditional rollators and walkers simply aren't designed well. They require you to hunch over and shuffle your feet when you walk. This puts pressure on your back, your neck, your wrists and your hands. Over time, this makes walking uncomfortable and can result in a variety of health issues. That's all changed with the Perfect Walker. Its upright design

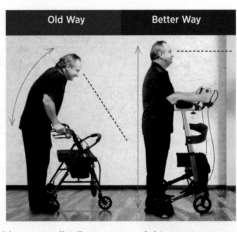

and padded elbow rests enable you to distribute your weight across your arms and shoulders, not your hands and wrists. Its unique frame gives you plenty of room to step, and the oversized wheels help you glide across the

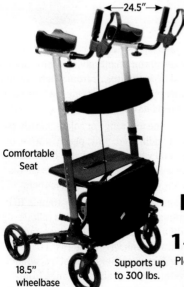

24.5"

Comfortable Seat

18.5" wheelbase for stability

Supports up to 300 lbs.

floor. Once you've reached your destination you can use the hand brakes to gently slow down, and there's even a handy seat with a storage compartment. Its sleek, lightweight design makes it easy to use indoors and out and it folds up for portability and storage.

Why spend another day hunched over and shuffling along. Call now, and find out how you can try out a Perfect Walker for yourself... in your own home. You'll be glad you did.

Perfect Walker

Call now Toll-Free

1-888-233-1651

Please mention promotion code
112420 when ordering.

Which Holiday Cactus Do You Have?
CHRISTMAS? THANKSGIVING? EASTER?

Christmas cactuses are a very popular and common houseplant. Many people have plants that are generations old. But did you know that all Christmas cactuses are not the same? You may actually have a Thanksgiving or an Easter cactus instead of a Christmas cactus! Although they look very similar, they're three distinct plants.

Unfortunately, the confusion between these three holiday succulents is perpetuated by the fact that they're often mislabeled in garden centers. And since they all bloom in late fall or winter, this further adds to the confusion. It's nice to know which one you truly have.

THANKSGIVING CACTUS

(*Schlumbergera truncata*)

Leaves
You can tell the Thanksgiving cactus apart from the Christmas cactus by the shape of its leaves. The leaf segments, called "phylloclades," are serrated or "toothed" with pointy spines (2-4 on each side).

This is why these succulents are referred to as "Crab Claw Cactus." The end of the last segment is slightly concave with a point on each side, thus resembling a crab claw.

Flowers
Flowers of the Thanksgiving cactus are produced from the tips or from where the leaf segments join. They resemble a long tube, appearing as if a flower within a flower.

They come in a range of colors, mostly pastels, including red, pink, peach, purple, orange, and white, and typically bloom around Thanksgiving. The blooms on this cactus contain yellow pollen-bearing anthers.

The anthers, the part of the stamen that contains the pollen, provide a telltale sign for differentiating the Christmas cactus from the Thanksgiving cactus. Thanksgiving cactus anthers are yellow, while Christmas cactus anthers range from pink to purplish-brown.

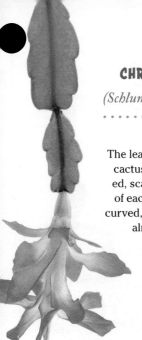

CHRISTMAS CACTUS

(Schlumbergera bridgesii)

Leaves

The leaves of the Christmas cactus have a more rounded, scalloped edge. The tip of each segment is slightly curved, but they can appear almost straight across.

Flowers

The flowers of the Christmas cactus are usually white or pink and bloom in December.

EASTER CACTUS *(Hatiora gaertneri)*

Believe it or not, there's also an Easter cactus, which blooms in—you guessed it—spring!

Leaves

These succulents have leaves with small bristles and a thick ridge on one side.

Flowers

The flowers have more of a star shape. They're native to the nontropical forests of Brazil. Exercise caution, though, when watering as this cactus is much more sensitive to over- or under-watering than its Thanksgiving and Christmas cousins.

How to Encourage Your Holiday Cacti to Bloom

If you're hoping to get blooms in time for Thanksgiving or Christmas, you'll need to begin temperature treatments several weeks before. Your plant will need 12 to 14 hours of total darkness along with cool nighttime temperatures of 60-65°F for about 3-4 weeks in order for buds to form.

One way to do this is to place the plant in a dark closet from 6 p.m. to 8 a.m. Or you can cover the plant with a large paper bag in the same time frame. Once you see buds, you can resume normal lighting but keep the plants cool.

If you keep the plant in a continuously cool room (around 50-60°F) in September and October, chances are excellent that it will produce flowers, although you'll notice growth will be slower. If temps are too cool, you'll find that the buds may drop off. So it's a bit of a balancing act.

Whichever "holiday" cactus you have, these flowering plants are a great houseplant that, with a little care and attention, can add color and joy to your home. Many people share cuttings with family members as they propagate easily, so in and of itself, these cacti could become the gift you give for whichever holiday you want.

By Richard Lederer

IF-THEN ILLOGIC

If the plural of tooth is teeth, shouldn't the plural of booth be beeth?
If the plural of goose is geese, shouldn't the plural of moose be meese?
If the plural of index is indices, shouldn't the plural of Kleenex be Kleenices?

Think About It...

If a megaphone makes your voice bigger,
what does a microphone do?

If a firefighter fights fire, what does a freedom fighter fight?

If adults commit adultery, do infants commit infantry?

If pro and con are opposites, is congress the opposite of progress?

If olive oil is made from olives, corn oil from corn, and
vegetable oil from vegetables, what is baby oil made from?

If a vegetarian eats vegetables, what does a humanitarian consume?

If a weightlifter lifts weights, what does a shoplifter lift?

If a cow is unable to produce milk, is it a milk dud or an udder failure?

If you don't pay your exorcist, do you get repossessed?

If you jump off a Paris bridge, are you in Seine?

How Does the *Farmers' Almanac* Predict the Weather?

Each and every year since 1818, the *Farmers' Almanac* has been offering long-range weather predictions that are known to be amazingly accurate. In this day and age in which weather is found at a click of a button, the *Farmers' Almanac* continues to offer over a year's worth of weather forecasts in one printed book.

People find the *Almanac's* long-range forecast especially useful when planning their days ahead, particularly when preparing for vacations, special events, weddings, heating bills, and more. Many businesses consult the *Farmers' Almanac's* outlook for their planning as well. And what's really amazing is that these weather predictions are quite accurate.

So how does the *Farmers' Almanac* do it?

The editors of the *Farmers' Almanac* firmly deny using any type of computer satellite tracking equipment, weather lore, or groundhogs. What they will admit to is using a specific and reliable set of rules that were developed back in 1818 by David Young, the *Almanac's* first editor. These rules have been altered slightly and turned into a formula that is both mathematical and astronomical. The formula takes things like sunspot activity, position of the planets, tidal action of the Moon, and a variety of other factors into consideration.

The only person who knows the exact formula is the *Almanac's* weather prognosticator, who goes by the pseudonym "Caleb Weatherbee." To protect this reliable formula and proprietary, the *Almanac* editors prefer to keep both Caleb's true identity and the formula a closely guarded brand secret.

While some may ask how a 204-year-old publication can still make such accurate weather forecasts, the *Farmers' Almanac* editors like to remind everyone that this formula has been time-tested, challenged, and approved for nearly two centuries. The *Farmers' Almanac* is the oldest source of consecutively published weather forecasts, even older than the National Weather Service.

Unlike your local news, government, or commercial weather service, the *Almanac's* forecasts are calculated in advance. Once the latest edition of the *Farmers' Almanac* is printed, the editors never go back to change or update its forecasts the way other local sources do.

Though weather forecasting, and long-range forecasting in particular, remains an inexact science, longtime *Almanac* followers claim that our forecasts are 80%–85% accurate. Check out the "On the Money" page at **FarmersAlmanac.com/on-the-money** to see some of the past weather events the *Farmers' Almanac* has accurately called for.

The maps below reflect an overall overview of the *Farmers' Almanac* weather predictions for winter (January–March) and summer (June–August) for the United States.

WINTER 2020-21: *Winter of the Great Divide*
Cold and snowy in the north, drought in the west, and everything crazy in between.

SUMMER 2021: *Thunder-Filled, Stormy Summer Ahead!*

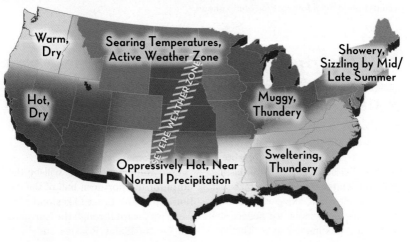

Get the complete forecast for the year ahead, including spring & fall weather maps, at **FarmersAlmanac.com/weather**

2021 Weather Outlook

Every year since 1818, we have provided long-range weather predictions that help you plan ahead. These forecasts are based on a mathematical and astronomical formula that is guided by the rules set forth by our founding editor. This formula has been altered slightly over the years, but it remains very much the same as the one our original editor, David Young, created for accurately predicting the weather up to two years in advance.

Traditionally, people who follow our forecasts closely say that their accuracy runs in the neighborhood of 75 to 80%. But, we remind everyone that our predictions are long-range and are meant to give you a good idea of what might come your way in the next year. We also bow to Mother Nature, who loves to throw us a curve ball or two (such as this past winter's abnormal Arctic Oscillation). However, we always stand by our predictions, just as we have for over two centuries. So it is with great anticipation that we release our official forecast for what's ahead.

Winter of the GREAT DIVIDE

As we go to press, there are indications from NOAA that a La Niña is brewing for the latter half of 2020, lasting until the winter of 2021. If we take that into consideration, along with our own tried-and-true formula, we believe the winter will be summed up as "The Winter of the Great Divide: Cold and snowy in the north, drought in the west, and everything crazy in between."

Frosty Comeback

Cold winter conditions will be the norm for the northern half of the nation—from the Great Lakes and Midwest, westward through the Northern and Central Plains, Rockies, and Pacific Northwest.

In New Mexico, Texas, Oklahoma east into Arkansas, and Louisiana,

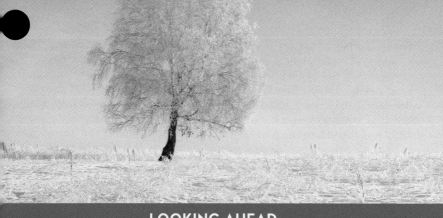

LOOKING AHEAD:
A Summary of What to Expect for Winter 2020-21 and Beyond

Mother Nature will mix intervals of tranquil weather with occasional shots of cold and wintry precipitation.

Snowy weather is anticipated in the Great Lakes, and above-normal snowfall is forecast for parts of the western Dakotas, northern portions of Colorado and Utah, as well as Wyoming, Montana, Idaho, and central and eastern sections of Washington and Oregon.

Right along the Pacific Coastal Plain, from northern California and points north through western portions of Oregon and Washington, rainy and wet weather seems to be the rule.

The southeastern part of the country, excluding the Tennessee Valley, will experience average precipitation levels, with temperatures chillier than normal. Showers are scheduled for Super Bowl LV in Tampa.

Winter's "wild card" will be the region covering the Tennessee and lower Ohio River valleys, north and east up through New England, where we can expect a rather intense weather system. This weather system will keep the storms active, delivering a wintry mix of rainy, icy and/or snowy weather throughout the season.

Snow Way Out

Over the Mid-Atlantic and Northeast coastal plain, we are "red-flagging" the second week of February for possible blizzard conditions, with the big cities, from Washington, D.C. to Boston, possibly in line for 1-2 feet of snow. Another comes during the third week of February, when we're forecasting a Southern Plains winter storm, which will bring a copious amount of snow, sleet, and rain. And finally, we anticipate another for much of the eastern half of the country during the final week of March. This storm will track from the nation's midsection to central New England and bring a significant late-season snowfall to the north of its track, and showers and thunderstorms to the south.

(continued)

Soaked Spring

Spring 2021 will be mild and wet for most parts of the country, with plenty of thunderstorms, especially over the central and eastern states during late April. In some cases, a few storms might give rise to tornadic activity.

Temperatures will be slow to warm for the Great Lakes and South Central States. The Southwest will be dry and warm, while the Northwest will see spells of mild, albeit still wet, conditions. This wet weather pattern could hinder a number of special outdoor events, including the Easter Parade in New York City, Patriots' Day in Boston, the Masters Golf Tournament in Georgia, two of the three jewels in horse racing's "Triple Crown" (the Preakness in Maryland and Belmont Stakes in New York), and the Indianapolis 500.

Toward the end of May, an early spell of heat could blanket much of the eastern U.S. Unfortunately, it looks like unsettled weather over the Great Lakes and northeast U.S. could "cast a shadow" on a dawn solar eclipse on June 10th.

Thunder-Filled Summer

Summer looks to be stormy, with a greater-than-average frequency and a larger coverage area. Many of these storms will be strong, particularly over the eastern-third of the nation. These storms may be severe and spawn some widespread tornadoes over the middle part of the country during June and July.

Portions of the Central and Southern Rockies and Great Plains could also experience higher-than-normal thunderstorm activity. Summer temperatures will run above-normal for about two-thirds of the country, especially in the South and East. While typically the hottest weather can be expected in late July or early August, this year's summer heat could peak in late August, into early September.

Across the Southwest, summer is typically hot and dry, but this summer could turn out to be exceptionally parched, except for monsoon showers occurring in July and August over Arizona and New Mexico.

Hurricanes?

As for tropical activity, we are forecasting a hurricane threat for Florida during the first week of August. That system is expected to weaken as it tracks north, mostly just inland from the coast in the days that follow. Another hurricane threat is expected in the final days of August near the Texas/Louisiana Gulf Coast. A hurricane could provide south Florida with a glancing blow during the second week of October; the Bahamas could also be threatened by this system.

Hurricane season runs from June 1 to November 30, with traditional peak activity on September 10.

Fall Warmth Turns Stormy

The weather will transition from rather warm conditions in September to an unusually agitated and turbulent October. October, in much of the country, is the clearest and most tranquil month of the year. There is an old saying in New England, for instance, that October usually has 19 fair days. That might normally be true, but with quite a few cloudy, windy, and showery days, 2021 will be the exception, not the rule. This will set the stage for November, which will only be an extension of October's unsettled weather pattern, except it will be turning colder. Watch for some snow to enter the picture, especially over higher terrain areas.

Carpe Diem!

Caleb Weatherbee

The trouble with **opportunity** is that it often comes **disguised** as hard work.

LIFE BEGINS THE DAY YOU START A GARDEN.

Fascinating conversation is the art of telling people a little less than they want to know.

ENJOY THE LITTLE THINGS

There are so many of them

its better to STUMBLE than not to START

Every next stage in your life will require a slightly different you.

Just because things aren't going the way you planned, doesn't mean they aren't going the way they should.

A BEND IN THE ROAD ISN'T THE END OF THE ROAD... UNLESS YOU FAIL TO MAKE THE TURN

FARMERS' ALMANAC®

SINCE 1818

Plan Your Day. Grow Your Life.

ORIGINATOR: David Young, Philom. (1781–1852)

EDITOR: Peter Geiger, Philom.

MANAGING EDITOR: Sondra Duncan, Philom.

ART DIRECTOR: Allison Vallin

PROGNOSTICATOR: Caleb Weatherbee

WEB CONTENT EDITOR: Susan Higgins

DIGITAL MARKETING MANAGER: Frank Pagano

ASTRONOMICAL CALCULATIONS & FORMATTING:
Q++Studio: www.qppstudio.net

CUSTOMER SERVICE: Patrick Travers

ADMINISTRATIVE SUPPORT: David Marshall

COPYEDITORS/PROOFREADERS:
Shelby Forbes, PhD, Rescue Edit
Tracy Crump Editing Services
Michelle Nati

CONTACT: Questions@FarmersAlmanac.com

PUBLISHER: Almanac Publishing Company
P.O. Box 1609, Lewiston, ME 04241 USA

Phone: 207-755-2000

DISPLAY ADVERTISING:
Fox Associates
adinfo.farmersalmanac@foxrep.com
1- 800-440-0231

CLASSIFIEDS:
Bob Farmer - Bob@BobFarmer.com

www.FarmersAlmanac.com

A LOOK BACK AT THE POLAR COASTER WINTER 2019-20

LAST YEAR IN REVIEW

Ahh, winter. It's the one season of the year that seems to make everyone eager and anxious, often at the same time. While each edition of the *Farmers' Almanac* contains all four seasons' worth of weather predictions, it's the winter that gets the most attention, complaints, and a few accolades.

SO HOW DID WE DO?

Last year was definitely one of our more challenging years. When we released the 2019-2020 overview, we suggested that it would be a "Polar Coaster Winter," filled with so many ups and downs on the thermometer that you might feel as if you were on a roller coaster. Our outlook also called for frigid and frosty conditions for two-thirds of the country, with only the far west experiencing near-normal temperatures.

Winter 2019/20 was quite a ride, and often one on the proverbial Polar Coaster, especially in the Rockies and parts of the Great Lakes. But in other areas, the winter was more of a dud, a vacation from the traditional cold and snowy conditions many areas of the country normally experience.

SO WHAT HAPPENED?

Here are some season highlights:

Some might be tempted to place the blame on global warming, thinking perhaps that "typical" wintry conditions may have been in short supply. However, there was plenty of frigidity to go around. But it was stuck up north, and only on rare occasions did that refrigerated air make it all the way south last winter. The chief reason for this holding pattern was the "AO," or as it's better known to meteorologists, the "Arctic Oscillation" (see page 70).

Arctic Oscillation refers to an atmospheric circulation pattern over the polar latitudes of the Northern Hemisphere. It serves to orient the storm-steering upper level jet stream, as well as the positioning of the polar vortex.

When the configuration of the AO is said to be "negative," it means that upper level jet stream winds can cause frigid air to flow freely southward and push cold air into the United States. Sometimes, the polar vortex becomes displaced from its normal position over northern Canada and is pushed much farther to the south, into the midwestern, central, southern, and northeastern United States. This, in turn, ushers in bitterly cold temperatures all the way down to normally warm locations. When the AO is in its positive phase, a ring of strong winds circulating around the North Pole acts to confine colder air across polar regions, keeping the cold way up north.

LAST WINTER

The Arctic Oscillation was strongly positive for most of last winter, particularly in January and February. This strengthened the jet stream and kept the polar vortex centered over the North Pole, trapping the colder temperatures in the Arctic.

To better explain the AO, think of a bottle of seltzer water, which in this case represents the supply of cold air over the Northern Hemisphere for 2019-20. There were very few times when the bottle cap was opened, so to speak, with some of the seltzer (cold air) spilling out. In other words, the frigid air remained "bottled up."

The good news? The cold air that remained constant over the polar regions helped form rapid ice growth across the Bering Sea in February, where sea ice extent expanded to 100% above average for the month. This was the first February since 2013 when the Bering Sea ice extent was not below average. Good news, since loss of Arctic sea ice in recent years has been the primary threat to polar bears.

COLD WEATHER APPEARANCE

Despite the generally mild winter temperatures across the nation, there was one noteworthy period of bitterly cold temperatures. On Valentine's Day, the Ohio River Valley region suffered brutally cold temperatures, with readings plummeting to a low of -2°F at Chicago O'Hare Airport. (*For more cold statistics about last winter go to* **FarmersAmanac.com**)

ONE DAMP THING AFTER ANOTHER

We had targeted much of the eastern part of the country for copious amounts of precipitation, and indeed, much-above-average precipitation was observed from the Southeast into the Great Lakes. Alabama and Geor-

gia ranked wettest on record for winter precipitation, while South Carolina ranked second wettest.

Storms that we had "red-flagged" all developed on schedule (Jan. 7-8, Jan. 12, Jan. 25), but with a lack of any cold air to interact with, more rain than snow fell. A snowstorm predicted to track south of Long Island around Feb. 7 cut across central New York and New England instead. The storm became incredibly intense, with a barometric pressure of 28.64," which is the equivalent of a category 2 hurricane!

AND SNOW ON AND SNOW FORTH

And yet, in spite of the unseasonable warmth that covered much of the country, there were not just a few locations that saw more than their fair share of snow. Much of the Rockies, Northern Plains, western Great Lakes, and northern New England received average to above-average snowfall during the winter, which we did predict in last year's outlook.

WEIRD WINTER

This past winter was weird and hard to predict. Our long-range forecasts are created to help people plan ahead. Unfortunately, unusual phenomenon, such as the Arctic Oscillation, can and do pop up late in the season, and cannot be accounted for when we are formulating our predictions. The AO can be forecast, but only in the very short term, a few weeks out at most. This and other factors are important reminders for not only us, but your local meteorologists; predicting the weather is an imperfect science. But we will continue to do our best to advise you on what's to come this winter, spring, summer, and fall ahead. (See page 62.)

ATMOSPHERIC PHENOMENA
That Can & Do Affect Winter Weather

ARCTIC OSCILLATION (AO)

What is it: A climate index of the state of the atmospheric circulation (winds) moving over & around the Arctic.

Effects: Shown to have a big influence on temperatures across the eastern two-thirds of the United States during the winter months. When the AO is positive, a ring of strong winds circulating around the North Pole acts to confine colder air across polar regions. The negative phase allows cold air to plunge into the Midwestern, Eastern United States.

Recent years: Years of a negative phase brought frigid temps in the East during the winters of 2013-14 & 14-15. A positive phase brought a mild winter in 2020.

Other: During the positive phase of the AO, cold air remains over polar regions, leading to generally milder temps across the U.S.

LA NIÑA

What is it: An unusual cooling of the surface water of large parts of the tropical Pacific Ocean.

Effects: Wetter than normal for Pacific NW and Midwest. Snowier & colder than normal conditions for the Northeast. Drier than normal across the southern U.S. Above normal temps Texas & all points east. Colder-than-normal Pacific NW and Plains states.

Recent years: Recent La Niña years occurred in 2005-06, 2007-08, 2008-09, 2010-12, 2016, & 2017-18. NOAA says the La Niña of 1999-2000 was the warmest on record (since 1900) for the U.S.

Other: The name was first used in 1932 by Sir Gilbert Walker in an attempt to predict India's year-to-year rainfall fluctuations.

LA NADA

What is it: The midpoint between El Niño & La Niña & occurs when temperatures are near average in the Pacific Ocean.

Effects: With no major weather influencer in overall control, making long-term forecasts is a little more challenging. Thanks to La Nada, it could be cold & snowy, mild and dry—or all of the above. In short, a La Nada winter is full of uncertainties when it comes to anticipating long-term outlooks.

Recent years: More often than not, it seems a La Nada pattern leads to some anomalous weather.

Other: La Nadas do not last very long, particularly when transitioning from an El Niño to a La Niña.

NORTH ATLANTIC OSCILLATION (NAO)

What is it: Fluctuations in the difference of atmospheric pressure over the North Atlantic Ocean between a persistent storm near Iceland & high pressure centered near the Azores.

Effects: A positive NAO index phase shows a stronger than usual subtropical high pressure center & a deeper than normal Icelandic low. When this occurs, the eastern U.S. experiences mild & wet winter conditions. The negative NAO index phase shows a weak subtropical high & a weak Icelandic low. The US East Coast experiences more cold air outbreaks & snowy weather conditions.

Recent years: Last year saw a near-record positive NAO index, resulting in a very mild & wet winter for the eastern U.S. The NAO index registered negative in 2014 & 2015, leading to cold/snowy weather for the East Coast.

Other: The NAO was discovered through several studies in the late 19th & early 20th centuries.

EL NIÑO

What is it: An unusual warming of the surface water of large parts of the tropical Pacific Ocean.

Effects: An unusual warming of the surface water of large parts of the tropical Pacific Ocean.

Recent years: Major El Niño events were recorded in: 1790-93, 1828, 1876-78, 1891, 1925-26, 1972-73, 1982-83, 1997-98, and 2014-16.

Other: The name comes from a Spanish-language term referring to the Christ child; it peaks around Christmas.

POLAR VORTEX

What is it: The polar vortex is a large area of low pressure & cold air surrounding both of the Earth's poles..

Effects: In winter, the polar vortex at the North Pole expands, sending cold air southward. This happens fairly regularly & is often associated with outbreaks of cold temperatures in the United States.

Recent years: During the winters of 2013-14 & 2014-15, very cold, snowy conditions occurred in the North-central & Northeast.

Other: Polar vortexes are not something new. The term "polar vortex" has only recently been popularized, bringing attention to a weather feature that has always been present.

 FarmersAlmanac.com/atmosphere-definition

ENERGAIRE® IONIZER CLEARS THE AIR OF SMOKE, POLLEN, POLLUTION.

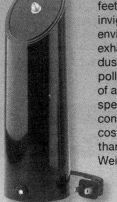

EnergAire continuously purifies up to 4,000 cubic feet (a large room) of air and makes it breathable and invigorating. Restores natural ion balance to unhealthy environments caused by industrial pollution, automobile exhaust, central air-conditioning, and heating, smoke, dust, pollen, animal fur . . . removes microscopic pollution particles not removed by any other method of air purification. EnergAire was rated Number One for speed of removal of cigarette smoke by the leading U.S. consumer protection magazine. It has no noisy fan, no costly filter, and requires no maintenance. Uses less than 2 watts. 9" high. 3" diameter. Weighs less than 1 pound.

$69.95

RODAR® ULTRASOUND GETS RID OF RATS, MICE, BATS, ROACHES, OTHER PESTS.

RODAR is the superpowerful professional ultrasonic pest repeller with up to 60 or more times the power of other devices — and power is what makes RODAR so effective. RODAR ultrasound equals a jet engine — noise unbearable to pests but at frequencies humans and pets cannot hear. RODAR units are completely safe. RODAR drives pests out and keeps them from getting in. Handsome simulated walnut cabinet. Uses less than 5 watts. 5-5/8" high. Weight 1-1/2 pounds.

$99.95

TO ORDER: Send cost for unit(s) plus $10.00 each for shipping and handling (in Mass. add 6.25% tax) by check, money order, MasterCard, Visa, or Discover number and expiration date to:

MICRON CORPORATION
Dept. 736 • 89 Access Road • Norwood, MA 02062
CALL TOLL-FREE 1-800-456-0734
www.MicronCorp.com/almanac

90-Day Money-Back Guarantee — 12-Month Warranty!

By
Amber
Kanuckel

That can send a driver screaming. It does happen, and it's not as uncommon as you might think. And it doesn't necessarily happen to cars that have been put in storage or parked for extended periods. It only takes a few hours for a rodent to weasel into a vehicle, which means it can happen to the car you drive every day, any time of year. So now what?

MOUSE IN YOUR HOUSE—CAR?

If you have noticed signs of rodents in your vehicle—droppings, bird seed on the seats, particles flying through the air when you turn on the heat or A/C—or you've even seen the critter in the flesh, here's what to do and tips on how to prevent an infestation in the future.

HOW TO GET AND KEEP THEM OUT:

• **Honk the horn!** Nobody likes to listen to blaring car horns, and rodents are no exception. Honk a few times to see if the noise encourages them to leave.

• **Use temperature to your advantage.** Part of what makes a car so attractive is warmth in the winter and shade in the summer. In the summer, park the car in sunlight and roll up the windows. The heat should drive the pesky critters away. In cold weather, open the hood to make the warm spots around the engine less inviting.

• **Try scents.** A few scents work well to chase off rodents. Make sachets with cedar wood chips and place in spots around the car where they could be making their entrance. You can also tuck a few peppermint-oil-soaked cotton balls in vents or wherever you see evidence that rodents have been.

• **Mousetraps are always effective**, provided you have the space to place them and there is no chance of injuring passengers. Place traps under the seats or in the footwells to capture invaders while the car is parked, but make sure that you remove them before you put the car in motion.

• Predator urine will also do the trick.
It may sound like a gross solution, but if you're at your wit's end, predator urine is sure to chase rodents away. You can buy it in dried granules, which you can place in sachets wherever you see signs of rodent infestation. Before you resort to this step, try bundles of cat or dog hair—the scent might be enough to drive mice and other rodents away.

Prevention Is Key!

The shelter that a car offers automatically makes it attractive to rodents, but there are a few things you can do to minimize an infestation.

———

Park your car away from other rodent attractors, like dumpsters, bird feeders, and sources of water.

———

If you keep pet food in the garage where you park your vehicle, consider storing the food in hard plastic storage bins or elsewhere.

———

Pick up dropped food inside the vehicle and clear out garbage and discarded food wrappers daily.

———

Vacuum regularly.

Like What You're Reading?

Be sure to go to
FarmersAlmanac.com
for

★ *More Weather Stories*
★ *Seasonal Weather Maps*
★ *Recipes & Cooking Tips*
★ *Lore-Trivia*
★ *Healthy Living Advice*
★ *Gardening Tips*
★ *Fishing Tales*
★ *And much, more!*

Only a click away!

Sign up for **FREE** newsletters!

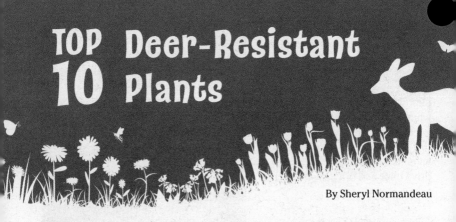

TOP 10 Deer-Resistant Plants

By Sheryl Normandeau

When hungry, deer will eat nearly any plant, but there are a few selections that gardeners can plant that are more off-putting than others to the four-legged ungulates.

In general, deer are not fond of plants with waxy or sharp textures, those that are fuzzy or dry, or any that have a strong odor. They will usually leave these plants alone, unless winter weather is particularly harsh or there are severe drought conditions. While no plant is completely deer proof, deterring them goes a long way. Why not consider adding these 10 beautiful, deer-resistant flowers and plants to your garden this year?

Roses (*Rosa spp.***)** are the top pick for deer resistance due to their heavily thorned stems. Some cultivars are strongly perfumed, which may further discourage deer. Shrub roses are an excellent selection for beautiful hedges that keep the critters away.

Hawthorns (*Crataegus spp.***)** are small trees with attractive white blossoms and edible fruit. There are some thornless varieties, but most sport one-inch long thorns from the trunk and branches. Poisonous plants are not usually on the menu either.

Foxglove (*Digitalis spp.***)** has showy, tubular, often speckled blooms. Several cultivars exist in a wide range of colors. Most foxgloves are short-lived biennials that may reseed themselves. There are some perennial varieties, as well. All parts of foxglove plants are poisonous.

Monkshood (*Aconitum napellus***)** is an attractive herbaceous perennial with dark purple blooms shaped like a monk's cowl. The deadly poison from monkshood was used in ancient Greece and Rome on the tips of weapons such as javelins and darts.

Sea Holly (*Eryngium spp.***)** is often mistaken for globe thistle (*Echinops spp.*, also a good deer-resistant selection). Sea holly is highly tolerant of drought and salinic soils. While sea holly doesn't have thorns or spines, most cultivars are uncomfortably abrasive in texture.

Lamb's Ear (*Stachys byzantina***)** is the opposite of abrasive: instead, it is a plant with leaves as soft as sheep's wool. Eating lamb's ear is like eating a blanket, which is why deer tend to leave them alone. The soft, gray-green

(continued)

leaves are highly attractive in the garden, and the pink, short-lived blooms that are borne on tall, furry stalks are conversation-starting oddities.

Cotoneaster (*Cotoneaster spp.*) is commonly used as a hedging plant, but some species, such as rockspray (*C. horizontalis*), are good specimen plants in a low border. Small, leathery leaves are unpalatable, and the berries, while sometimes consumed by birds, are dry and not edible for humans nor favored by deer.

Junipers (*Juniperus spp.*) come in tall, upright, and low-growing ground cover varieties. They are strongly scented and flavored and difficult for deer to gnaw on due to their sharp needles. Groundcover junipers range in color from yellow to green to blue, and are an attractive choice for many types of landscapes.

Chives (*Allium schoenoprasum*) have a propensity to reseed freely, but in a deer-resistant garden, they are welcome additions when interplanted with other ornamentals or edibles. As a bonus, there are several delicious dishes that use chives, from eggs to salads, and the flowers provide an onion-flavored zing to oils and vinegars.

Lavender (*Lavandala spp.*) offers a desirable scent, and it doesn't hurt that the plants are extremely beautiful as well, with stalks of deep purple flowers. Deer, however, will usually pass on this useful herb.

Bear in mind that deer may sample young, tender foliage and flowers while leaving mature plants alone. Additionally, trees may be subjected to antler rubbing instead of eating, which can do quite a bit of damage to the bark and lower branches. (Try using chicken wire wraps around the lower parts of the trunks to prevent this problem.)

Be sure to check out our Gardening By The Moon calendar at FarmersAlmanac.com and on page 166 to see when to plant.

Homemade DEER Repellent

Sometimes deer will eat just about everything, including the things they aren't supposed to! For extra protection, try this homemade repellent. The deer do not like the smell of these ingredients, so it keeps them away.

COMBINE:
3 Tbsp hot sauce
3 raw eggs
3 Tbsp minced garlic

Blend in a blender.

Add mixture to 1 gallon of water in a spray bottle and use it to spray your plants.

Be sure to reapply the deer repellent after rain.

By Tiffany Means

Animals With Accidental Green Thumbs

Have you ever taken a moment to admire your garden work and noticed plant shoots springing up where you didn't seed them? It's a puzzle that likely left you wondering: how on earth did those get over there? The short answer is the wildlife wandering through your garden beds and backyard could be to blame.

From seed sowers to weed whackers, here are five creatures who are unintentional pros at helping your garden grow.

SONGBIRDS

Birds eat seeds. But when dining at feeders and bird baths, they also spill them. If left on the ground, birdseed will sprout where it lands, creating impromptu patches of wildflowers and weeds among the grass.

HUMMINGBIRDS

Like bees and butterflies, hummingbirds are "pollinators," meaning they help flowers and trees reproduce. Hummingbirds pollinate plants through the simple act of eating. As the tiny birds stick their needlelike bills into trumpet vine, fuchsia, and foxglove blooms to sip nectar, pollen is disturbed within the flower. It sticks to hummingbirds' bills and is transferred to new blooms as the tiny birds visit neighboring flowers. While pollination doesn't make flowers bloom, as many as 80% of plants require it to bear fruit or to produce new seeds that grow new plants.

SQUIRRELS & CHIPMUNKS

To sustain themselves when plants are scarce during cooler months, squirrels—and their striped cousins, chipmunks—feverishly gather and store seeds and nuts (acorns, walnuts, tulip and crocus bulbs, etc.). But if squirrels and chipmunks work up such a fuss that they drop seeds before burying them or forget where they hid a secret stash, these misplaced meals might reappear as "surprise" sunflowers or saplings in flowerpots and lawns.

EARTHWORMS

Earthworms are nature's soil tillers. As they journey underground, burrowing through dirt, they loosen compact soil. This not only aerates the soil, making oxygen and other nutrients more accessible to plants, it also allows for better drainage since water is able to filter more quickly down to the roots.

Earthworms also aid in composting—they eat bacteria, fungi, and small organisms in dirt, making it richer in nutrients and help neutralize soil pH.

TURTLES & TORTOISES

Terrestrial turtles, freshwater turtles, and tortoises occasionally creep into gardens in search of cool, damp spots to rest and refuel. While turtles may eat garden lettuces, fruits, and vegetables if given the chance, they also make meals of destructive garden insects (like caterpillars and slugs) and intruder-weeds (like dandelions, clover, and mallow).

DEER, RABBITS, & BEARS

These creatures are often unwelcome visitors to gardens and backyards, but despite taste testing foliage and fruits, their activities aren't entirely destructive. After fruits are eaten, their hard, inner seeds pass through these animals' digestive tracts and make their way back to the earth (albeit miles away from a garden) via the animals' feces. This manner of seed scattering is quite common and is especially beneficial for the propagation and livelihood of native plants and wildflowers that are unique to local regions.

BEST DAYS TO SET EGGS

According to Moon lore and Almanac *tradition, for best results you should "set" eggs (place under a hen or in an incubator) during the specific phases of the Moon shown on the dates below. A chick usually takes about **21 days** to hatch.*

JANUARY 5, 6, 23, 24   **JULY** 24, 25

FEBRUARY 1-3, 20   **AUGUST** 21, 22, 29

MARCH 1, 2, 28-30   **SEPT.** 17, 18, 25-27

APRIL 24-26   **OCT.** 14, 15, 23, 24

MAY 3, 4, 22, 23, 31   **NOV.** 19, 20

JUNE 1, 18, 19, 27, 28   **DEC.** 16-18, 26

ANIMAL GESTATION & INCUBATION

*This table shows the **average** period of time between impregnation and birth of the young, called "incubation" in egg-laying animals.*

Referred to As	Average # of Young	Gestation in Days
Elephant	1	640–645
Giraffe	1	395–425
Donkey	1	340–420
Horse	1	340–365
Seal	3	350
Cow	1	284
Human	1	280
Monkey	1	164
Goat	1–2	150
Sheep	1–2	148
Pig	10	114
Lion	2–4	108
Cat	4–6	58–63
Dog	6–8	58–60
Fox	5–8	51–53
Rabbit	4–8	33
Rat	10	22
Mouse	10	22
Goose	15–18	28–35
Turkey	12–15	28
Duck	9–12	26–28
Hen	12–15	21

A Good Reason to Raise Chickens

They—along with Guinea fowl—will eat almost anything, including ticks! Researchers in South Africa found that in tick-infested areas, chickens will eat as many as 10 ticks per hour. If you have a fenced-in yard or enough space to let them roam, just a few hens will put a massive dent in the tick population while supplying you with farm fresh eggs.

Our Favorite Uses for Eggshells

Don't throw out or compost those empty eggshells just yet! Here are some great uses for them:

• Use crushed eggshells as a calcium- and mineral-rich additive to wild bird feed and chicken feed.

• Add eggshells to ground coffee before brewing. The shells help reduce the bitter taste.

• As a soil additive for houseplants, eggshells add minerals and help keep soil loose and aerated.

• Scatter crushed eggshells around your vegetables and flowers. The smell of the eggs deter deer and repel slugs, snails, and cutworms.

• Use empty shells with soapy water as a natural abrasive for pots and pans, especially when camping.

• Add to your garden to keep cats from using your garden as an outdoor litter box. Cats don't like the sharpness under their tender paws.

PROTECT YOUR LAND

PROTECT YOUR FAMILY

Always call or click **811** and work with pipeline and utility operators to locate underground lines.

Hitting a pipeline or underground utility can impact your family for generations. Underground lines can be located less than 12 inches below the surface due to topsoil removal, erosion and weather. Never assume the location or depth of underground lines.

Always call or click 811 or contact the pipeline or utility line operator to discuss your project and to check the location and depth of underground lines before you deep plow, till, rip, install a fence or drain tiles. Operators will locate the pipeline, perform a depth and safety analysis and work with you to help protect you, your land and the pipeline or underground utility line. Operators will typically request to be on-site during projects directly near the underground line to provide safety guidance regarding clearances and backfilling procedures.

The safety information on the following pages provide general guidance regarding how to safely work near underground pipelines and utility lines. This safety guide is designed to increase awareness regarding the safety risks associated with excavation-type activities near underground pipelines and utility lines, and to facilitate project planning and coordination with pipeline and utility line operators.

Pipeline Operators for Ag Safety

Get the facts at **FarmSafe811.org**

Land Contour Modifications

Land contour projects near underground pipelines and utility lines, including the installation of ponds, lakes and drainage ditches, require expert engineering in planning and implementation to protect land, water and underground pipeline and utility line infrastructure. A plan should be developed and provided to the pipeline or utility line operator in advance to initiate discussion regarding potential impact to the integrity and safety of underground lines. Call or click 811 to initiate contact with all impacted pipeline and utility line operators and to discuss the land contour modifications you are planning.

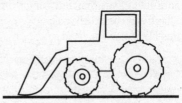

When considering land contour modifications, no substantial amount of soil can be removed or added directly near underground pipelines or utility lines. Project requirements should be designed to maintain the current pipeline or utility line depth of cover or as advised by the operator. The edge of a proposed land contour modification should maintain a minimum clearance of at least 25 feet when parallel to a pipeline or utility line.

Drain Tile Installation

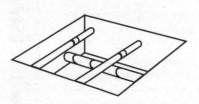

Cross at an angle as close to 90 degrees as possible and with at least 24 inches of separation.

When planning your field drain tile installation project, call or click 811 to check the location of pipelines and utility lines and to discuss your installation plans with pipeline and utility line operators. Advanced planning is key to allow sufficient time for operators to review the project design, verify pipeline depths and operational requirements.

Generally, field drain tiles crossing a pipeline or utility line should be as near to 90 degrees (perpendicular to the line) as possible and clear the line by at least 24 inches. Solid tiles and plastic pipe are typically recommended when crossing a pipeline or utility line. Pea gravel is used to prevent settling.

Subsoiling, Deep Ripping or Deep Plowing

Due to erosion and topsoil removal, the existing depth of underground pipelines and utility lines may not support deep tillage activities, such as subsoiling, deep ripping or plowing.

Never assume the location or depth of pipelines or underground utility lines. Call or click 811 to initiate contact with pipeline and utility operators. Operators will locate the pipeline, perform a depth and safety analysis and work with you to ensure that you, your land and the pipeline or utility line stay safe.

Safety Guidelines

 Step 1: Call or click 811 before agricultural excavation activities.

Never rely on pipeline markers to identify the location of pipelines or utility lines. Markers indicate the general, but not exact, location of pipelines or utility lines.

Always call or click 811 at least two to three working days before you deep plow, tile, scrape or dig. 811 is a **free service** in most states that will notify pipeline and underground utility operators of your planned work. For larger projects, contact the operator during the planning phase to allow time to ensure safety for you and the pipeline or utility line.

 Step 2: Wait for Operators to Mark Lines

Identify the location where you will be digging using white paint or coordinate a time to meet with the operator to discuss your project. Wait for operators to locate their lines before beginning your project. Operators may request to be on-site when you dig.

 Step 3: Dig with Hand-Digging Tools Near the Line and Backfill Properly

Dig with care using appropriate hand digging or vacuum-digging tools near pipelines and underground utilities. For your safety, backhoes, augers and other mechanical equipment should not be used when digging within 24 inches of the outside edge of pipelines or utility lines. Don't remove flags, stakes or paint marks until you've finished digging. Carefully backfill and compact the soil.

 Step 4: Notify Operator Regarding Damage or Leaks

Never operate mechanical equipment in an area where you suspect a leak. Immediately notify operator if you dent, scrape or hit a pipeline while digging so that it can be inspected and repaired, if needed, to prevent future damage. If you suspect a pipeline leak, immediately leave the area in an upwind direction and warn others to stay away. From a safe location, call 911 and the operator.

Got leaves?
Branches?
Grass clippings?

Turn them into
your best garden yet!

By Amy
Grisak

For many homeowners, dealing with landscape debris, including brush, branches, grass clippings, and dead trees, is a challenging task. This is where hugelkultur (pronounced hoo-gul-culture) comes to the rescue, turning a trip to the dump with environmentally unfriendly bagged organic matter into the foundation of a productive, self-watering garden.

Hugelkultur, a centuries-old technique, roughly translated means "mound culture" (think raised bed garden). "The difference between a hugelkultur raised bed and a regular raised bed is that hugelkultur includes wood in the soil. This wood will rot over the years and provide parking spaces for water and nutrients," says Paul Wheaton, permaculture mad scientist and the force behind permies.com, a site dedicated to sharing ideas and tips on homesteading and permaculture utilizing natural systems to create a more harmonious landscape.

The Main Benefits of Hugelkultur

For Wheaton, hugelkultur fits perfectly into his goal of having an abundant garden with less maintenance and fewer additional resources, such as fertilizer or even water. "When it [the mound] gets to be about three years old, with a tall enough hugelkultur, it will hold so much water that you will no longer need to irrigate," he says. "Imagine going on vacation and returning to a garden that is even lusher than when you left. And you didn't have to arrange with somebody to care for it!"

The ideal hugelkultur bed uses large chunks of wood, even logs and stumps, to create a veritable bio-sponge that holds moisture and provides nutrients for years as it decomposes. This atmosphere also creates a healthy web of fungi, insects, and microbes. On the flip side, in areas where too much water is an issue, the height of the bed prevents plants from drowning.

In colder climates, hugelkultur beds are often used to extend the growing season since the composting wood and debris increases the heat at root level, allowing additional growing time.

How to Build A Hugelkultur Bed

Building a hugelkultur bed doesn't have to be precise since nature never is, but there is a general way to build the structure for maximum efficiency.

To create these debris-heavy beds, start with an area at least 3' x 6', although larger is even better.

Some gardeners dig a foot or more into the ground to start the foundation below the soil line to keep everything in place, but it's not necessary. These can be truly no-dig raised beds with carefully stacked wood placed directly on top of the ground.

TOP LAYER

Add more compost, topsoil, and mulch if you have copious amounts of it. The point of permaculture is to use what you have on hand, so only use mulch if you have ample amounts of spray-free grass, straw, or other mulch materials.

• • • • • • • • • • • • • •

FOURTH LAYER

These materials fill in the gaps of the hill. You can use manure, compost, and subsoil (if available), which is the soil roughly 6-12 inches deep, which is found below the topsoil. It's typically higher in clay or sand, yet has less nutrients than the topsoil. If you dug a trench to build the hugelkultur bed, use this material to create this particular layer on the pile.

• • • • • • • • • • • • • •

THIRD LAYER

Twigs and garden debris

• • • • • • • • • • • • • •

SECOND LAYER

Smaller branches and untreated lumber
(This is a great way to use half-rotten lumber.)

• • • • • • • • • • • • • •

BOTTOM LAYER

Large stumps, tree trunks, or large branches

(continued)

Situate the largest chunks of wood at the bottom, and gradually add the smaller-diameter branches and debris as you neatly stack the pile.

Next add a layer of nitrogen-rich material—leaves, grass clippings (as long as the lawn was not sprayed), kitchen scraps, manure, or any other organic matter to the spaces at the top of the pile.

Depending on the leftover spaces within the pile, add less desirable subsoil (this can be the soil removed if you dug the foot-deep trench), then shovel on 3-4 inches of compost, followed by an inch or two of topsoil.

The life span of the hugelkultur bed partly depends upon the tree varieties used. Cottonwood, oak, apple, maple, and birch are the most desirable as they are slow to decompose. Pine, fir, spruce, and cherry also work well, but they won't last quite as long. *Avoid black locust and black walnut because they take forever to break down and inhibit growth.

"Now that our hugelkultur beds are getting to be about four years old, they are becoming exceptionally lush. Rhubarb, potatoes, fruit trees, and grains seem to be doing the best. But we expect next year to be even lusher still," says Paul.

By taking a little effort to build a Hugelkultur bed, not only are you utilizing otherwise wasted products, you're turning it into a garden that grows better every year.

The Invention of the Year

The world's lightest and most portable mobility device

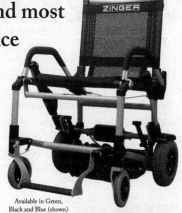

Once in a lifetime, a product comes along that truly moves people. Introducing the future of personal transportation... The Zinger.

Throughout the ages, there have been many important advances in mobility. Canes, walkers, rollators, and scooters were created to help people with mobility issues get around and retain their independence. Lately, however, there haven't been any new improvements to these existing products or developments in this field. Until now. Recently, an innovative design engineer who's developed one of the world's most popular products created a completely new breakthrough... a personal electric vehicle. It's called the *Zinger*, and there is nothing out there quite like it.

The first thing you'll notice about the *Zinger* is its unique look. It doesn't look like a scooter. Its sleek, lightweight yet durable frame is made with aircraft grade aluminum. It weighs only 47.2 lbs but can handle a passenger that's up to 275 lbs! It features one-touch folding and unfolding– when folded it can be wheeled around like a suitcase and fits easily into a backseat or trunk. Then, there are the steering levers. They enable the *Zinger* to move forward, backward, turn on a dime and even pull right up to a table or desk. With its compact yet powerful motor it

Available in Green, Black and Blue (shown)

The Zinger folds to a mere 10 inches.

can go up to 6 miles an hour and its rechargeable battery can go up to 8 miles on a single charge. With its low center of gravity and inflatable tires it can handle rugged terrain and is virtually tip-proof. Think about it, you can take your *Zinger* almost anywhere, so you don't have to let mobility issues rule your life.

Why take our word for it. You can try the *Zinger* out for yourself with our exclusive home trial. Call now, and find out how you can try out a *Zinger* of your very own.

Zinger Chair®

Call now and receive a utility basket absolutely FREE with your order.

1-888-810-1944

Please mention code 112421 when ordering.

WHAT IN THE WORLD IS
WORKAMPING?

By Glenn Morris

CAMPING. For millions in the country, it's a vacation that's affordable and rewarding, as it enables you to reconnect with nature and disconnect from the confines of technology and urban areas.

WORKING. No definition needed here, as we are all familiar with the idea that, as an adult, working is part of life, especially if you want to take vacations.

But what happens when you combine the two? You get Workamping—a growing niche in the travel/leisure market that's appealing to retirees and younger folks alike.

IMAGINE THIS . . .

George, a park volunteer, stopped traffic for a wildlife moment in Yellowstone National Park—200 bison were thundering across the road. He chatted with camera-wielding onlookers: "We don't know why they cross; they just do." He is retired and now spends summers in Yellowstone as a volunteer.

"How does that work? Where do you live?"

"In an RV," he said.

More people like George are exploiting the fact that a recreational vehicle (RV) is both a living space and the key to living and working in beautiful places around the country.

Jody Anderson Duquette, Executive Director of *Workamper News*, defines it clearly. "Workamping is doing any kind of part-time or full-time work while living in an RV."

As a practical matter, Workamping provides the means to extend one's stay in a selected location. Employers

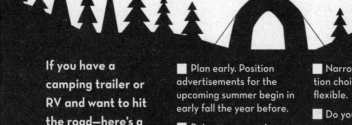

If you have a camping trailer or RV and want to hit the road—here's a checklist to help turn work camping dreams into reality.

■ Plan early. Position advertisements for the upcoming summer begin in early fall the year before.

■ Put your resume in order. Highlight skills and experiences that are relevant. Everybody who has worked has skills to offer!

■ Narrow your destination choices but remain flexible.

■ Do you want to work for wages or volunteer? How many hours each week?

■ Do you need to receive an RV site as part of your compensation?

and potential employees come to an agreement on terms, such as hours of work and where employees can park their RVs.

YEAR-ROUND OPPORTUNITIES

Workamping opportunities range from volunteering as a park host to full-season employment managing a concession store or campground—whatever is needed, wherever. Positions include jobs as park service vendors who staff the stores, hotels, restaurants, and campgrounds. Private RV campgrounds also look for seasonal help.

You could work as a sous chef, a handyman, a retail clerk, or a campground caretaker. Or volunteer to be a field guide at a national wildlife refuge. Prospective workampers can easily search opportunities by organization or state.

GROWING IN NUMBERS

This niche is growing: a Kampgrounds Of America (KOA) survey counted 7 million more campers today than in 2014.

A *Workamper News* survey notes that 77% of respondents were between 51-70 years old, and 70% of these were full-time RVers! (Full-time RVers live on the road; they have no "sticks and bricks" permanent home, a choice that presents particular problems for licensing, voting, paying taxes, etc.)

To learn more about this camping plus working lifestyle, check out the following resources: *Workamper News* (www.workamper. com), along with other organizations such as Escapees RV Club (www.escapees.com) and RV-Dreams (www.RV-Dreams.com), are packed with information for "workamping wannabes."

Sometimes work-kampers can even mean managing a Christmas tree lot, as Michael and Deb Roe found out in November 2019, when they trailered from near Yosemite National Park to Santa Cruz, California to work on-site for five weeks.

"We lived on the lot, hired the employees, and ran the business for a salary," Mike recalled. "We sold 1,620 freshly cut trees shipped in from Oregon. It was hard work but great fun. Everybody is happy buying Christmas trees."

■ Be aware of dress and grooming requirements. Pack clothes for the destination.

■ Determine how long you can stay. Opportunities are contingent upon your availability.

■ Make a travel budget; include the carrying costs of your permanent home.

■ If you are bidding for semi-permanent employment, be realistic about your salary needs.

■ Confirm the availability of internet/wifi connectivity at possible destinations.

■ Engage a mail forwarding service.

■ Automate banking and bill paying or set up online banking services.

Natural device stops a cold before it starts

N ew research shows you can stop a cold in its tracks if you take one simple step with a new device when you feel a cold about to start.

Colds start after cold viruses get in your nose. Viruses multiply fast. If you don't stop them early, they spread and cause misery.

But scientists have found a quick way to kill a virus - touch it with copper. Researchers at labs and universities agree, copper is "antimicrobial." It kills microbes, such as viruses and bacteria, just by touch.

That's why ancient Greeks and Egyptians used copper to purify water and heal wounds. They didn't know about viruses and bacteria, but now we do.

Scientists say the high conductance of copper disrupts the electrical balance in a microbe cell and destroys the cell in seconds.

Tests by the EPA (Environmental Protection Agency) show germs die fast on copper. So some hospitals tried copper for touch surfaces like faucets and doorknobs. This cut the spread of MRSA and other illnesses by over half, and saved lives.

The strong scientific evidence gave inventor Doug Cornell an idea. When he felt a cold about to start he fashioned a smooth copper probe and rubbed it gently in his nose for 60 seconds.

"It worked!" he exclaimed. "The cold never got going." It worked again every time. He has not had a single cold for 7 years since.

He asked relatives and friends to try it. They said it worked for them, too, so he patented CopperZap™ and put it on the market.

Soon hundreds of people had tried it and given feedback. Nearly 100% said the copper stops colds if used

New research: Copper stops colds if used early.

within 3 hours after the first sign. Even up to 2 days, if they still get the cold it is milder than usual and they feel better.

Users wrote things like, "It stopped my cold right away," and "Is it supposed to work that fast?"

"What a wonderful thing," wrote Physician's Assistant Julie. "No more colds for me!"

Pat McAllister, age 70, received one for Christmas and called it "one of the best presents ever. This little jewel really works." Now thousands

(advertisement)

of users have simply stopped getting colds.

People often use CopperZap preventively. Frequent flier Karen Gauci used to get colds after crowded flights. Though skeptical, she tried it several times a day on travel days for 2 months. "Sixteen flights and not a sniffle!" she exclaimed.

Businesswoman Rosaleen says when people are sick around her she uses CopperZap morning and night. "It saved me last holidays," she said. "The kids had colds going round and round, but not me."

Many users say it also helps with sinuses. Attorney Donna Blight had a 2-day sinus headache. When her CopperZap arrived, she tried it. "I am shocked!" she said. "My head cleared, no more headache, no more congestion."

Some users say copper stops nighttime stuffiness if used just before bed. One man said, "Best sleep I've had in years."

Copper can also stop flu if used early and for several days. Lab technicians placed 25 million live flu viruses on a CopperZap. No viruses were found alive soon after.

People have used it on cold sores and say it can completely prevent ugly outbreaks. You can also rub it gently on wounds, cuts, or lesions to combat infections.

The handle is curved and finely textured to improve contact. It kills germs picked up on fingers and hands to protect you and your family.

Copper even kills deadly germs that have become resistant to anti-

Sinus trouble, cold sores, stuffiness.

biotics. If you are near sick people, a moment of handling it may keep serious infection away. It may even save a life.

The EPA says copper works even when tarnished. It kills hundreds of different disease germs so it can prevent serious or even fatal illness.

CopperZap is made in the U.S. of pure copper. It has a 90-day full money back guarantee when used as directed to stop a cold. It is $69.95. Get $10 off each CopperZap with code **FMA3** at www.CopperZap.com or call toll-free 1-888-411-6114.

Buy once, use forever.

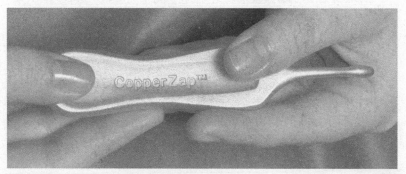

Just think of the way a hawk glides, a hummingbird flits, an owl hoots in the night, or a songbird ushers in the day. Birds delight and entertain us. They're so ubiquitous that we take them for granted. But we would surely miss them if they were gone.

That's why reports about the dramatic 29% decrease in the North American bird population since 1970 have been so alarming. That's a loss of nearly three billion birds.

This devastating news came from a study published in the journal *Science* that was co-authored by representatives from seven leading bird and environment institutions in the U.S. and Canada. Data for the study was gathered by scientists, citizen-scientists (people like you and me who participated in bird-monitoring projects), and a weather-radar network that showed a significant drop in the biomass of migratory birds in the last 10 years.

The birds we're losing aren't necessarily endangered or rare species, and they aren't limited to one area or type of habitat. Forests have seen the most substantial decline, yet grasslands have seen significant losses as well.

This population decline has implications far greater than depriving us of the pleasure we receive from birds, however. Given the intricacies of the natural world, major losses within any class of animals disrupts the balance of ecosystems. For example, if the population of insect-eating birds drops, will the insect population increase exponentially? If so, what does this mean for agriculture and habitat?

Where Are All The Birds?

By Jean Grigsby

Why is this happening?

Scientists have identified loss of habitat as the chief reason for the decline in the bird population. The first step in most construction projects is removing all of the vegetation on the lot. The typical way to harvest wood is by clearcutting a given area of the forest. These activities result in a deficiency of places where birds can eat, breed, and nest.

Our feline friends also share much of the responsibility. Feral and domesticated cats kill more than two billion birds each year in the U.S. In Canada, where there are fewer cats overall, feral and domesticated cats still kill between 100 million and 350 million birds annually.

It's important to note that the reported loss of nearly three billion birds is on balance. This means that both the births and deaths of birds have been tracked to account for the total population loss. So the answer, as some have suggested, is not to kill all the cats. Cats are but one facet of a complex problem that requires a multifaceted solution.

Collisions with man-made objects also account for a vast number of bird deaths. Airplanes, buildings, cars, communication towers, trucks, utility lines, wind turbines, and windows all pose life-threatening risks for birds.

Reasons to be hopeful:

We've all heard the stories of species being brought back from the edge of extinction. Most famously, the bald eagle, the only eagle species unique to North America, was once on the brink and is now flourishing. The bald eagle population reached an all-time low in the U.S. in the 1960s. Thankfully, the bald eagle population has surged since the 1970s, due in part to the passage of the Endangered Species Act (ESA) and the ban on DDT.

WAYS TO HELP

Keep cats under control.

Keep your pet cat indoors. If you're looking for a new cat, adopt one from an animal welfare organization or shelter. And do your part to keep the cat population under control by spaying or neutering your cat.

Treat your windows.

The reflective quality of windows makes them a danger to birds. Birds see the reflections as extensions of their habitat and fly right into windows. Break up the reflections by using screens or stickers— even string will work. Do this yourself or have it done for you.

Be a thoughtful resident of the planet.

Engage in good environmental practices (don't litter, recycle, try to use natural weed killers and fertilizer). A healthy environment considerably improves the odds of restoring the bird population.

(continued)

Become a citizen scientist

Participating in bird-monitoring projects is a great way to help protect birds. For example, anyone can participate in the Great Backyard Bird Count, which was one of the first online projects to collect wild bird data and display it in almost real time. All bird organizations have citizen-science projects in one form or another.

IF YOU'D LIKE TO DO MORE, HERE ARE SOME EXTRA STEPS:

Support bird organizations

They need your support in the form of donations, memberships, and volunteer service to continue their efforts to study and protect birds. The www.3billionbirds. org website is a great place to start gathering more information. The National Audubon Society (www.audubon.org) and Environment and Climate Change Canada (https://www.canada.ca/en/environ-ment-climate-change.html) websites also have great information to get you going.

Speak up, step up

Policy work is a key way to help birds. Local ordinances may need to be changed to protect bird habitat; state agencies may issue calls to hear from citizens on environmental matters; and members of Congress may need to be contacted to support upcoming legislation. There's lots to do, so get involved.

The good news is that birds are tremendously hardy creatures. If we do our part to help protect them and improve the quality of their lives, we won't have to reminisce about the bird song that used to fill the air. All we'll have to do is listen.

Can Birds Predict the Weather?

~ ROOSTERS ~

Around the farm, roosters and hens
give clues about the weather:

If the rooster crows on going to bed,
You may rise with a watery head.

Also written as,

If a rooster crows at night,
there will be rain by morning.

People have observed that an approaching
storm makes birds restless.
And it was believed when a rooster can't rest,
he tends to crow more.

~ WILD BIRDS ~

There are other observations
about wild bird behavior:

If birds fly low, expect rain and a blow.

Or *If birds fly low, then rain we shall know.*

A drop in air pressure causes air to become
"heavier," making it difficult for birds to fly at
higher altitudes. When birds fly low in the sky,
you can be certain a weather system is approaching. This is because bad weather is associated
with low pressure. The arrival of low pressure
can also cause certain birds to hunt for insects
that are flying lower to the ground for the same
reason. This proverb doesn't only apply to heavy
precipitation and wind, but also imminent winter
weather, which can also cause birds to fly low.

Birds on a telephone wire predict the coming of rain.

This old saying is often disputed. While birds in
migration will often stop over in an area to wait
out a bad storm in their path, there's no real
evidence that birds just resting on a wire indicate
any sort of bad weather approaching. But if you
notice a sudden increase in the number of birds in
your town—whether they're on telephone wires or
not—it could mean that a downpour is on the way.

MORE FEATHERED FORECASTERS

One crow flying alone is a
sign of foul weather; but if
crows fly in pairs, expect
fine weather.

If crows fly south, a severe
winter may be expected; if
they fly north, the reverse.

When chickens pick up
small stones and pebbles
and are more noisy than
usual, expect rain.

Roosters are said to clap
their wings in an unusual
manner, and hens rub in the
dust and seem very uneasy
when rain is coming.

During rain if chickens pay
no attention to it, you may
expect a continued rain; if
they run to shelter, it won't
last long. (You would think
the opposite is true!)

The severity of winter is
determined by how far down
the feathers have grown on a
partridge's legs.

Barred owls calling late into
the fall signal a rough winter.

Check out more weather lore
on FarmersAlmanac.com

4 Infuriating & Frightening Invasive Species in the Country

On land and in the air, destructive, gross, and just plain scary invasive species wreak havoc across the fruited plain.

By Jim Kneiszel

The rampant spread of invasive species across North America brings about the extinction of beneficial native plants and animals, severely alters the landscape to threaten wildlife and agriculture, and ultimately brings harm to humans.

And it's all our fault!

Through either intentional or accidental release, people are to blame for the many invasives that are causing environmental, health, and economic mayhem across the land. And in many cases, there's not a lot we can do to stop the problem from growing.

Sure, it may have seemed harmless to release a few exotic birds during a ceremony in a park. And nobody thought that crate of fur-bearing little animals would cause any problems. But in a few years, the sky is being blackened by swarms of obnoxious birds and the ground is crawling with giant scurrying rodents.

According to the Center for Invasive Species and Ecosystem Health, the US suffers $120 billion in economic losses caused by these non-native invaders. And the National Wildlife Federation reports more than 42 percent of threatened or endangered species are at risk because of invasive species.

Here are the tales of a few of the most frightening and infuriating invasive species making their relentless spread across the US and what—if anything—you can do to stop them.

FERAL PIG
(*Sus scrofa*)

What they are: A cross between the Eurasian boar and the domestic swine. Adults typically weigh up to 300 pounds and have bristly hair that comes in many color combinations as well as a rubbery snout and menacing lower tusks used for fighting.

How they got here: The boars were brought from Europe to the US in small numbers, starting about 300 years ago, but the population only started to explode when hunters brought the animals to Texas in the past century. Then hunters sometimes trapped the animals to introduce them to new regions. It is estimated that they now have made it into 47 US states, and their population may exceed 6 million.

What's the big deal: Feral pigs maraud across the countryside, leaving in their wake billions of dollars in property damage in the form of rooting, wallowing, and feeding on farm crops. The nocturnal beasts eat everything from acorns to a wide variety of animals, wipe out native nesting birds' eggs, spread disease to livestock, cause traffic crashes, and compete for habitat with native species of all kinds. With sharp tusks, the aggressive swine are known to charge humans. They thrive in many climates, and sows typically produce up to 10-12 young per year. Where they are most common, the hogs are starting to encroach on residential areas.

How to eradicate them: Wild hogs are hunted for pest control, sport, and food. Dozens can be corralled and killed in baited enclosures, and shooting them from helicopters is becoming a popular pastime. Hunters are encouraged to kill as many of the pigs as possible and are often paid by ranchers to clear areas of the pest. But that's not enough. Researchers are developing new poisons and swine contraception in an attempt to slow their spread.

NUTRIA
(*Myocastor coypus*)

What they are: Furry, dark-colored, semi-aquatic rodents with menacing bright orange buckteeth used for foraging. They can weigh up to 20 pounds and stretch over 2 feet long.

(continued)

How they got here: Beginning in the early 1900s, fur farmers imported the native South American nutria. Later, as the fur farming industry declined, the animals were released into the wild or escaped captivity during floods in Louisiana. They are now found in abundance in 40 US states.

What's the big deal: Bearing some resemblance to native muskrats and beavers, nutria thrive in the swampy areas where land meets water. Able to eat up to 20 percent of their body weight daily and use large, webbed claws to burrow into shoreline banks, they quickly mow down thousands of acres of vegetation, eliminating critical marshland wildlife habitat, particularly in places like Louisiana. They damage sugarcane, rice, corn, milo, and sugar beet crops as well as other vegetables and grains. They are infected with pathogens and parasites that can be transmitted to livestock through their feces via the drinking supply. Their effects upon humans include "swimmer's itch," which is derived from waterways contaminated with nutria feces.

How to eradicate them: The fur market has collapsed for the most part, but nutria provide hunting sport and a food resource in some parts of Louisiana. Some states now pay trappers and hunters about $5 per nutria tail as part of an eradication initiative. But the approximately 350,000 tails collected in Louisiana in one year is just a drop in the bucket for an invasive species that continues to reproduce in huge numbers. A female can mate 3-4 times a year and produce up to 14 offspring each time.

EUROPEAN STARLING
(*Sternus vulgaris*)

What they are: An aggressive, glossy black songbird that develops white spots in wintertime.

How they got here: In 1890, a group of literary enthusiasts imported and released 100 pairs of the birds in New York's Central Park in an effort to bring all animals mentioned in Shakespeare's plays to America. Over the next century, their numbers exploded to more than a billion, according to estimates, and they now reside in great numbers in every corner of North America.

What's the big deal: Starlings are the most prolific invasive bird species in the US, and they sure like to throw their weight around. They push native birds, such as bluebirds, owls, and woodpeckers, out of their favored nesting sites; they compete aggressively for food; and swarms of starlings cause all sorts of problems. For instance, starling swarms have caused thousands of airplane-bird collisions. In fact, in 1960, 62 people were killed over Boston when the plane they were in struck a flock of starlings and crashed.

(continued)

For the BIG JOBS, bring on the POWER of
DR® Chippers & Shredders!

CHIP

SHRED

POWER. Engines up to 13.5 HP for the rigors of continuous wood chipping.

CAPACITY. Chip branches up to 5.75" in diameter and shred cuttings up to 1.5" thick.

SELECTION. Models for yard, farm, and ranch—including PTO and towable units.

Seven models to choose from!

1B208X © 2020

They also cause millions of dollars in crop damage every year as they descend on grain, fruit, and berry crops. What's more is that the droppings from large roosts of starlings threaten the health of farm animals and humans alike. And backyard birders curse the starling as it takes over their feeders.

How to eradicate them: There are no restrictions on killing starlings, and target shooters and farmers do their best to reduce the population. Some attempts have been made to scare the birds away with sound and trapping programs, but it's a losing battle as females continue to reliably produce hardy offspring every year.

AFRICANIZED "KILLER" BEE

(*Apis mellifera scutellata*)

What they are: An aggressive bee hybrid of an African bee and the docile European honeybee, slightly smaller than the European bee but with a similar appearance. Unlike the European honeybee, however, the Africanized bee does not produce a lot of honey.

How they got here: Entomologists in 1950s Brazil looking to build the honey industry imported the African bees because of a poor long-term survival rate among European honeybees. In 1957, a few dozen African queen bees were accidentally released, and they quickly produced hybrids after mating with honeybees. They spread north to Central America, then Mexico, and finally to the US in 1985, arriving first in California. They are now flourishing throughout the southern US.

What's the big deal: The sting of the Africanized bee is no worse than other bees, but they aggressively swarm and are quick to attack if they feel threatened. Queens can mate with several male drones at a time and store the sperm for a lifetime to keep producing new generations. They can take over honeybee hives but often take up residence in man-made crevices like cracks in houses, old tires, and abandoned cars. Easily provoked, the so-called killer bees will swarm at a moment's notice and chase targets for a quarter mile or more and sting relentlessly. Mass stings can result in serious illness or death. It is estimated that 1,000 people have been killed by Africanized bees.

How to eradicate them: Bees in general are beneficial insects that pollinate plants and crops, and the European variety creates delicious honey. So it's tough to selectively eradicate the Africanized bees. Rather, experts recommend tidying areas to eliminate favored habitat and calling a pest management professional. If pursued by a swarm of bees, run away in a zigzag pattern and seek shelter indoors. Do not jump into a body of water, as the bees will wait for their target to surface and attack.

In 1822, the Reverend Clement Clarke Moore, a literature professor at a theological seminary in New York City, wrote for his children what many believe is the best-known poem in the English language, "A Visit from Saint Nicholas."

The poem, better known as "The Night Before Christmas" from its first line, powerfully influenced the iconography of Santa Claus—his plump and jolly white-bearded look, his means of transportation, the names of his reindeer, and the tradition of delivering toys to boys and girls on Christmas Eve. On that night, many parents read this poem to their children.

Later in the 19th century, another New Yorker, Thomas Nast, expanded upon the image of Santa Claus with his artist's pen and brush. Known as the "Father of the American Cartoon," Nast recalled that, when he was a little boy in southern Germany, a fat old man gave toys and cakes to children every Christmas. So, when he sketched and painted Santa, his portraits looked like the kindly old man of his childhood.

Santa Claus had been represented in various ways, but Nast, influenced by the "right jolly old elf" depicted in Moore's poem, created the figure we now know today. Over the course of 30 years of drawing for *Harper's Weekly* magazine, he baked into our culture his image of Santa Claus—his jolly girth, his white beard and moustache, his bright red-and-white-trimmed coat, trousers, and hat, his black belt and boots, and his sack of toys. He also drew Mrs. Claus and set the Clauses' workshop at the North Pole.

Reinventing Christmas

By Richard Lederer

Across the sea in England, a boy named Charles Dickens was born into an impoverished family. His father served a term in debtors' prison, and Charles worked as a child laborer in a London boot-blacking factory. Despite such unpromising origins, he rose to prominence, later becoming the best-selling writer of his time and one of the most perennial and quotable writers of all time. In fact, Dickens' rags-to-riches life became more fantastic than any of his stories written in just six short weeks.

In 1843, Dickens gave the world *A Christmas Carol*—a Christmas present with astounding and enduring influence. The story's glowing message—the importance of charity and goodwill toward all—struck a chord with 19th century England as well as the United States, and made Christmas even more meaningful.

The impact of Dickens's *A Christmas Carol* was truly far-reaching. For instance, although Christmases in eastern England are rarely snowy, Dickens's backdrop of a blizzardy London stuck with readers and helped create the expectation of a "White Christmas."

And think of how we're apt to call anyone who is not in the Christmas spirit a "Scrooge" and give them a sarcastic "Bah! Humbug!" Most of us know that we owe this phrase to Charles Dickens, but hardly anyone realizes that he also popularized the greeting "Merry Christmas."

In Dickens's tale, Ebenezer Scrooge's visiting nephew greets his uncle with this phrase in the very first chapter. In all his curmudgeonly glory, Scrooge fires back, "'Merry Christmas!' What right have you to be merry? Every idiot who goes about with 'Merry Christmas' on his lips should be boiled with his own pudding and buried with a stake of holly through his heart!" After appearing in that exchange, "Merry Christmas" became lodged in both readers' minds and hearts.

Without Charles Dickens's slim stack of messy manuscript pages, which later came to be known as *A Christmas Carol*, Christmas today might still be a relatively minor holiday with no snow, no carolers, and no families gathered for turkey dinners.

Native American LEGENDS & Lore of Stars

By Amy Grisak

Many of us know the night sky by the Greek and Roman stories describing the constellations, but for eons, the indigenous people of North America shared their own stories and traditions to teach lessons and explain the world around them.

The descriptive names are indicators of a much deeper story behind them, such as the Belly Button of the Sky. According to the Blackfeet tradition, when Feather Woman dug out the large turnip in the sky, the resulting hole was called the Belly Button because it never moved.

One key difference in Native American star stories is they are primarily oral traditions, changing according to the audience and the teller. Details are added or left out, depending on the listeners, and often one tale leads to another, blending together like the stars themselves. Time is also irrelevant.

While the stories might differ from region to region, the sky connects us all. It makes sense for us to recognize these names and learn some of the stories behind them to gain a better appreciation for our beautiful night sky.

[Big Dipper ✴ Fisher ✴ Ojibwe]

When the great hunter, Fisher, traveled to Skyland to bring summer to his people, he was fatally shot by the Sky People during his escape. When the arrow struck him, he turned over on his back and began to fall. But the spirits turned him into stars that change with the seasons. In the winter, it appears he is falling backward, but during the summer he is once again on his feet.

[Pleiades ✴ The Boys ✴ Cherokee]

There were seven boys who constantly played the gatayu'sti game, neglecting everything else. Their mothers scolded them, but it didn't stop them. One day they played and prayed to the spirits to help them since they felt their parents didn't treat them well. Soon they found themselves off the ground drifting to the sky. Even when their mothers called for them, they floated into the sky until they became the seven stars of the Pleiades.

[Polaris ✴ North Star ✴ Paiute]

Na-gah was a mountain sheep who loved to climb, which made his father very proud. One day he found a peak he thought he could not climb. After much effort, he found a hole in the mountain that led him to the top, but rocks rolled into the hole and trapped him on the high peak. His father was very sad that his son could never return so he made him into a star that didn't move so everyone could see it.

[Milky Way ✴ Wolf Trail ✴ Blackfeet]

According to the Blackfeet tradition, wolves were the first earth beings to take pity on the people of the plains. When the wolves found the starving people, they made themselves look like men and brought them back to their camp where they taught them how to work with the other animals to survive. The wolves disappeared in the spring, but the people saw them every winter in the Wolf Trail, what is called the Milky Way.

Learn more about Native American Moon names as well as star legends on FarmersAlmanac.com

WHAT MAKES A MOON
"SUPER"?

No, it's not a cape or its ability to leap tall buildings. It does have to do with how close the Moon is to the Earth as well as its orbit.

A Supermoon is caused by the shape of the Moon's orbit, which is not a perfect circle but an ellipse, or oval, shape. As the Moon orbits the Earth each month, it reaches a point farthest from Earth called the *apogee* and a point closest called the *perigee*.

According to how most people define a Supermoon, it occurs when the Moon **is at least 90% of the way to its perigee position at the same time it is in its "full" or "new" phase.** An extreme Supermoon is when a full or new Moon happens at the same time the Moon is at perigee.

Why New And Full Phases?

The reason these two Moon phases are singled out is because each of them means that the Sun, Earth, and Moon are in alignment. When the Moon is **full**, it sits exactly on the opposite side of the Earth from the Sun. When the Moon is **new**, it sits between the Earth and the Sun. In both cases, the gravitational pull from these two bodies—the Moon and the Sun—combine to create higher-than-normal tides called "spring tides," on Earth. When the Moon is also at perigee at this time, the effect is magnified into what is known as a *proxigean spring tide*.

A new Moon at perigee isn't very exciting to look at because in this phase, the Moon does not reflect the Sun's light, so it is invisible to the naked eye. Therefore, full Supermoons get all the attention.

There are four or five Supermoon events each year, half of which are full Supermoons. Extreme Supermoons are rare and occur at intervals ranging from as little as a year to 20 years or more.

Not All Supermoons Are Created Equal!

Just as the Moon's orbit isn't a perfect circle, it also varies slightly from month to month and year to year. Its perigee one month may be slightly farther from the Earth than its perigee the next month. The Moon's average distance from the Earth is 235,000 miles, and its average *farthest* distance is 248,000 miles.

2021 Super Full Moon Dates:
April 26 and May 26

FULL MOONS

Year/Month	Date	Full Moon Name	Time (est/edt)
2020/September	2nd	Full Corn Moon	1:22 am
2020/October	1st	Full Harvest Moon	5:05 pm
2020/October	31st	Full Blue Moon	10:49 am
2020/November	30th	Full Beaver Moon	4:30 am
2020/December	29th	Full Cold Moon	10:28 pm
2021/January	28th	Full Wolf Moon	2:16 pm
2021/February	27th	Full Snow Moon	3:17 am
2021/March	28th	Full Worm Moon	2:48 pm
2021/April	26th	Full Pink Moon	11:32 pm
2021/May	26th	Full Flower Moon	7:14 am
2021/June	24th	Full Strawberry Moon	2:40 pm
2021/July	23rd	Full Buck Moon	10:37 pm
2021/August	22nd	Full Sturgeon Moon	8:02 am
2021/September	20th	Full Harvest Moon	7:55 pm
2021/October	20th	Full Hunter's Moon	10:57 am
2021/November	19th	Full Beaver Moon	3:57 am
2021/December	18th	Full Cold Moon	11:35 pm

THE LUNAR CYCLE

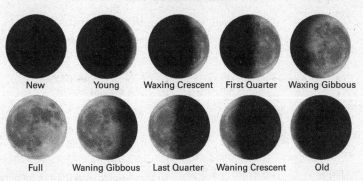

New · Young · Waxing Crescent · First Quarter · Waxing Gibbous

Full · Waning Gibbous · Last Quarter · Waning Crescent · Old

New Moon The Moon is not illuminated by direct sunlight.

Waxing Crescent The Moon is partly, but less than one-half, illuminated by direct sunlight while the illuminated part is increasing.

First Quarter One-half of the Moon appears illuminated by direct sunlight while the illuminated part is increasing.

Waxing Gibbous The Moon is more than one-half, but not fully, illuminated by direct sunlight while the illuminated part is increasing.

Full Moon The Moon is fully illuminated by direct sunlight.

Waning Gibbous The Moon is less than fully, but more than one-half, illuminated by direct sunlight while the illuminated part is decreasing.

Last Quarter One-half of the Moon appears illuminated by direct sunlight while the illuminated part is decreasing.

Waning Crescent The Moon is partly, but less than one-half, illuminated by direct sunlight while the illuminated part is decreasing.

ANNUAL METEOR SHOWERS

This table lists some of the best-known meteor showers.
All times given are listed in local time.

Name	Maximum Activity	Average Hourly Rate	Best Direction and Time to View	Speed
Quadrantids	Jan 3–4	60–200	Northeast 4–6 am	Medium
Lyrids	Apr 21–22	10–20	Overhead 2–4 am	Swift streaks
Eta Aquarids	May 4–5	20–40	Southeast 2–4 am	Very swift, long paths
Delta Aquarids	Jul 28–29	15–25	South 1–3 am	Slow, long paths
Perseids	Aug 11–13	50–100	Overhead 2–4 am	Very swift, rich display
Orionids	Oct 21–22	15–25	South 2–4 am	Swift streaks
South Taurids	Nov 2–4	10–20	South 1–3 am	Very slow, bright
North Taurids	Nov 12–14	10–20	South 12–2 am	Slow fireballs
Leonids	Nov 16-17	25–50	S/Southeast 4–6 am	Very swift
Geminids	Dec 13–14	60–120	Overhead 1–3 am	Medium
Ursids	Dec 22–23	15–25	North All night	Medium

METEOR-WATCHING TIPS:

- **Comfortable seating**
- **Dress in warm layers (even in the summer!)**
- **Clear, unobstructed view**
- **Little to no light pollution (including from the gibbous or full Moon)**

 *For meteor alerts, follow us on **Facebook!***

OBSERVING THE VISIBLE PLANETS

QUICK-VIEW TABLE FOR 2021

*Apparitions that are the brightest and easiest to spot.

PLANET	WHEN VISIBLE			WHEN BRIGHTEST	
	MORNINGS	EVENINGS	FAINT OR INVISIBLE	MORNINGS	EVENINGS
Mercury	Feb. 28 to Mar. 20 Jun. 27 to Jul. 16 Oct. 18 to Nov. 1	Jan. 15 to Jan. 31 May 3 to May 24 Aug. 31 to Sep. 21	Except for periods around the dates listed in the adjacent columns	Oct. 18 to Nov. 1*	May 3 to May 24*
Venus	Jan. 1 to Jan. 23	May 24 to Dec. 31	Jan. 24 to May 23	Jan. 1 to Jan. 23	Dec. 1 to Dec. 13
Mars	Nov. 24 to Dec. 31	Jan. 1 to Aug. 22	Aug. 23 to Nov. 23	Dec. 28 to Dec. 31	Jan. 1 to Jan. 4
Jupiter	Feb. 17 to Aug. 19	Jan. 1 to Jan. 9 Aug. 20 to Dec. 31	Jan.10 to Feb. 16	Aug. 8 to Aug. 19	Aug. 20 to Sep. 2
Saturn	Feb. 10 to Aug. 1	Jan. 1 to Jan. 9 Aug. 2 to Dec. 31	Jan. 7 to Feb. 9	Aug. 1	Aug. 2 to Aug. 4
Uranus	May 16 to Nov. 3	Jan. 1 to Apr. 12 Nov. 4 to Dec. 31	Apr. 13 to May 15	Aug. 28 to Nov. 3	Nov. 4 to Dec. 31
Neptune	Mar. 27 to Sep. 13	Jan. 1 to Feb. 23 Sep. 14 to Dec. 31	Feb. 24 to Mar. 26	Jul. 19 to Sep. 13	Sep. 14 to Nov. 8

 STARRY-EYED?

Be sure to follow *Farmers' Almanac* on Facebook for easy-to-follow night sky graphics!

And visit **FarmersAlmanac.com** for more information on visible planets.

ECLIPSES OF THE SUN AND MOON IN 2021

Times listed are Eastern. Daylight Saving Time is taken into account for Eclipses I and II.

I. MAY 26 — Total Eclipse of the MOON

This eclipse favors the Pacific Rim, the geographic area surrounding the Pacific Ocean, which covers the western shores of North and South America, as well as the shores of Australia, eastern Asia, and the Pacific islands. Hawaiians get a great view of this eclipse. Across North America, western regions will be able to see the total phase and a part of the closing partial stages before moonset intervenes. Central regions will be able to watch the start of the partial stages up to (or almost to) totality before the Moon sets. Eastern regions must be content with a small scallop of darkness appearing on the Moon's left-hand edge, or just a faint shading–the result of the Earth's penumbral shadow. The Canadian Maritime provinces will be completely shut out as the eclipse begins after the Moon has already set. The Moon will pass well to the north of the center of the Earth's dark umbra; the uppermost part of the Moon will be only 21 miles (34 km) from its outer edge. That's why totality will last only 15 minutes.

Moon Enters Penumbra: 4:48 am • **Moon Enters Umbra:** 5:45 am
Total Eclipse Begins: 7:11 am • **Mid-Eclipse:** 7:20 am • **Total Eclipse Ends:** 7:26 am
Moon Leaves Umbra: 8:52 am • **Moon Leaves Penumbra:** 9:50 am
Magnitude of the Eclipse: 1.0095

II. JUNE 10 — Annular Eclipse of the SUN

Because at this moment in time the Moon is situated at a distance of 251,200 miles (404,300 km) from the Earth, its disk will appear somewhat smaller than the Sun, 5.7 percent smaller, to be exact. As such, when the Moon passes squarely in front of the Sun, it will not totally cover it, but instead a ring of sunlight will remain visible. Hence, the term "annular" eclipse, derived from the Latin "annulus," meaning "ring-shaped." Call it a "penny-on-nickel effect," with the nickel representing the Sun and the penny, the Moon.

This will be a rather unusual eclipse in that the path of annularity tracks in a strange manner, moving northeast and then north at first. Then it moves in a northwest direction, through central and northern Canada and northwest Greenland, past the North Pole, and finally ending over northeast Siberia. Because the Moon's shadow is striking the Earth at a very oblique angle, the path width is abnormally large: averaging about 380 miles (600 km) wide.

In the province of Ontario, those located in Wabakimi Provincial Park will be able to see the rising Sun appear not as a circle of orange light, but rather as a ring. After passing over James Bay and southern and eastern portions of Hudson Bay, the path moves over northern Quebec. And after crossing the Hudson Strait, the path of annularity moves over Nunavut, the newest, largest, and northernmost territory of Canada. The Inuit hamlet of Pangnirtung, home to 1,500 inhabitants, played host to a total eclipse of the Sun in 1979 and will now have an opportunity to see an annular eclipse lasting for 2 minutes 38 seconds, beginning at 6:10 a.m. EDT.

The point of greatest eclipse occurs not far from tiny Hans Island, a small, uninhabited barren knoll located in the center of the Kennedy Channel of Nares Strait. It is here that the ring phase will last the longest: 3 minutes 51 seconds. About 20 minutes later, the shadow sideswipes the North Pole, then turns northwest, to leave the Earth's surface a little over a half hour later over the Kolyma region of the Russian Far East.

For those in New York State, New England, or southern portions of Ontario and Quebec, there will be an opportunity to see a most unusual sunrise this morning as the Sun will rise looking like a crescent with cusps pointed upward. Toronto will see 86 percent of the Sun's diameter eclipsed, Montreal, 85 percent, and New York and Boston, 80 percent. The closing stages of the eclipse will be visible from Minnesota, the Great Lakes, and Ohio Valley, as well as the Carolinas and Mid-Atlantic States.

But, be careful! Staring at the sun with unprotected eyes or inadequate filters during the partial stages can cause severe retinal damage or blindness.

Partial Eclipse Begins: 4:12 am • **Annular Eclipse Begins:** 5:50 am
Greatest Eclipse: 6:42 am • **Annular Eclipse Ends:** 7:34 am
Partial Eclipse Ends: 9:11 am
Magnitude Duration of Annularity: 3 minutes 51.2 seconds

III. NOVEMBER 19 — Partial Eclipse of the MOON

America is in a very good position to see this lunar eclipse. It will take place in the predawn hours with the visible stages ending before moonset. The Moon will slide through the southern portion of the Earth's dark umbra, and at greatest eclipse, all but 2.5 percent of the moon's diameter will be immersed in the shadow. Because some of the sunlight striking the Earth is diffused and scattered by our atmosphere, the Earth's shadow is not completely dark; enough of this light reaches the Moon to give it a faint coppery glow. Combined with the remaining uneclipsed yellow sliver, this will create what some call the "Japanese lantern effect," a strikingly beautiful sight for the naked eye. Prior to moonset, the very beginning stages of the eclipse will be visible from the United Kingdom and parts of northern Europe. Eastern Asia and Australia will also see it after moonrise later that evening.

Moon Enters Penumbra: 1:02 am • **Moon Enters Umbra:** 2:19 am
Greatest Eclipse: 4:04 am • **Moon Leaves Umbra:** 5:47 am
Moon Leaves Penumbra: 7:04 am • **Magnitude of the Eclipse:** 0.974

(continued)

IV. DECEMBER 4 — Total Eclipse of the SUN

The final eclipse of 2021 will be visible only from the icy continent of Antarctica. The path of totality, averaging 265 miles (427 km) wide, will sweep inland south-southwest from the Weddell Sea, passing over Berkner Island and the Filchner-Ronne Ice Shelf. Then the path continues across West Antarctica, darkening the Executive Committee Range (a mountain range consisting of five major volcanoes), before moving offshore at the Ross Sea. For even the most ardent eclipse chaser, this will prove to be a tough assignment; although a few hardy souls did see the last total solar eclipse visible here (in 2003) from the ground, others overflew this frozen land in commercial aircraft.

An associated small partial eclipse can be glimpsed from parts of South Africa, Namibia, and Botswana as well as Tasmania and southern sections of New South Wales and Victoria in Australia and a small slice of southernmost New Zealand and adjacent Stewart Island.

Partial Eclipse Begins: 12:29 am
Total Eclipse Begins: 2:00 am
Greatest Eclipse: 2:33 am
Total Eclipse Ends: 3:06 am
Partial Eclipse Ends: 4:37 am
Maximum Duration of Totality:
1 minute 54.4 seconds

STARRY-EYED? Be sure to follow *Farmers' Almanac* on Facebook for easy-to-follow night sky graphics!

Visit **FarmersAlmanac.com** for more information on visible planets.

DO NOT USE sunglasses, photographic filters, old color film negatives, or—what was considered to be the old standby—smoked glass to watch the Sun.

You CAN, however, use a rectangular piece of welder's glass, designated as "shade 14," which can be bought at a welder's supply shop in sizes that will cover both eyes. The Sun appears green when viewed through a filter of this type. You can view the eclipse for short periods through this filter.

The safest way to watch the eclipse is to turn your back on it—literally, not figuratively—by making a pinhole projector. Use two sheets of cardboard with a small hole in one. The perforated sheet is held up to the Sun, projecting the light through it onto the other sheet which is held beneath the "projector" in its shadow.

All About **Mercury Retrograde**

The term retrograde comes from the Latin word *retrogradus*, which literally means "backward step." As the name suggests, retrograde is when a planet appears to go backward in its orbit, as viewed from Earth. Astronomers refer to this as "apparent retrograde motion," because it is an optical illusion.

Backward Motion?

Every planet in our solar system travels in the same direction in its journey around the Sun, and none of them ever pause or turn back in the opposite direction. Yet, all of them appear to do just that from time to time.

Because of the Earth's daily rotation, the objects appear to move from east to west through the night sky. While the location of the stars relative to the Earth is fixed, at least from our vantage point, the other planets in our solar system all orbit the Sun at varying speeds. The outer planets—Mars, Jupiter, Saturn, Uranus, and Neptune—all take longer to orbit the Sun than the Earth does, because their orbits are larger. Because of this, the Earth often laps these planets in its journey around the Sun. When the Earth overtakes an outer planet, that planet appears to travel backward, as compared to the stars, for a time. *(Picture two cars on the highway going in the same direction in different lanes. If one car is driving faster than the other, the slower car will appear to go backward from the perspective of a person in the faster car.)*

Why Dread It?

Astrologers believe that the Moon, stars, planets, and Sun affect events here on Earth, and that each planet in our solar system rules a different aspect of life. Like the Greek messenger god it was named for, Mercury is said to govern transportation and communication.

Those who dread Mercury's retrograde motion say that, when the planet travels backward, its power to positively influence these domains is stifled, leading to chaos. Believers in the malevolent power of Mercury retrograde blame the phenomenon for everything from arguments to lost mail or luggage to car accidents, and warn people to hold back on conducting important business during this time.

Of course, few of us can afford to hide under our beds for three weeks, so for most people, life goes on as usual during Mercury retrograde. And if you choose to be more cautious during this time, well, a little extra caution never hurt anyone.

Mercury Retrograde in 2021:

January 30—February 19
May 29—June 21
September 27—October 17

ASTROLOGY AND ASTRONOMY EXPLAINED

ASTROLOGY interprets the influence that the Sun and Moon have while they are in a specific zodiacal constellation, and is based on the concept that there are 12 signs of the zodiac, measuring 30° each, along the astrological circle.

Because the astrological placement doesn't take into account the precession of the equinoxes (the "wobble" that the Earth's axis experiences over a 26,000-year interval), the Moon's place according to astrology differs from its physical place according to astronomy. For your convenience, we provide both the astrological place of the Moon and the physical, or astronomical, place of the Moon, which is listed on the Calendar Pages under the Moon's Place column.

ASTRONOMY is the scientific interpretation of matter in space. The Moon can wander into a few astronomical constellations that are not members of the zodiac. These constellations include: Sextans, the Sextant (SXT); and Ophiuchus, the Serpent Bearer (OPH). Thus, you will see these abbreviations under the Moon's Place listing on the Calendar Pages.

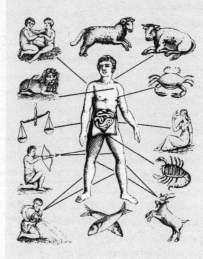

RAM
ARIES (ARI)
Head & Face
March 20 at 5:37 am
to April 19 at 4:33 pm

TWINS
GEMINI (GEM)
Arms
May 20 at 3:37 pm
to June 20 at 11:32 pm

LION
LEO (LEO)
Heart
July 22 at 10:26 am
to Aug. 22 at 5:35 pm

BALANCE
LIBRA (LIB)
Reins
Sept. 22 at 3:21 pm
to Oct. 23 at 12:51 am

ARCHER
SAGITTARIUS (SAG)
Thighs
Nov. 21 at 9:34 pm
to Dec. 21 at 10:59 am

WATER BEARER
AQUARIUS (AQU)
Legs
Jan. 19 at 3:40 pm
to Feb. 18 at 5:44 am

BULL
TAURUS (TAU)
Neck
April 19 at 4:33 am
to May 20 at 3:37 pm

CRAB
CANCER (CAN)
Breast
June 20 at 11:32 pm
to July 22 at 10:26 am

VIRGIN
VIRGO (VIR)
Bowels
Aug. 22 at 5:35 pm
to Sept. 22 at 3:21 pm

SCORPION
SCORPIO (SCO)
Secrets
Oct. 23 at 12:51 am
to Nov. 21 at 9:34 pm

GOAT
CAPRICORN (CAP)
Knees
Dec. 21 at 10:59 am
to Jan. 19 at 9:39 pm

FISHES
PISCES (PSC)
Feet
Feb. 18 at 5:44 am
to March 20 at 5:37 am

THE MAN OF MANY SIGNS

Astrologers associate the signs of the zodiac with specific parts of the body, believing that these signs have an effect on those parts. The dates listed on both sides are the Sun's place in each astrological sign.

This is not to be confused with the Moon's place in the zodiac, which is used for calculating our charts and calendars.

MOON'S ASTROLOGICAL PLACE IN THE ZODIAC

**The signs listed below are based on astrological calculations for 2020–2021.
Use these signs for all planting and other Almanac traditions.**

NOTE: The Moon's Place column on the Calendar Pages gives the astronomical position.

	SEP	OCT	NOV	DEC	JAN	FEB	MAR	APR	MAY	JUN	JUL	AUG	SEP	OCT	NOV	DEC
1	PSC	ARI	TAU	CAN	LEO	LIB	LIB	SAG	CAP	PSC	ARI	TAU	CAN	LEO	LIB	SCO
2	PSC	ARI	GEM	CAN	VIR	LIB	SCO	SAG	AQU	PSC	ARI	GEM	CAN	LEO	LIB	SCO
3	ARI	TAU	GEM	CAN	VIR	SCO	SCO	CAP	AQU	ARI	TAU	GEM	LEO	VIR	SCO	SAG
4	ARI	TAU	CAN	LEO	VIR	SCO	SAG	CAP	PSC	ARI	TAU	CAN	LEO	VIR	SCO	SAG
5	ARI	TAU	CAN	LEO	LIB	SAG	SAG	AQU	PSC	ARI	GEM	CAN	VIR	LIB	SAG	CAP
6	TAU	GEM	CAN	VIR	LIB	SAG	CAP	AQU	PSC	TAU	GEM	CAN	VIR	LIB	SAG	CAP
7	TAU	GEM	LEO	VIR	SCO	CAP	CAP	PSC	ARI	TAU	GEM	LEO	LIB	SCO	CAP	AQU
8	GEM	CAN	LEO	LIB	SCO	CAP	CAP	PSC	ARI	GEM	CAN	LEO	LIB	SCO	CAP	AQU
9	GEM	CAN	VIR	LIB	SAG	AQU	AQU	PSC	TAU	GEM	CAN	VIR	LIB	SAG	AQU	PSC
10	GEM	LEO	VIR	SCO	SAG	AQU	AQU	ARI	TAU	GEM	LEO	VIR	SCO	SAG	AQU	PSC
11	CAN	LEO	LIB	SCO	CAP	AQU	PSC	ARI	TAU	CAN	LEO	LIB	SCO	CAP	AQU	ARI
12	CAN	LEO	LIB	SAG	CAP	PSC	PSC	TAU	GEM	CAN	LEO	LIB	SAG	CAP	PSC	ARI
13	LEO	VIR	SCO	SAG	AQU	PSC	ARI	TAU	GEM	LEO	VIR	SCO	SAG	AQU	PSC	ARI
14	LEO	VIR	SCO	CAP	AQU	ARI	ARI	TAU	CAN	LEO	VIR	SCO	CAP	AQU	ARI	TAU
15	VIR	LIB	SAG	CAP	PSC	ARI	ARI	GEM	CAN	VIR	LIB	SAG	CAP	PSC	ARI	TAU
16	VIR	LIB	SAG	CAP	PSC	TAU	TAU	GEM	CAN	VIR	LIB	SAG	AQU	PSC	TAU	GEM
17	LIB	SCO	CAP	AQU	PSC	TAU	TAU	CAN	LEO	VIR	SCO	SAG	AQU	PSC	TAU	GEM
18	LIB	SCO	CAP	AQU	ARI	TAU	GEM	CAN	LEO	LIB	SCO	CAP	PSC	ARI	TAU	GEM
19	SCO	SAG	AQU	PSC	ARI	GEM	GEM	CAN	VIR	LIB	SAG	CAP	PSC	ARI	GEM	CAN
20	SCO	SAG	AQU	PSC	TAU	GEM	GEM	LEO	VIR	SCO	SAG	AQU	ARI	TAU	GEM	CAN
21	SAG	CAP	PSC	ARI	TAU	CAN	CAN	LEO	LIB	SCO	CAP	AQU	ARI	TAU	CAN	LEO
22	SAG	CAP	PSC	ARI	TAU	CAN	CAN	VIR	LIB	SAG	CAP	PSC	ARI	TAU	CAN	LEO
23	CAP	AQU	PSC	ARI	GEM	CAN	LEO	VIR	SCO	SAG	AQU	PSC	TAU	GEM	CAN	LEO
24	CAP	AQU	ARI	TAU	GEM	LEO	LEO	LIB	SCO	CAP	AQU	ARI	TAU	GEM	LEO	VIR
25	CAP	PSC	ARI	TAU	CAN	LEO	VIR	LIB	SAG	CAP	PSC	ARI	GEM	CAN	LEO	VIR
26	AQU	PSC	TAU	GEM	CAN	VIR	VIR	SCO	SAG	AQU	PSC	ARI	GEM	CAN	VIR	LIB
27	AQU	PSC	TAU	GEM	LEO	VIR	VIR	SCO	CAP	AQU	PSC	TAU	GEM	CAN	VIR	LIB
28	PSC	ARI	TAU	GEM	LEO	LIB	LIB	SAG	CAP	PSC	ARI	TAU	CAN	LEO	VIR	SCO
29	PSC	ARI	GEM	CAN	LEO		LIB	SAG	CAP	PSC	ARI	GEM	CAN	LEO	LIB	SCO
30	ARI	TAU	GEM	CAN	VIR		SCO	CAP	AQU	ARI	TAU	GEM	LEO	VIR	LIB	SAG
31		TAU		LEO	VIR		SCO		AQU		TAU	GEM		VIR		SAG

BEST DAYS IN 2021

The best days listed here are based on both the phase of the Moon and its position in the zodiac. Many people believe that if you do the tasks on the dates listed, you will get the best results possible.

	JAN	FEB	MAR	APR	MAY	JUN
COOKING/BAKING						
BAKE	18, 19, 25, 26	14, 15, 21-23	13-15, 21, 22	11, 17-19, 24, 25	14-16, 21, 22	11, 12, 18, 19
BREW	NO GOOD DAYS	NO GOOD DAYS	11, 12	7-9	4-6	1, 2, 28, 29
CAN FRUITS & VEGETABLES	7, 8	3, 4	2, 3, 11, 12, 30, 31	7-9, 26, 27	4-6	1, 2, 28, 29
DRY FRUITS & VEGETABLES	1, 28, 29	NO GOOD DAYS	4	1, 2, 28, 29	26	30
JAMS/JELLIES	7, 8	3, 4, 9, 10	2, 3, 9, 10, 30, 31	5, 6, 26, 27	2, 3, 9, 10, 30, 31	6, 7, 26, 27
HEALTH & BEAUTY						
CUT HAIR TO INCREASE GROWTH	15-17, 20-22, 25, 26	12, 13, 16-18, 21-23	16, 17, 21, 22	12-14, 17-19	11, 14-16, 23, 24	11, 12, 20, 21
CUT HAIR TO SLOW GROWTH	1, 5, 6, 9, 10, 28, 29	1, 2, 5, 6, 9, 10, 28	1, 4, 5, 9, 10, 28, 29	1, 2, 5, 6, 10, 28, 29	2, 3, 7, 8, 26, 30, 31	3-5, 8, 9, 26, 27, 30
QUIT SMOKING	1-4, 9, 10, 28-31	5, 6, 9, 10, 27	4, 5, 9, 10	1, 2, 5, 6, 10, 28, 29	2, 3, 7, 8, 26, 30, 31	3-5, 8, 9, 26, 27, 30
START DIET TO GAIN WEIGHT	15-17, 25, 26	12, 13, 21-23	21, 22	17-19	14-16	11, 12
START DIET TO LOSE WEIGHT	1-4, 9, 10, 28-31	5, 6, 9, 10, 27	4, 5, 9, 10	1, 2, 5, 6, 10, 28, 29	2, 3, 7, 8, 26, 30, 31	3-5, 26, 27, 30
PARENTING						
POTTY TRAIN	9-17	5-13	4-12	1-9, 28-30	1-6, 25-31	1, 2, 22-29
WEAN HUMANS OR ANIMALS	9-17	5-13	4-12	1-9, 28-30	1-6, 25-31	1, 2, 22-29
HOME MAINTENANCE						
DEMOLITION	1, 9, 10, 28, 29	5, 6	4, 5	1, 2, 10, 28, 29	7, 8, 26	3-5, 30
PAINT	1, 13, 14, 20-22, 27-29	9-11, 16-18, 24, 25	9, 10, 16, 17, 23, 24	5, 6, 12-14, 20, 21	2, 3, 9-11, 17, 18, 30, 31	6, 7, 13, 14, 26, 27
WASH WINDOWS	9, 10	5, 6	4, 5	1, 2, 28, 29	25, 26	22, 23
WASH WOODEN FLOORS	1, 9, 10, 28, 29	5, 6, 9, 10	4, 5, 9, 10	1, 2, 5, 6, 10, 28, 29	2, 3, 7, 8, 26, 30, 31	3-5, 8, 9, 26, 27, 30
WAX FLOORS	15-17, 20-22, 25, 26	12, 13, 16-18, 21-23, 26	16, 17, 21, 22, 25-27	12-14, 17-19, 22-25	11, 14-16, 19-24	11, 12, 15-21

BEST DAYS IN 2021

The best days listed here are based on both the phase of the Moon and its position in the zodiac. Many people believe that if you do the tasks on the dates listed, you will get the best results possible.

JUL	AUG	SEP	OCT	NOV	DEC	
COOKING/BAKING						
9, 15, 16, 21, 22	11, 12, 18, 19	7-9, 14, 15	6, 11, 12, 18, 19	7, 8, 14, 15	5, 6, 11-13	**BAKE**
8, 25-27	4-6, 22, 23	1, 2, 28, 29	25-27	21-23	19, 20	**BREW**
8, 25-27	4-6, 22, 23	1, 2, 28, 29	25-27	3, 21-23	1, 2, 19, 20, 28, 29	**CAN FRUITS & VEGETABLES**
28, 29	24-26	20-22	NO GOOD DAYS	24, 25	21-23	**DRY FRUITS & VEGETABLES**
3, 4, 23, 24, 30, 31	1, 27, 28	23, 24	20-22	3	1, 2, 28, 29	**JAMS/JELLIES**
HEALTH & BEAUTY						
9, 17, 18, 21, 22	13, 14, 18, 19	10, 11, 14, 15, 18, 19	7, 8, 11, 12, 15-17	4, 7, 8, 12, 13, 16-18	5, 6, 9, 10, 14, 15	**CUT HAIR TO INCREASE GROWTH**
1, 2, 5-7, 23, 24, 28, 29	2, 3, 7, 24-26, 29-31	3, 4, 20-22, 25-27, 30	1, 2, 5, 23, 24, 28, 29	1, 2, 19, 20, 24, 25, 29, 30	3, 18, 21-23, 26, 27, 30, 31	**CUT HAIR TO SLOW GROWTH**
1, 2, 5-7, 23, 24, 28, 29	2, 3, 7, 24-26, 29-31	3-5, 20-22, 25-27, 30	1-4, 23, 24, 28-31	19, 20, 24-28	3, 18, 21-25, 30, 31	**QUIT SMOKING**
9	NO GOOD DAYS	18, 19	15-17	12, 13	9, 10	**START DIET TO GAIN WEIGHT**
1, 2, 23, 24, 28, 29	7, 24-26	3-5, 20-22, 30	1-4, 28-31	24-28	3, 21-25, 30, 31	**START DIET TO LOSE WEIGHT**
PARENTING						
19-27	15-23	12-19	9-17	5-13	3-10, 30, 31	**POTTY TRAIN**
19-27	15-23	12-19	9-17	5-13	3-10, 30, 31	**WEAN HUMANS OR ANIMALS**
HOME MAINTENANCE						
1, 2, 28, 29	7, 24-26	3, 4, 20-22, 30	1, 2, 28, 29	24, 25	3, 21-23, 30, 31	**DEMOLITION**
3, 4, 10-12, 23, 24, 30, 31	1, 7, 8, 20, 21, 27, 28	3, 4, 16, 17, 23, 24, 30	1, 2, 13, 14, 20-22, 28, 29	9-11, 16-18, 24, 25	7, 8, 14, 15, 21-23	**PAINT**
19, 20	15-17	12, 13	9, 10	5, 6	3, 4, 30, 31	**WASH WINDOWS**
1, 2, 5-7, 23, 24, 28, 29	2, 3, 7, 24-26, 29-31	3, 4, 20-22, 25-27, 30	1, 2, 23, 24, 28, 29	19, 20, 24, 25	3, 18, 21-23, 30, 31	**WASH WOODEN FLOORS**
9, 13-18, 21, 22	9-14, 18, 19	6-11, 14, 15, 18, 19	6-8, 11, 12, 15-17	4, 7, 8, 12, 13, 16-18	5, 6, 9, 10, 14, 15	**WAX FLOORS**

BEST DAYS IN 2021

The best days listed here are based on both the phase of the Moon and its position in the zodiac. Many people believe that if you do the tasks on the dates listed, you will get the best results possible.

	JAN	FEB	MAR	APR	MAY	JUN
OUTDOOR CHORES						
Cut Firewood	13-27	11-26	13-27	11-25	11-25	10-23
Dig Holes	13-27	11-26	13-27	11-25	11-25	10-23
Dig Post Holes	1, 28, 29	9, 10	9, 10	5, 6	2, 3, 9, 10, 30, 31	6, 7, 26, 27
Harvest	9, 10	5, 6, 9, 10	5, 9, 10	5, 6, 10	3, 7, 8	3-5, 8, 9
Kill Plant Pests	1-4, 9, 10, 13, 14, 18, 19, 23, 24, 27-31	5, 6, 9-11, 14, 15, 19, 20, 24-27	4, 5, 9, 10, 13-15, 18-20, 23-27	1, 2, 5, 6, 10, 11, 15, 16, 20-23, 28, 29	2, 3, 7, 8, 12, 13, 17-20, 25, 26, 30, 31	3-5, 8-10, 13-17, 22, 23, 26, 27, 30
Mow to Increase Growth	13-27	11-26	13-27	11-25	11-25	10-23
Mow to Slow Growth	1-12, 28-31	1-10, 27, 28	1-12, 28-31	1-10, 26-30	1-10, 26-31	1-9, 24-30
Pick Apples & Pears	1, 9, 10, 28, 29	5, 6	4, 5	1, 2, 10, 28, 29	7, 8, 26	3-5, 30
Prune Trees	7, 8, 11, 12	3, 4, 7, 8	2, 3, 6-8, 30, 31	3, 4, 26, 27, 30	1, 27-29	24, 25
FARM/ANIMAL						
Castrate Farm Animals	9-17	5-13	4-12	1-9, 28-30	1-6, 25-31	1, 2, 22-29
Hunt	NO GOOD DAYS	3	2, 3, 30, 31	26, 27	NO GOOD DAYS	1, 28, 29
Slaughter	30	27, 28	1, 28-30	26-28	26-28	24-26
ADVERTISE, TRAVEL, & MORE						
Advertise to Sell	9, 10, 20-22	5, 6, 16-18	4, 5, 16, 17	1, 2, 12-14, 28, 29	9-11, 25, 26	6, 7, 22, 23
Ask for a Loan	1, 28, 29	NO GOOD DAYS	NO GOOD DAYS	NO GOOD DAYS	9, 10	6, 7
Buy a Home	NO GOOD DAYS	16-18	16, 17	12-14, 17-19	11, 14-18	11-14
Get Married	6, 15-17, 20-22, 25-27	12, 13, 16-18, 21-25	11, 12, 16, 17, 21-24	7-9, 12-14, 17-21, 24, 25	4-6, 9-11, 14-18, 21, 22	2, 6, 7, 11-14, 18, 19
Travel for Pleasure	23, 24, 27	19, 20, 24, 25	18-20, 23, 24	15, 16, 20, 21	12, 13, 17, 18, 25	10, 13, 14, 22, 23

BEST DAYS IN 2021

*The best days listed here are based on both the phase of the Moon and its position in the zodiac.
Many people believe that if you do the tasks on the dates listed, you will get the best results possible.*

JUL	AUG	SEP	OCT	NOV	DEC	
OUTDOOR CHORES						
9-22	8-21	6-19	6-19	4-18	4-17	**CUT FIREWOOD**
9-22	8-21	6-19	6-19	4-18	4-17	**DIG HOLES**
3, 4, 23, 24, 30, 31	1, 7, 27, 28	3, 4, 23, 24, 30	1, 2, 20-22, 28, 29	24, 25	21-23	**DIG POST HOLES**
1, 2, 5-7	2, 3, 7, 30, 31	3-5, 30	1-4, 28-31	27, 28	3, 30, 31	**HARVEST**
1, 2, 5-7, 10-14, 19, 20, 23, 24, 28, 29	2, 3, 7-10, 15-17, 20, 21, 24-26, 29-31	3-6, 12, 13, 16, 17, 20-22, 25-27, 30	1-4, 9, 10, 13, 14, 18, 19, 23, 24, 28-31	5, 6, 9-11, 14, 15, 19, 20, 24-28	3, 4, 7, 8, 11-13, 16-18, 21-25, 30, 31	**KILL PLANT PESTS**
9-22	8-21	6-19	6-19	4-18	4-17	**MOW TO INCREASE GROWTH**
1-8, 23-31	1-7, 22-31	1-5, 20-30	1-5, 20-31	1-3, 19-30	1-3, 18-31	**MOW TO SLOW GROWTH**
1, 2, 28, 29	7, 24-26	3, 4, 20-22, 30	1, 2, 28, 29	24, 25	3, 21-23, 30, 31	**PICK APPLES & PEARS**
NO GOOD DAYS	NO GOOD DAYS	NO GOOD DAYS	NO GOOD DAYS	3	1, 2, 28, 29	**PRUNE TREES**
FARM/ANIMAL						
19-27	15-23	12-19	9-17	5-13	3-10, 30, 31	**CASTRATE FARM ANIMALS**
25-27	22, 23	NO GOOD DAYS	25-27	21-23	19, 20	**HUNT**
23-25	22-24	20-22	20-22	19-21	18-20	**SLAUGHTER**
ADVERTISE, TRAVEL, & MORE						
3, 4, 19, 20, 30, 31	1, 15-17, 27, 28	12, 13, 23, 24	9, 10, 20-22	5, 6, 16-18	3, 4, 14, 15, 30, 31	**ADVERTISE TO SELL**
3, 4, 30, 31	1, 7, 27, 28	3, 4, 23, 24, 30	1, 2, 20-22, 28, 29	24, 25	21-23	**ASK FOR A LOAN**
9-12	8	NO GOOD DAYS	NO GOOD DAYS	NO GOOD DAYS	NO GOOD DAYS	**BUY A HOME**
3, 4, 8-12, 15, 16, 31	1, 4-8, 11, 12	1-4, 7-9, 18, 19, 28-30	1, 2, 5, 6, 15-17, 28, 29	1, 2, 12, 13, 16-18, 29, 30	9, 10, 14, 15, 26, 27	**GET MARRIED**
10-12, 19, 20	8, 15-17	12, 13	9, 10	5, 6	4, 16, 17	**TRAVEL FOR PLEASURE**

FARMERS' ALMANAC 2021 FISHING CALENDAR

What is the best day to fish?

Some say that the best day is any day you can cast a line in the water!

Experience does show that there are certain days and times when fish tend to be more active, making the fishing much better. Our Fishing Calendar is based on the Moon phase, the zodiac sign the Moon is in, and our experience. Local conditions, tides, and weather may affect your fishing success.

	January Fishing Condition	Best Time	February Fishing Condition	Best Time	March Fishing Condition	Best Time	April Fishing Condition	Best Time	May Fishing Condition	Best Time	June Fishing Condition	Best Time
1	F	E	P	E	F	E	P	E	F	E	B	E
2	F	E	P	E	B	E	P	E	G	E	B	M
3	F	E	G	E	G	E	F	E	G	M	P	M
4	F	E	G	M	P	E	F	M	B	M	P	M
5	P	E	P	M	P	M	G	M	B	M	P	M
6	P	M	P	M	F	M	G	M	B	M	F	M
7	G	M	F	M	F	M	B	M	P	M	F	M
8	G	M	F	M	F	M	B	M	P	M	P	M
9	P	M	F	M	G	M	G	M	P	M	P	M
10	P	M	F	M	G	M	P	M	P	M	P	E
11	P	M	F	E	G	M	P	E	P	E	G	E
12	P	M	G	E	G	M	P	E	P	E	G	E
13	F	E	G	E	P	E	P	E	P	E	P	E
14	F	E	P	E	P	E	F	E	B	E	P	E
15	G	E	P	E	P	E	P	E	B	E	F	E
16	B	E	F	E	F	E	P	E	B	E	F	E
17	B	E	F	E	F	E	B	E	P	E	F	M
18	P	E	F	E	P	E	B	E	P	E	P	M
19	P	E	P	M	P	E	B	E	F	M	P	M
20	F	M	P	M	P	E	P	M	F	M	G	M
21	F	M	B	M	B	M	P	M	P	M	B	M
22	F	M	B	M	B	M	F	M	P	M	F	M
23	P	M	B	M	P	M	G	M	B	M	F	M
24	P	M	F	M	P	M	F	M	B	M	G	E
25	B	M	F	M	G	M	F	M	F	M	G	E
26	B	M	G	M	G	M	B	E	F	E	B	E
27	F	M	G	E	G	M	B	E	G	E	B	E
28	F	E	F	E	F	E	F	E	G	E	B	E
29	F	E			F	E	F	E	G	E	B	E
30	G	E			B	E	F	E	G	E	P	E
31	G	E			B	E			G	E		

FARMERS' ALMANAC 2021 FISHING CALENDAR

CALENDAR KEY: *Fishing Condition:* This column lists the overall rating for the entire day, based on our formula. **B=Best** means that you will catch something almost every time you cast your line in the water. **G=Good** means that you will catch enough fish that day to feel gratified. **F=Fair** means that you may catch one or two fish, but you will have to work hard to do so. **P=Poor** means the fish will either steal all your bait or will not even touch your line. *Best Time:* This column lists the best time of the day when fish will be biting: **M=Morning** or **E=Evening**. To view online, visit **FarmersAlmanac.com.**

	July Fishing Condition	July Best Time	August Fishing Condition	August Best Time	September Fishing Condition	September Best Time	October Fishing Condition	October Best Time	November Fishing Condition	November Best Time	December Fishing Condition	December Best Time
1	P	M	F	M	B	M	P	M	P	M	G	M
2	P	M	P	M	B	M	P	M	P	M	F	M
3	F	M	P	M	P	M	F	M	F	M	P	M
4	F	M	B	M	P	M	P	M	F	E	P	E
5	P	M	B	M	P	M	P	M	P	E	P	E
6	P	M	G	M	P	E	P	E	P	E	P	E
7	P	M	P	M	P	E	F	E	F	E	G	E
8	G	M	P	E	P	E	F	E	F	E	G	E
9	G	E	P	E	P	E	P	E	G	E	B	E
10	P	E	P	E	G	E	P	E	G	E	B	M
11	P	E	P	E	G	E	F	E	G	M	P	M
12	P	E	P	E	P	E	F	M	B	M	P	M
13	F	E	G	E	P	M	G	M	B	M	P	M
14	F	E	G	E	F	M	G	M	P	M	F	M
15	P	E	P	M	F	M	B	M	P	M	G	M
16	P	E	P	M	G	M	B	M	G	M	F	M
17	G	M	P	M	B	M	B	M	G	M	F	M
18	G	M	F	M	B	M	F	M	G	M	F	E
19	P	M	G	M	B	M	F	M	F	E	B	E
20	F	M	B	M	F	E	G	E	F	E	B	E
21	G	M	B	M	F	E	G	E	B	E	F	E
22	G	M	B	E	F	E	G	E	B	E	F	E
23	B	E	B	E	G	E	F	E	B	E	P	E
24	B	E	F	E	F	E	P	E	P	E	F	E
25	B	E	F	E	F	E	B	E	P	E	F	E
26	B	E	P	E	P	E	B	E	F	E	P	M
27	B	E	F	E	P	E	B	E	F	M	P	M
28	P	E	F	E	B	M	P	M	F	M	G	M
29	P	E	P	E	B	M	P	M	P	M	G	M
30	F	E	P	M	P	M	F	M	P	M	P	M
31	F	M	P	M			F	M			P	M

By Francesca Duval

COULD CHICKENS BE THE ANSWER?

Earth-Friendly Reasons to Raise Chickens

We are at a unique point in time. Our busy lives have invited the creation and dependency on a plethora of disposable, single-use plastics and time-saving conveniences that also carry with them the unfortunate side effect of ecological uncertainty. Plastics are filling our oceans; unnecessary food waste is piling up in our landfills; and our produce and protein are being transported from miles away before they show up in our grocery stores. At times, it may feel overwhelming and hard to figure out what you can do to help or where to start to make positive changes to our environment. Chickens, however, may just be the answer we were looking for.

Humans have lived alongside chickens for thousands of years. When explorers set sail across the seas, chickens were brought along. Small, easy to care for, and remarkably scrappy, humble hens are a great addition to anyone's life. With a small amount of space, food, water, and protection, they give you eggs, protein, fertilizer, pest control, company, and a window into the natural world.

FOOD WASTE

There is nothing on planet Earth that is more adept at turning kitchen and food waste into consumable protein than a chicken. A small flock of six birds could easily keep up with the food waste made by a family of four. Instead of sending table scraps to the landfill to turn into harmful methane gases, keep a metal compost container with charcoal filters (which help reduce odors) on your countertop, and set the food aside for the hens. You will be amazed at how fast the compost container fills.

Chickens can eat almost anything from the kitchen, with the exception of bone, citrus, banana peels, coffee grounds, and avocados. (You may consider a second compost bin for these compostable items.) As a thank you for food scraps, hens will produce rich and delicious eggs, which can be collected daily.

FOOD FOR YOU

The act of daily egg collection and simple chores involved in caring for chickens make for a lovely family affair. Children and adults of all ages delight in beautiful eggs produced by the hens, and they get us out of the house and away from computer screens. And as most now know, experiencing fresh air and connecting with nature provides a powerful boost to our mental and emotional health. Whether you have a postage-stamp-sized yard or hundreds of acres on a homestead, anyone can feel the wonder of visiting a hen's nesting box.

CHICKEN COOPS

To make cleaning and egg-collecting more ergonomic, a coop that is raised off the ground is advisable. A raised coop also offers the added benefit of providing shade for the birds in the summertime and shelter from aerial attacks from hawks and flying predators. At the same time, a coop and run should be constructed with gopher wire to protect the hens from land predators. The tight, heavy wire will also work to keep rodents out. Traditional "chicken wire," unfortunately, does not do the trick when it comes to deterring pests.

If you live on a large piece of land, try a mobile coop to rotationally graze your chickens. One way to create a mobile coop is to place a coop atop a trailer that can be pulled by a tractor. Then you can easily move the coop to different areas of your property. This allows you to move the chickens to fields or grass patches that need revitalization; the chickens will leave their nitrogen-rich droppings in your fields, thus fertilizing them, while feasting on ticks and thereby keeping the insect population in check.

Include bedding for the birds to nest, with something as simple as straw. The bedding will catch their droppings, and once cleaned out of the coop, it can be composted in a compost pile. No compost pile? No problem! Reach out to your local trash company and ask if they have a special weekly collection bin for yard waste, sometimes called a "green waste bin." Or put some feelers out for gardeners or people with more land, as they may gladly take the used straw.

If you make your own compost, the nitrogen-rich hen droppings coupled with the carbon of the straw make for amazing soil that works well in garden beds. That means you won't have to buy soil—bagged in plastic that eventually ends up in a landfill or worse, our waterways. You can make exceptional soil right at home! That incredible soil can then be used to nourish seedlings and plant starts of all sorts.

Chickens, if raised properly, can be a small-scale answer to becoming more ecologically minded. People often think that the ecological devastation facing our planet is too great a problem, and their contributions can't make a difference. Any positive change we make for the environment is a step in the right direction, and no change is too small. Because, eventually, all of those small changes add up to something great.

*Franchesca Duval owns and operates Alchemist Farm in
northern California, a humane, plastic-free chicken and quail hatchery.
She can be found at: alchemistfarm.com | Instagram & Facebook @AlchemistFarm*

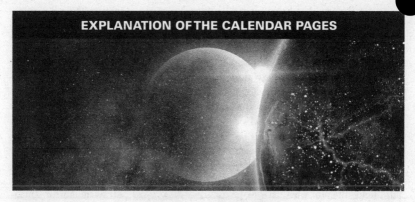

EXPLANATION OF THE CALENDAR PAGES

Times Listed

The astronomical times listed for daily sunrise/sunset, moonrise/moonset, solar noon, length of day, and twilight are based on: northern states 40°N latitude, 75°W longitude (near Philadelphia, PA) and southern states 35°N latitude, 90°W longitude (near Memphis, TN). NOTE: Times listed for the southern states are in Central Time, with adjustments made for Daylight Saving Time.

Adjustments

The times for the rising and setting of the Sun and Moon are calculated for an observer located exactly on one of the standard meridians (in North America: Eastern–75° West; Central–90° West; Mountain–105° West; Pacific–120° West). If your longitude is very close to one of these, then luck is with you, and you can use the printed times for the rising and setting of the Sun and Moon without any correction.

If your longitude is different from one of these standard meridians, you need to add four minutes to the times listed on the Calendar Page for each degree of longitude that you are west of your time zone meridian. Or subtract four minutes for each degree you are east of it. For example, Boston, Massachusetts (longitude 71°) is 4 degrees east of the Eastern Time meridian. So, for Boston, subtract 16 minutes from the times obtained from the Calendar Pages. The result is in Eastern Standard Time or Eastern Daylight Time, depending on the time of year.

The above calculations will yield approximate local times for the rising and setting of the Sun and Moon, but will ignore the less important difference between your latitude and those of the Calendar Pages (35° and 40° North), as well as the character of your local horizon.

Earliest Moonrise/Moonset

Times listed in this column of the Calendar Pages are based on the earliest visible moonset or moonrise of the day. Moonrise and moonset are when the upper limb appears or disappears above/below the horizon. The arrow up means the Moon is rising, and the arrow down means it's setting. There are dates when neither moonrise nor moonset occurs during darkness. These dates are identified with the word "None" on the Calendar Pages.

EXPLANATION OF THE CALENDAR PAGES

Moon's Place

This column shows the astronomical position of the Moon at 7:00 am EST/DST. As the Moon travels in the night sky, in addition to the 12 well-known zodiac constellations, it will also enter 5 other constellations: Auriga (AUR), located to the north of Taurus; Cetus (CET), a large constellation bordering the southern part of Pisces; Ophiuchus (OPH), a large complex constellation whose lower portion reaches into the zodiac immediately adjacent to Scorpius and Sagittarius; Orion (ORI), a constellation that straddles the celestial equator and whose northern extremities border Gemini and Taurus; and Sextants (SXT), a faint and unimpressive star pattern whose northwest corner comes very close to the ecliptic in Leo.

Rise, Set, and Culmination Times for Stars and Planets

As with the rising and setting times of the Sun and Moon, you need to take your longitude into consideration and adjust accordingly. This rule also pertains to the culmination or meridian passage ("mer.") time of a given object for the Moon's southing or meridian passage.

Twilight and Length of Days

Across the calendars, and even with the Sunday Liturgical Calendar, you will find the average length of day and length of astronomical twilight beginning Sunday. These calendars are calculated for 35 and 40 degrees North latitude, based on the Sun being 8.5 degrees below the horizon, which roughly corresponds to the ambient light from a full Moon on a cloudless night.

The "Calendar Pages" are across from our monthly weather predictions (starting on page 130). On these pages, you will find many important celestial events, dates, and times.

HURRICANE TIPS

BEFORE HURRICANE SEASON:

- Develop or review a family hurricane safety plan
- Find out where official shelters are located
- Learn safe routes inland
- Ensure that you have enough nonperishable food and water on hand

IF A HURRICANE WATCH HAS BEEN ISSUED:

- Prepare to cover all windows and doors, preferably with plywood
- Prepare disaster supply kit
- Move lightweight objects inside
- Fuel and service family vehicles
- Have extra cash on hand

IF A HURRICANE WARNING HAS BEEN ISSUED:

- Complete preparation activities
- Follow instructions issued by local officials
- If told to evacuate, do so immediately
- Leave mobile homes
- Notify family living outside the warned area of your plans
- Fill the bathtub and large containers with water for sanitary purposes
- Turn off propane tanks
- Unplug small appliances

DURING A STORM:

- Stay inside
- Stay away from windows and doors (even if boarded)
- Move to small interior room on the first floor

AFTER A STORM:

- Wait until an area is declared safe before returning
- Don't drive into flooded roadways
- Don't allow children to play in flooded areas
- Use flashlights (not candles) for emergency lighting
- Beware of downed power lines that may be electrically charged
- Use telephone only for emergency calls

DISASTER SUPPLY KIT:

- ☐ A 3-day supply of water (1 gallon per person per day)
- ☐ Food that won't spoil (canned and dried goods)
- ☐ Prescription medicines
- ☐ Toiletries
- ☐ First aid kit
- ☐ Battery-powered radio
- ☐ Flashlight, extra batteries
- ☐ Extra set of clothing and shoes for each person
- ☐ One blanket or sleeping bag per person
- ☐ Hand (manual) can opener
- ☐ Special items for infants, elderly, or disabled family members

In addition, have the following readily available and sealed in a moisture-proof package:

☐ Identification ☐ Valuable papers (insurance) ☐ Extra money or a credit card

Source: *National Weather Service and the National Oceanic and Atmospheric Administration*

2021 Atlantic Hurricane Names				
Ana	Elsa	Ida	Mindy	Rose
Bill	Fred	Julian	Nicholas	Sam
Claudette	Grace	Kate	Odette	Teresa
Danny	Henri	Larry	Peter	Victor
				Wanda

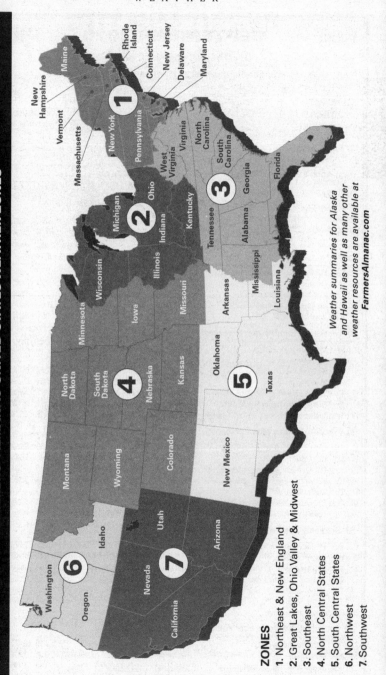

FARMERS' ALMANAC UNITED STATES WEATHER ZONES

Weather summaries for Alaska and Hawaii as well as many other weather resources are available at
FarmersAlmanac.com

ZONES

1. Northeast & New England
2. Great Lakes, Ohio Valley & Midwest
3. Southeast
4. North Central States
5. South Central States
6. Northwest
7. Southwest

SEPTEMBER 2020

9th Month — SEPTEMBER 2020 — **30 Days**

VIRGO
August 22 to
September 21

LIBRA
September 22 to
October 21

NOW AUTUMN'S GOLDEN STORES BEHOLD, WITH FRUIT EACH TREE IS CROWNED;
PEACHES IN SUITS OF RED OR GOLD, EACH TWIG BOWS TOWARD THE GROUND.

MOON'S PHASES
EASTERN DAYLIGHT TIME

○ Full Moon	2nd	1:22 am
◑ Last Quarter	10th	5:26 am
● New Moon	17th	7:00 am
◐ First Quarter	23rd	9:55 pm

Subtract 1 hour for CDT, 2 hours for MDT,
and 3 hours for PDT.

SUN ON MERIDIAN CIVIL TIME

Day	H:MM:SS
1st	13:00:16
8th	12:57:55
15th	12:55:27
22nd	12:52:58
29th	12:50:34

MOON'S PLACE AT 7am ASTRONOMICALLY

			CALENDAR FOR NORTHERN STATES (EDT) 40°N. Lat. 75°W. Long.				CALENDAR FOR SOUTHERN STATES (CDT) 35°N. Lat. 90°W. Long.			
DATE	**ASTRONOMY, HOLIDAYS, AND EVENTS**		**SUN RISES**	**SUN SETS**	**EARLIEST MOONRISE MOONSET**	**MOON'S MERIDIAN PASSAGE**	**SUN RISES**	**SUN SETS**	**EARLIEST MOONRISE MOONSET**	**MOON'S MERIDIAN PASSAGE**
1 Tu	Pullman sleeping car invented, 1859	AQU	6:28	7:31	5:36ă	12:21a	6:33	7:26	5:48ă	12:23a
2 We	Great Fire of London, 1666	AQU	6:29	7:29	8:09p̂	1:07a	6:34	7:25	8:06p̂	1:08a
3 Th	ATM machine 1st used, 1969	AQU	6:30	7:28	8:34p̂	1:50a	6:34	7:23	8:33p̂	1:51a
4 Fr	Los Angeles, CA, founded, 1781	CET	6:31	7:26	8:58p̂	2:31a	6:35	7:22	8:59p̂	2:33a
5 Sa	Jesse James born, 1847	PSC	6:32	7:24	9:21p̂	3:12a	6:36	7:21	9:26p̂	3:13a

36. Fourteenth Sunday after Pentecost — Day's Length: 12h 50m / Astron. Twilight: 1h 21m — Day's Length: 12h 43m / Astron. Twilight: 1h 16m

6 Su	Moon at apogee 2:20am	PSC	6:33	7:23	9:46p̂	3:52a	6:37	7:19	9:53p̂	3:54a
7 Mo	Labor Day	ARI	6:34	7:21	10:13p̂	4:34a	6:37	7:18	10:23p̂	4:36a
8 Tu	Buddy Holly born, 1936	TAU	6:35	7:20	10:43p̂	5:17a	6:38	7:16	10:56p̂	5:19a
9 We	Mars retrograde	TAU	6:36	7:18	11:19p̂	6:03a	6:39	7:15	11:35p̂	6:05a
10 Th	Traditional peak of hurricane season	TAU	6:36	7:16	None	6:52a	6:39	7:13	None	6:54a
11 Fr	Halley's Comet rediscovered, 1909	GEM	6:37	7:15	12:02ă	7:44a	6:40	7:12	12:19ă	7:46a
12 Sa	Jupiter direct	GEM	6:38	7:13	12:52ă	8:38a	6:41	7:11	1:11ă	8:41a

37. Fifteenth Sunday after Pentecost — Day's Length: 12h 32m / Astron. Twilight: 1h 21m — Day's Length: 12h 28m / Astron. Twilight: 1h 15m

13 Su	Willie Mays hit 500th HR, 1965	CAN	6:39	7:11	1:51ă	9:35a	6:42	7:09	2:09ă	9:37a
14 Mo	Holy Cross Day	CAN	6:40	7:10	2:58ă	10:31a	6:42	7:08	3:14ă	10:34a
15 Tu	Darwin reached Galapagos Islands, 1835	LEO	6:41	7:08	4:10ă	11:27a	6:43	7:06	4:23ă	11:30a
16 We	Ember Day; San Felipe hurricane, 1928	LEO	6:42	7:06	5:24ă	12:22p	6:44	7:05	5:35ă	12:24p
17 Th	Citizenship Day	VIR	6:43	7:05	6:40ă	1:16p	6:45	7:03	6:47ă	1:18p
18 Fr	Ember Day; Moon at perigee 9:41am	VIR	6:44	7:03	8:11p̂	2:09p	6:45	7:02	8:14p̂	2:11p
19 Sa	Rosh Hashanah; Ember Day	VIR	6:45	7:01	8:42p̂	3:02p	6:46	7:00	8:49p̂	3:04p

38. Sixteenth Sunday after Pentecost — Day's Length: 12h 14m / Astron. Twilight: 1h 20m — Day's Length: 12h 12m / Astron. Twilight: 1h 15m

20 Su	Dr. Joyce Brothers born, 1928	LIB	6:46	7:00	9:16p̂	3:56p	6:47	6:59	9:27p̂	3:58p
21 Mo	Fast of Gedaliah	LIB	6:47	6:58	9:54p̂	4:52p	6:47	6:58	10:08p̂	4:54p
22 Tu	Autumnal equinox (1st day of fall) 9:31am	OPH	6:48	6:56	10:38p̂	5:48p	6:48	6:56	10:54p̂	5:51p
23 We	Lewis & Clark completed journey, 1806	OPH	6:49	6:55	11:28p̂	6:46p	6:49	6:55	11:46p̂	6:48p
24 Th	Moon, Jupiter best visible in the SW 9:38pm	SAG	6:50	6:53	None	7:43p	6:50	6:53	None	7:45p
25 Fr	Moon, Saturn best visible in the S 10:03pm	SAG	6:51	6:51	12:23ă	8:38p	6:50	6:52	12:42ă	8:40p
26 Sa	Fall Astronomy Day	CAP	6:52	6:50	1:23ă	9:30p	6:51	6:50	1:41ă	9:32p

39. Seventeenth Sunday after Pentecost — Day's Length: 11h 56m / Astron. Twilight: 1h 20m — Day's Length: 11h 57m / Astron. Twilight: 1h 14m

27 Su	Gold Star Mother's Day	CAP	6:53	6:48	2:26ă	10:19p	6:52	6:49	2:41ă	10:21p
28 Mo	Yom Kippur	AQU	6:54	6:47	3:28ă	11:05p	6:53	6:48	3:41ă	11:06p
29 Tu	Michaelmas Day; Saturn direct	AQU	6:55	6:45	4:30ă	11:48p	6:53	6:46	4:40ă	11:50p
30 We	1st Edison hydroelectric plant, 1882	AQU	6:56	6:43	5:30ă	None	6:54	6:45	5:37ă	None

SEPTEMBER 2020 WEATHER FORECAST

ZONE 1 Northeast & New England
1–3: Thunderstorms, then becoming pleasant. **4–7:** Improving weather for Labor Day; scattered showers and thunderstorms, then fair. **8–11:** Clearing, cooler weather. **12–15:** Hurricane threat from Virginia Capes/Delmarva to Cape Cod on to eastern Maine. **16–19:** Fair, then showers. **20–23:** Mostly fair skies developing. **24–27:** Locally heavy showers/thunderstorms. **28–30:** Clear.

ZONE 2 Great Lakes, Ohio Valley & Midwest
1–3: Fair. **4–7:** Showers persist through Labor Day. **8–11:** Severe thunderstorms, tornado possibility. **12–15:** Thunderstorms in Kentucky and Ohio Valley, followed by clearing. **16–19:** Fair, then scattered showers. **20–23:** Mostly fair. **24–27:** Locally heavy showers and thunderstorms from the Great Lakes, points east. **28–30:** Fair/quite cool.

ZONE 3 Southeast
1–3: Thunderstorms clear the Atlantic Coast, then turning fair. **4–7:** Potentially stormy Labor Day weekend; widespread thunderstorms. **8–11:** Fair skies. **12–15:** Thunderstorms from Tennessee Valley and points east. Hurricane threat for Outer Banks of North Carolina. **16–19:** Rain/showers. **20–23:** Mostly fair skies. **24–27:** Showery and thundery. **28–30:** Gradually clearing.

ZONE 4 North Central States
1–3: Fair. **4–7:** Showers through holiday weekend. **8–11:** Severe thunderstorms Rockies, points east. Possible tornado weather for parts of Kansas/Missouri/Iowa. **12–15:** Clearing skies, pleasant. **16–19:** Turning unsettled Rockies and across Plains, then fair. **20–23:** Fair, then scattered showers/thunderstorms over the Rockies. **24–27:** Thunderstorms Colorado; squalls over the Plains. **28–30:** Fair skies, unseasonably chilly.

ZONE 5 South Central States
1–3: Clearing. **4–7:** Mixed bag for Labor Day, windy in New Mexico. Scattered showers Texas and points east, then fair. **8–11:** Severe thunderstorms from Rockies through Plains, tornado weather possible. Tropical storm threat Texas and Louisiana Gulf Coast. **12–15:** Clearing and pleasant. **16–19:** Turning unsettled; showers over Rockies and Plains, then fair. **20–23:** Fair, then scattered showers/thunderstorms. **24–27:** Thunderstorms for Colorado; squalls for Plains. Windy, locally heavy showers New Mexico to Texas. Thunder showers Louisiana, Arkansas. **28–30:** Fair and unseasonably chilly.

ZONE 6 Northwest
1–3: Fair. **4–7:** Showery for holiday weekend. **8–11:** Continued unsettled with a few more showers. **12–15:** Clearing, pleasant. **16–19:** Turning unsettled, showers Washington, Oregon. **20–23:** Fair, followed by scattered showers. **24–27:** More scattered showers. **28–30:** Fair skies and quite cool.

ZONE 7 Southwest
1–3: Fair skies. **4–7:** Showers. Windy conditions Arizona. **8–11:** Mixed clouds and Sun; a few showers and possible thunderstorms. **12–15:** Clearing skies, pleasant. **16–19:** Threatening weather; few showers. **20–23:** Fair, then scattered showers/a few thunderstorms; windy with a few showers for California and Nevada. **24–27:** Thunderstorms Utah, then clearing. Fair weather elsewhere. **28–30:** Fair skies, unseasonably chilly.

OCTOBER 2020

10th Month   **OCTOBER 2020**   **31 Days**

LIBRA
September 22 to
October 21

SCORPIO
October 22 to
November 20

AND NOW THE FROST IS SEEN IN MORN, OVERSPREADING FIELDS WITH WHITE;
THE FARMER GATHERS IN HIS CORN, WITH PLEASURE AND DELIGHT.

MOON'S PHASES EASTERN DAYLIGHT TIME		
○ Full Moon	1st	5:05 pm
◑ Last Quarter	9th	8:40 pm
● New Moon	16th	3:31 pm
◐ First Quarter	23rd	9:23 am
○ Full Moon	31st	10:49 am

Subtract 1 hour for CDT, 2 hours for MDT, and 3 hours for PDT.

SUN ON MERIDIAN CIVIL TIME	
Day	H:MM:SS
1st	12:49:55
8th	12:47:50
15th	12:46:07
22nd	12:44:52
29th	12:44:10

CALENDAR FOR NORTHERN STATES (EDT) — 40°N. Lat. 75°W. Long.

CALENDAR FOR SOUTHERN STATES (CDT) — 35°N. Lat. 90°W. Long.

DATE		ASTRONOMY, HOLIDAYS, AND EVENTS	MOON'S PLACE AT 7am ASTRONOMICALLY	SUN RISES	SUN SETS	EARLIEST MOONRISE MOONSET	MOON'S MERIDIAN PASSAGE	SUN RISES	SUN SETS	EARLIEST MOONRISE MOONSET	MOON'S MERIDIAN PASSAGE
1	Th	1st Mississippi River steamboat, 1911	PSC	6:57	6:42	6:29ă	12:30a	6:55	6:43	6:33ă	12:31a
2	Fr	Groucho Marx born, 1890	CET	6:58	6:40	7:25p̄	1:10a	6:56	6:42	7:29p̄	1:12a
3	Sa	Succot; Moon at apogee 1:07pm	PSC	6:59	6:38	7:49p̄	1:51a	6:56	6:41	7:55p̄	1:52a
40. Eighteenth Sunday after Pentecost				Day's Length: 11h 37m Astron. Twilight: 1h 20m				Day's Length: 11h 42m Astron. Twilight: 1h 15m			
4	Su	1st volunteer fire department, 1648	ARI	7:00	6:37	8:15p̄	2:32a	6:57	6:39	8:24p̄	2:34a
5	Mo	Ray Kroc born, 1902	ARI	7:01	6:35	8:44p̄	3:14a	6:58	6:38	8:56p̄	3:16a
6	Tu	Jane Eyre 1st published in London, 1847	TAU	7:02	6:34	9:17p̄	3:59a	6:59	6:36	9:32p̄	4:01a
7	We	Desmond Tutu born, 1931	TAU	7:03	6:32	9:56p̄	4:46a	7:00	6:35	10:13p̄	4:48a
8	Th	Cats opened on Broadway, 1982	TAU	7:04	6:31	10:43p̄	5:36a	7:00	6:34	11:01p̄	5:38a
9	Fr	Fire Prevention Day	GEM	7:05	6:29	11:37p̄	6:29a	7:01	6:32	11:55p̄	6:31a
10	Sa	U.S. Naval Academy est., 1845	GEM	7:06	6:27	None	7:23a	7:02	6:31	None	7:25a
41. Nineteenth Sunday after Pentecost				Day's Length: 11h 19m Astron. Twilight: 1h 20m				Day's Length: 11h 27m Astron. Twilight: 1h 15m			
11	Su	Simchat Torah	CAN	7:07	6:26	12:38ă	8:18a	7:03	6:30	12:56ă	8:20a
12	Mo	**Columbus Day**	LEO	7:08	6:24	1:46ă	9:12a	7:04	6:28	2:01ă	9:14a
13	Tu	Mercury retrograde; Mars in opposition	LEO	7:09	6:23	2:58ă	10:06a	7:04	6:27	3:10ă	10:08a
14	We	George Eastman patented photo film, 1884	LEO	7:10	6:21	4:12ă	10:59a	7:05	6:26	4:20ă	11:02a
15	Th	Virgil born, 70 BC	VIR	7:11	6:20	5:27ă	11:52a	7:06	6:25	5:32ă	11:55a
16	Fr	Moon at perigee 7:39pm	VIR	7:12	6:18	6:43ă	12:46p	7:07	6:23	6:45ă	12:48p
17	Sa	Pope John Paul I born, 1912	VIR	7:13	6:17	7:10p̄	1:40p	7:08	6:22	7:19p̄	1:43p
42. Twentieth Sunday after Pentecost				Day's Length: 11h 02m Astron. Twilight: 1h 21m				Day's Length: 11h 12m Astron. Twilight: 1h 15m			
18	Su	Saturn in eastern quadrature	LIB	7:14	6:16	7:47p̄	2:37p	7:09	6:21	8:00p̄	2:39p
19	Mo	John Jay, 1st U.S. Chief Justice, 1789	SCO	7:15	6:14	8:30p̄	3:35p	7:10	6:20	8:45p̄	3:38p
20	Tu	John Dewey born, 1859	OPH	7:16	6:13	9:18p̄	4:35p	7:10	6:18	9:36p̄	4:38p
21	We	Guggenheim Museum opened, 1959	SAG	7:17	6:11	10:14p̄	5:34p	7:11	6:17	10:33p̄	5:37p
22	Th	Moon, Jupiter, Saturn best visible SW 8:36pm	SAG	7:18	6:10	11:14p̄	6:32p	7:12	6:16	11:33p̄	6:34p
23	Fr	1st use of aircraft in war, 1911	CAP	7:19	6:09	None	7:26p	7:13	6:15	None	7:28p
24	Sa	United Nations Day; United Nations est., 1945	CAP	7:20	6:07	12:18ă	8:16p	7:14	6:14	12:34ă	8:19p
43. Twenty-first Sunday after Pentecost				Day's Length: 10h 44m Astron. Twilight: 1h 22m				Day's Length: 10h 58m Astron. Twilight: 1h 16m			
25	Su	Mercury in inferior conjunction	CAP	7:22	6:06	1:21ă	9:03p	7:15	6:13	1:35ă	9:05p
26	Mo	1st electric generator, Hoover Dam, 1936	AQU	7:23	6:05	2:23ă	9:47p	7:16	6:12	2:34ă	9:49p
27	Tu	Theodore Roosevelt born, 1858	AQU	7:24	6:03	3:24ă	10:29p	7:17	6:10	3:32ă	10:31p
28	We	Harvard University founded, 1636	PSC	7:25	6:02	4:23ă	11:10p	7:18	6:09	4:28ă	11:11p
29	Th	Statue of Liberty dedicated, 1886	CET	7:26	6:01	5:21ă	11:50p	7:19	6:08	5:23ă	11:52p
30	Fr	Moon at apogee 2:28pm	PSC	7:27	6:00	6:19ă	None	7:19	6:07	6:18ă	None
31	Sa	Halloween; 1st All Hallows' Eve, 834	CET	7:28	5:58	7:18ă	12:31a	7:20	6:06	7:14ă	12:32a

OCTOBER 2020 WEATHER FORECAST

ZONE 1 Northeast & New England

1–3: Fair, then scattered rain showers. **4–7:** Fair/pleasant, some unseasonably cold mornings. **8–11:** Heavy showers and gusty thunderstorms, followed by clearing, cool weather. **12–15:** Pleasant weather returns. **16–19:** Showers, then clearing. **20–23:** Rainy/milder. **24–27:** Thunderstorms, then becoming clear. **28–31:** Fair skies, followed by showers.

ZONE 2 Great Lakes, Ohio Valley & Midwest

1–3: Gusty showers. **4–7:** Fair/pleasant, followed by increasingly cloudy skies. **8–11:** Heavy showers/thunderstorms. **12–15:** Partly sunny, pleasant. **16–19:** Showers Great Lakes and points east. **20–23:** Gusty winds, showers. **24–27:** Clearing and colder. **28–31:** Fair, then showers Michigan/Ohio, points east.

ZONE 3 Southeast

1–3: Fair, then turning unsettled. **4–7:** Pleasant. **8–11:** Heavy rains, followed by clearing and cool conditions. **12–15:** Pleasant weather. **16–19:** Cold rain, then fair. **20–23:** Pleasant, then rain along the Gulf Coast. **24–27:** Clearing, quite cool. **28–31:** Fair skies.

ZONE 4 North Central States

1–3: Light rain, mixed with snow over mountains of Montana; gusty winds and showers across Plains. **4–7:** Fair, then stormy, rainy Rockies; rain showers/wet flurries Plains to Dakotas and Nebraska. **8–11:** Fair, chilly. **12–15:** Milder, then showers, wet flurries for the Rockies; showers across Plains. **16–19:** Mostly fair. **20–23:** Unsettled Rockies, Plains. **24–27:** Clearing and colder. **28–31:** Wet Rockies/Plains, then turning fair.

ZONE 5 South Central States

1–3: Gusty winds, showery. **4–7:** Fair, then turning stormy, showers. **8–11:** Fair and chilly. **12–15:** Milder, followed by showers. **16–19:** Mostly fair. **20–23:** Unsettled, Rockies and Plains. **24–27:** Clearing colder. **28–31:** Wet weather, followed by clearing skies.

ZONE 6 Northwest

1–3: Light rain, mixed with snow over the mountains of Idaho. **4–7:** Fair, then turning stormy. **8–11:** Fair and cool. **12–15:** Milder, then showers. **16–19:** Mostly fair weather. **20–23:** Unsettled from the Pacific Coast, spreading east. **24–27:** Clearing/chilly. **28–31:** Unsettled; showers for Washington and Oregon.

ZONE 7 Southwest

1–3: Unsettled conditions. **4–7:** Gusty winds and showery. **8–11:** Fair/chilly. **12–15:** Milder, then showers. **16–19:** Mostly fair skies. **20–23:** Unsettled from West Coast, points east. **24–27:** Clearing and turning colder. **28–31:** Unsettled and showery.

NOVEMBER 2020

11th Month — 30 Days

SCORPIO
October 22 to
November 20

SAGITTARIUS
November 21 to
December 20

TIME ON HIS WING FAST HASTES AWAY, AND CHILLS EACH WARM SUCCEED;
TO CAPRICORN SOL HASTES EACH DAY, SO NIGHTS THE DAY EXCEED.

MOON'S PHASES
EASTERN STANDARD TIME

☽ Last Quarter	8th	8:46 am
● New Moon	15th	12:07 am
☾ First Quarter	21st	11:45 pm
○ Full Moon	30th	4:30 am

SUN ON MERIDIAN
CIVIL TIME

Day	H:MM:SS
1st	11:44:03
8th	11:44:16
15th	11:45:11
22nd	11:46:47
29th	11:49:01

Subtract 1 hour for CST, 2 hours for MST, and 3 hours for PST.

MOON'S PLACE AT 7am ASTRONOMICALLY

CALENDAR FOR
NORTHERN STATES
(EST)
40°N. Lat.
75°W. Long.

CALENDAR FOR
SOUTHERN STATES
(CST)
35°N. Lat.
90°W. Long.

DATE	ASTRONOMY, HOLIDAYS, AND EVENTS		SUN RISES	SUN SETS	EARLIEST MOONRISE MOONSET	MOON'S MERIDIAN PASSAGE	SUN RISES	SUN SETS	EARLIEST MOONRISE MOONSET	MOON'S MERIDIAN PASSAGE
44. Twenty-second Sunday after Pentecost			Day's Length: 10h 28m — Astron. Twilight: 1h 23m				Day's Length: 10h 44m — Astron. Twilight: 1h 17m			
1	Su	Daylight Saving Time ends; All Saints' Day	ARI	6:29	4:57	5:46p	1:13a	6:21	5:05	5:57p	1:15a
2	Mo	All Souls' Day; Daniel Boone born, 1734	TAU	6:31	4:56	6:18p	12:57a	6:22	5:04	6:32p	12:59a
3	Tu	**Election Day;** Mercury direct	TAU	6:32	4:55	6:55p	1:43a	6:23	5:04	7:11p	1:45a
4	We	First female US Anglican bishop, 2006	TAU	6:33	4:54	7:38p	2:33a	6:24	5:03	7:56p	2:35a
5	Th	Guy Fawkes arrested, 1605	GEM	6:34	4:53	8:29p	3:24a	6:25	5:02	8:48p	3:26a
6	Fr	Jacob Schick patented electric shaver, 1923	GEM	6:35	4:52	9:27p	4:17a	6:26	5:01	9:45p	4:19a
7	Sa	1st airfreight shipment, 1910	CAN	6:36	4:51	10:31p	5:10a	6:27	5:00	10:47p	5:12a
45. Twenty-third Sunday after Pentecost			Day's Length: 10h 12m — Astron. Twilight: 1h 24m				Day's Length: 10h 31m — Astron. Twilight: 1h 18m			
8	Su	X-Ray Discovery Day, 1895	CAN	6:37	4:50	11:39p	6:03a	6:28	4:59	11:53p	6:05a
9	Mo	*Mayflower* spotted land, 1620	LEO	6:39	4:49	None	6:56a	6:29	4:58	None	6:58a
10	Tu	Wreck of *Edmund Fitzgerald*, 1975	LEO	6:40	4:48	12:49â	7:47a	6:30	4:58	1:00â	7:49a
11	We	**Veterans Day**	VIR	6:41	4:47	2:01â	8:38a	6:31	4:57	2:08â	8:40a
12	Th	Ellis Island closed, 1954	VIR	6:42	4:46	3:15â	9:29a	6:32	4:56	3:18â	9:32a
13	Fr	Mars direct	VIR	6:43	4:45	4:31â	10:22a	6:33	4:56	4:30â	10:25a
14	Sa	Moon at perigee 6:36am	LIB	6:44	4:44	5:48â	11:18a	6:34	4:55	5:44â	11:20a
46. Twenty-fourth Sunday after Pentecost			Day's Length: 9h 58m — Astron. Twilight: 1h 25m				Day's Length: 10h 20m — Astron. Twilight: 1h 19m			
15	Su	1st modern Olympics, 1859	LIB	6:45	4:44	5:18p	12:16p	6:35	4:54	5:32p	12:18p
16	Mo	Oklahoma admitted as 46th state, 1907	OPH	6:47	4:43	6:04p	1:16p	6:36	4:54	6:21p	1:19p
17	Tu	1st steamship through Panama Canal, 1913	SAG	6:48	4:42	6:58p	2:18p	6:37	4:53	7:17p	2:21p
18	We	Moon, Jupiter, Saturn visible SW 6:20pm	SAG	6:49	4:41	7:59p	3:19p	6:38	4:53	8:18p	3:21p
19	Th	Gettysburg Address, 1863	SAG	6:50	4:41	9:03p	4:16p	6:39	4:52	9:21p	4:19p
20	Fr	1st commercial teletype service, 1931	CAP	6:51	4:40	10:09p	5:10p	6:40	4:52	10:24p	5:12p
21	Sa	Mayflower Compact signed, 1620	CAP	6:52	4:39	11:13p	5:59p	6:41	4:51	11:25p	6:01p
47. Christ the King Sunday			Day's Length: 9h 46m — Astron. Twilight: 1h 26m				Day's Length: 10h 09m — Astron. Twilight: 1h 20m			
22	Su	President JFK assassinated, 1963	AQU	6:53	4:39	None	6:45p	6:42	4:51	None	6:47p
23	Mo	1st jukebox, 1889	AQU	6:54	4:38	12:15â	7:28p	6:42	4:50	12:24â	7:30p
24	Tu	Darwin's *Origin of Species* published, 1859	PSC	6:56	4:38	1:15â	8:09p	6:43	4:50	1:21â	8:10p
25	We	Moon, Mars best visible in the SW 9:49pm	CET	6:57	4:37	2:14â	8:49p	6:44	4:50	2:17â	8:51p
26	Th	**Thanksgiving Day;** Moon at apogee 7:18pm	PSC	6:58	4:37	3:12â	9:29p	6:45	4:49	3:12â	9:31p
27	Fr	Anders Celsius born, 1701	CET	6:59	4:37	4:10â	10:11p	6:46	4:49	4:07â	10:13p
28	Sa	Grand Ole Opry made radio debut, 1925	ARI	7:00	4:36	5:09â	10:54p	6:47	4:49	5:03â	10:56p
48. First Sunday of Advent			Day's Length: 9h 35m — Astron. Twilight: 1h 28m				Day's Length: 10h 01m — Astron. Twilight: 1h 21m			
29	Su	Central New England's worst ice storm, 1921	TAU	7:01	4:36	6:09â	11:40p	6:48	4:49	6:01â	11:42p
30	Mo	Hurricane season ends; Lunar eclipse 4:43am	TAU	7:02	4:36	4:54p	None	6:49	4:49	5:10p	None

NOVEMBER 2020 WEATHER FORECAST

ZONE 1 Northeast & New England

1–3: Fair and cold. Ideal conditions for runners in NYC Marathon. **4–7:** Stormy, heavy rains, perhaps mixed with sleet, wet snow in the mountains. **8–11:** Fair. **12–15:** Rain, then clearing. **16–19:** Increasingly cloudy with rain and (over mountains) snow. **20–23:** More rain and wet snow, then clearing/colder. **24–27:** Unsettled, light snow, flurries; clearing in time for Thanksgiving. Macy's parade in NYC goes off without a hitch. **28–30:** Mostly fair.

ZONE 2 Great Lakes, Ohio Valley & Midwest

1–3: Rain, wet snow for Great Lakes. **4–7:** Stormy for nation's midsection, which sweeps heavy precipitation up through the Ohio Valley, then fair and cold. **8–11:** Increasingly cloudy but pleasant. **12–15:** Some rain for Great Lakes, then fair. **16–19:** Storm emerging out of the southwest states dumps snow and rain up through Great Lakes. **20–23:** Fair and cold. **24–27:** Light snow through Great Lakes and Ohio Valley, followed by fair skies for Thanksgiving. **28–30:** Fair, then stormy.

ZONE 3 Southeast

1–3: Fair and pleasant. **4–7:** Unsettled, showery/thundery. **8–11:** Wet weather continues. **12–15:** Rain, then clearing. **16–19:** Breezy/pleasant. **20–23:** Rainy skies, then fair, colder. **24–27:** Quick changes during Thanksgiving holiday: fair, then rain, then quickly followed by clearing. **28–30:** Fair/milder.

ZONE 4 North Central States

1–3: Turning stormy Colorado, Plains. **4–7:** Stormy Missouri, then fair/cold. Clearing, cold elsewhere. **8–11:** Pleasant, then unsettled with strong winds, heavy precipitation for Rockies/Plains. Some wet snow for parts of Colorado, Kansas. **12–15:** Fair. **16–19:** Windy with snow for Colorado and Plains. **20–23:** Fair, cold. **24–27:** Light snow Rockies/Plains, points east for Thanksgiving. **28–30:** Fair, then turning stormy.

ZONE 5 South Central States

1–3: Stormy Southern Plains to Texas. **4–7:** Stormy Arkansas, then fair, cold. Clearing/cold elsewhere. **8–11:** Turning unsettled with gusty winds, heavy precipitation; some wet snow northern New Mexico, Texas/Oklahoma. **12–15:** Rain Texas and points east, followed by clearing. Fair elsewhere. **16–19:** Blustery with snow Plains States. **20–23:** Fair, cold. **24–27:** Generally unsettled for Thanksgiving; light snow Rockies, Plains. Fair, then rain for Texas. **28–30:** Fair, then stormy.

ZONE 6 Northwest

1–3: Mixed Sun, clouds; pleasant. **4–7:** Clearing, chilly. **8–11:** Pleasant, then unsettled. **12–15:** Fair. **16–19:** Blustery, with showers Washington and Oregon. **20–23:** Fair, chilly. **24–27:** Unsettled/showery for Thanksgiving time. **28–30:** Fair at first, then turning stormy.

ZONE 7 Southwest

1–3: Pleasant weather, except stormy for Utah. **4–7:** Clearing and cold. **8–11:** Pleasant, then unsettled; gusty winds and precipitation. Wet snow Nevada, Utah, and parts of Arizona. **12–15:** Fair skies. **16–19:** Gusty winds with heavy precipitation; snow for Utah. **20–23:** Fair, cold. **24–27:** Light snow Nevada, Utah, and parts of Arizona, then fair, cold. **28–30:** Fair, then stormy; snowstorm for Utah; showers and thunderstorms for Arizona.

DECEMBER 2020

12th Month | **31 Days**

SAGITTARIUS
November 21 to
December 20

CAPRICORN
December 21 to
January 18

COLD BLOWS THE WIND, THE FROZEN RAIN AND FLEECY SNOW DESCEND;
FOR, FREEZING WINTER'S COME AGAIN, AND SO THE YEAR DOES END.

MOON'S PHASES — EASTERN STANDARD TIME

◗ Last Quarter 7th 7:37 pm
● New Moon 14th 11:17 am
◑ First Quarter 21st 6:41 pm
○ Full Moon 29th 10:28 pm

Subtract 1 hour for CST, 2 hours for MST, and 3 hours for PST.

SUN ON MERIDIAN CIVIL TIME

Day	H:MM:SS
1st	11:49:45
8th	11:52:39
15th	11:55:56
22nd	11:59:24
29th	12:02:50

MOON'S PLACE AT 7am ASTRONOMICALLY

CALENDAR FOR NORTHERN STATES (EST) 40°N. Lat. 75°W. Long.

CALENDAR FOR SOUTHERN STATES (CST) 35°N. Lat. 90°W. Long.

DATE		ASTRONOMY, HOLIDAYS, AND EVENTS		SUN RISES	SUN SETS	EARLIEST MOONRISE MOONSET	MOON'S MERIDIAN PASSAGE	SUN RISES	SUN SETS	EARLIEST MOONRISE MOONSET	MOON'S MERIDIAN PASSAGE
1	Tu	Rosa Parks arrested, 1955	TAU	7:03	4:35	5:36p̱	12:29a	6:50	4:49	5:54p̱	12:31a
2	We	La Guardia Airport opened, 1939	GEM	7:04	4:35	6:25p̱	1:20a	6:51	4:48	6:44p̱	1:22a
3	Th	Alka Seltzer sold for 1st time, 1931	GEM	7:05	4:35	7:21p̱	2:13a	6:52	4:48	7:40p̱	2:15a
4	Fr	Edison invented phonograph, 1877	CAN	7:06	4:35	8:23p̱	3:06a	6:52	4:48	8:40p̱	3:09a
5	Sa	Walt Disney born, 1901	CAN	7:07	4:35	9:29p̱	3:59a	6:53	4:48	9:44p̱	4:02a

49. Second Sunday of Advent — Day's Length: 9h 27m / Astron. Twilight: 1h 28m — Day's Length: 9h 54m / Astron. Twilight: 1h 28m

DATE		ASTRONOMY, HOLIDAYS, AND EVENTS		SUN RISES	SUN SETS	EARLIEST MOONRISE MOONSET	MOON'S MERIDIAN PASSAGE	SUN RISES	SUN SETS	EARLIEST MOONRISE MOONSET	MOON'S MERIDIAN PASSAGE
6	Su	13th Amendment ratified, 1865	LEO	7:08	4:35	10:37p̱	4:51a	6:54	4:48	10:49p̱	4:53a
7	Mo	Pearl Harbor Day; Earliest sunset of 2020	LEO	7:08	4:35	11:46p̱	5:42a	6:55	4:48	11:55p̱	5:44a
8	Tu	Conception B.V.M.; Eli Whitney born, 1765	VIR	7:09	4:35	None	6:31a	6:56	4:49	None	6:33a
9	We	1st YMCA in North America, 1851	VIR	7:10	4:35	12:57â	7:20a	6:56	4:49	1:01â	7:22a
10	Th	Emily Dickinson born, 1830	VIR	7:11	4:35	2:08â	8:10a	6:57	4:49	2:09â	8:12a
11	Fr	Chanukah	LIB	7:12	4:35	3:22â	9:02a	6:58	4:49	3:19â	9:04a
12	Sa	Moon at perigee 3:34pm	LIB	7:13	4:35	4:38â	9:57a	6:59	4:49	4:31â	9:59a

50. Third Sunday of Advent — Day's Length: 9h 22m / Astron. Twilight: 1h 29m — Day's Length: 9h 50m / Astron. Twilight: 1h 22m

DATE		ASTRONOMY, HOLIDAYS, AND EVENTS		SUN RISES	SUN SETS	EARLIEST MOONRISE MOONSET	MOON'S MERIDIAN PASSAGE	SUN RISES	SUN SETS	EARLIEST MOONRISE MOONSET	MOON'S MERIDIAN PASSAGE
13	Su	Federal Reserve System est., 1913	SCO	7:13	4:36	5:54â	10:55a	6:59	4:50	5:45â	10:58a
14	Mo	Total central solar eclipse 11:13am (S.Amer.)	OPH	7:14	4:36	7:10â	11:57a	7:00	4:50	6:57â	11:59a
15	Tu	Prohibition ended, 1933	SAG	7:15	4:36	5:38p̱	12:59p	7:01	4:50	5:57p̱	1:01p
16	We	Ember Day	SAG	7:15	4:36	6:42p̱	2:00p	7:01	4:51	7:01p̱	2:02p
17	Th	FCC approved RCA's color TV specs, 1953	CAP	7:16	4:37	7:50p̱	2:57p	7:02	4:51	8:06p̱	2:59p
18	Fr	Ember Day; 1st U.S. Thanksgiving, 1777	CAP	7:17	4:37	8:57p̱	3:50p	7:03	4:51	9:11p̱	3:52p
19	Sa	Ember Day; Mercury in superior conjunction	AQU	7:17	4:38	10:02p̱	4:38p	7:03	4:52	10:12p̱	4:40p

51. Fourth Sunday of Advent — Day's Length: 9h 20m / Astron. Twilight: 1h 29m — Day's Length: 9h 49m / Astron. Twilight: 1h 22m

DATE		ASTRONOMY, HOLIDAYS, AND EVENTS		SUN RISES	SUN SETS	EARLIEST MOONRISE MOONSET	MOON'S MERIDIAN PASSAGE	SUN RISES	SUN SETS	EARLIEST MOONRISE MOONSET	MOON'S MERIDIAN PASSAGE
20	Su	Jupiter, Saturn best visible in SW 5:49pm	AQU	7:18	4:38	11:04p̱	5:23p	7:04	4:52	11:11p̱	5:25p
21	Mo	Winter solstice (1st day of winter) 5:02am	AQU	7:18	4:39	None	6:05p	7:04	4:53	None	6:07p
22	Tu	Jupiter, Saturn best visible in SW 5:47pm	CET	7:19	4:39	12:04â	6:46p	7:05	4:53	12:08â	6:48p
23	We	NASA approved to continue *Voyager 2*, 1981	CET	7:19	4:40	1:02â	7:26p	7:05	4:54	1:03â	7:28p
24	Th	Moon at apogee 11:26am	PSC	7:20	4:40	2:00â	8:07p	7:05	4:54	1:59â	8:09p
25	Fr	**Christmas Day**	ARI	7:20	4:41	2:59â	8:50p	7:06	4:55	2:54â	8:52p
26	Sa	Washington crossed the Delaware, 1776	TAU	7:20	4:42	3:59â	9:35p	7:06	4:56	3:51â	9:37p

52. First Sunday after Christmas — Day's Length: 9h 22m / Astron. Twilight: 1h 29m — Day's Length: 9h 50m / Astron. Twilight: 1h 22m

DATE		ASTRONOMY, HOLIDAYS, AND EVENTS		SUN RISES	SUN SETS	EARLIEST MOONRISE MOONSET	MOON'S MERIDIAN PASSAGE	SUN RISES	SUN SETS	EARLIEST MOONRISE MOONSET	MOON'S MERIDIAN PASSAGE
27	Su	*Howdy Doody* made TV debut, 1947	TAU	7:21	4:42	4:59â	10:23p	7:07	4:56	4:49â	10:25p
28	Mo	Woodrow Wilson born, 1856	TAU	7:21	4:43	6:00â	11:13p	7:07	4:57	5:48â	11:16p
29	Tu	Charles Goodyear born, 1800	TAU	7:21	4:44	6:59â	None	7:07	4:58	6:45â	None
30	We	Rudyard Kipling born, 1865	GEM	7:21	4:44	5:14p̱	12:07a	7:07	4:58	5:32p̱	12:09a
31	Th	New Year's Eve	GEM	7:22	4:45	6:15p̱	1:01a	7:08	4:59	6:33p̱	1:03a

DECEMBER 2020 WEATHER FORECAST

ZONE 1 Northeast & New England

1–3: Snow/rain. **4–7:** Mostly fair, cold. **8–11:** Light snow New England; showers Mid-Atlantic States, then clearing. **12–15:** Major East Coast storm. **16–19:** Blustery and cold, scattered flurries. **20–23:** Heavy rains near the coastal plains; ice/snow interior. **24–27:** Fair, cold Christmas. **28–31:** Strong weather front from west brings gusty winds and a wide variety of precipitation to close out the year.

ZONE 2 Great Lakes, Ohio Valley & Midwest

1–3: Snow Great Lakes area, with accumulations of 2-4". **4–7:** Fair/cold. **8–11:** Light snow, then turning fair. **12–15:** Stormy. **16–19:** Dry and turning colder. **20–23:** Light snow east through Ohio Valley, then becoming fair. **24–27:** Increasingly cloudy skies for Christmas. **28–31:** Intense Midwest storm delivers heavy wind, snow/mixed precipitation as 2020 comes to a close.

ZONE 3 Southeast

1–3: Rainy; some wet snow mixes in over higher terrain of Tennessee. **4–7:** Fair, cold. **8–11:** Cold showers, then clearing. **12–15:** Rainy. **16–19:** Rains clear, then fair, cold, with frosts to Florida. **20–23:** Rain/showers, then fair, colder. **24–27:** Fair and unseasonably cold Yuletide; frosts down to Gulf Coast. **28–31:** Windy and rainy South; wintry mix for the mountains of the Virginias, Carolinas, and Tennessee as the year winds down.

ZONE 4 North Central States

1–3: Big storm clears Dakotas/Nebraska area. **4–7:** Fair at first, then unsettled; wet for Rockies, Plains. **8–11:** Clearing skies Plains. **12–15:** Stormy Rockies, across Plains. **16–19:** Colder weather. **20–23:** Some snow or flurries. **24–27:** Fair, then stormy with heavy snow over Rockies, Plains. **28–31:** Clearing skies as we make the transition to 2021.

ZONE 5 South Central States

1–3: Gradually clearing skies. **4–7:** Fair at first, then unsettled with showers; wet for Rockies and Plains. **8–11:** Fair skies. **12–15:** Stormy in Rockies, across Plains; rain in Texas. **16–19:** Colder temperatures. **20–23:** Some showers of rain or wet snow. **24–27:** Fair, then stormy. **28–31:** Clearing skies Rockies, points east as we say goodbye to 2020.

ZONE 6 Northwest

1–3: Fair skies. **4–7:** Fair at first, then unsettled with showers. **8–11:** Clearing skies. **12–15:** Changeable, sun/clouds, risk of a passing shower. **16–19:** Chilly and dry. **20–23:** Showers Washington, Oregon. **24–27:** Very unsettled. **28–31:** Clearing as we ring out the old year and usher in the new.

ZONE 7 Southwest

1–3: Fair skies. **4–7:** Fair at first, then unsettled with showers Pacific Coast. **8–11:** Fair skies for California, points east. **12–15:** Milder under threatening skies. **16–19:** Colder weather moves in. **20–23:** Rain and (over mountainous terrain) snow, then clearing. **24–27:** Fair, then becoming very unsettled. **28–31:** Clearing weather moves in as we close the books on 2020.

JANUARY 2021

1st Month · 31 Days

CAPRICORN
December 21 to
January 18

AQUARIUS
January 19 to
February 17

NOW DREARY WINTER'S PIERCING COLD, FLOATS ON THE NORTHERN GALE,
AND TREES, THOUGH GREEN, LOOK DRY AND OLD; SNOW COVERS HILL AND DALE.

MOON'S PHASES
EASTERN STANDARD TIME

◑ Last Quarter	6th	4:37 am
● New Moon	13th	12:00 am
◐ First Quarter	20th	4:02 pm
○ Full Moon	28th	2:16 pm

Subtract 1 hour for CST, 2 hours for MST,
and 3 hours for PST.

SUN ON MERIDIAN
CIVIL TIME

Day	H:MM:SS
1st	12:04:16
8th	12:07:22
15th	12:10:04
22nd	12:12:11
29th	12:13:40

DATE	ASTRONOMY, HOLIDAYS, AND EVENTS	MOON'S PLACE AT 7am ASTRONOMICALLY	CALENDAR FOR NORTHERN STATES (EST) 40°N. Lat. 75°W. Long.				CALENDAR FOR SOUTHERN STATES (CST) 35°N. Lat. 90°W. Long.			
			SUN RISES	SUN SETS	EARLIEST MOONRISE MOONSET	MOON'S MERIDIAN PASSAGE	SUN RISES	SUN SETS	EARLIEST MOONRISE MOONSET	MOON'S MERIDIAN PASSAGE
1 Fr	**New Year's Day**	CAN	7:22	4:46	7:21p̄	1:55a	7:08	5:00	7:36p̄	1:57a
2 Sa	1st wire suspension bridge, 1842	LEO	7:22	4:47	8:29p̄	2:48a	7:08	5:01	8:42p̄	2:50a
53. Epiphany Sunday			Day's Length: 9h 26m Astron. Twilight: 1h 29m				Day's Length: 9h 53m Astron. Twilight: 1h 22m			
3 Su	J.R.R. Tolkien born, 1892	LEO	7:22	4:48	9:38p̄	3:39a	7:08	5:01	9:47p̄	3:41a
4 Mo	Latest sunrise of 2021	LEO	7:22	4:49	10:47p̄	4:29a	7:08	5:02	10:53p̄	4:31a
5 Tu	Golden Gate Bridge construction began, 1933	VIR	7:22	4:50	11:57p̄	5:17a	7:08	5:03	11:59p̄	5:19a
6 We	Epiphany	VIR	7:22	4:51	None	6:05a	7:08	5:04	None	6:07a
7 Th	Fire destroyed Jamestown, VA, 1608	VIR	7:22	4:52	1:08â	6:55a	7:08	5:05	1:06â	6:57a
8 Fr	Battle of New Orleans, 1815	LIB	7:21	4:52	2:20â	7:47a	7:08	5:06	2:15â	7:49a
9 Sa	Moon at perigee 10:27am	LIB	7:21	4:53	3:34â	8:42a	7:08	5:07	3:25â	8:44a
1. First Sunday after Epiphany			Day's Length: 9h 33m Astron. Twilight: 1h 28m				Day's Length: 9h 59m Astron. Twilight: 1h 21m			
10 Su	Baptism of Jesus	OPH	7:21	4:55	4:47â	9:40a	7:08	5:08	4:36â	9:42a
11 Mo	Moon, Venus best visible in the SE 6:46am	SAG	7:21	4:56	5:58â	10:40a	7:08	5:08	5:45â	10:43a
12 Tu	1st woman elected to U.S. Senate, 1932	SAG	7:21	4:57	7:02â	11:41a	7:08	5:09	6:48â	11:44a
13 We	1st appearance of Mickey Mouse, 1930	SAG	7:20	4:58	5:28p̄	12:40p	7:08	5:10	5:46p̄	12:43p
14 Th	Hal Roach born, 1892	CAP	7:20	4:59	6:36p̄	1:36p	7:07	5:11	6:51p̄	1:38p
15 Fr	Donkey chosen for Democratic Party, 1870	CAP	7:20	5:00	7:43p̄	2:28p	7:07	5:12	7:56p̄	2:30p
16 Sa	U.S. ratifies 18th Amendment, 1919	AQU	7:19	5:01	8:48p̄	3:15p	7:07	5:13	8:57p̄	3:17p
2. Second Sunday after Epiphany			Day's Length: 9h 43m Astron. Twilight: 1h 27m				Day's Length: 10h 08m Astron. Twilight: 1h 08m			
17 Su	Benjamin Franklin born, 1706	AQU	7:19	5:02	9:50p̄	3:59p	7:07	5:14	9:56p̄	4:01p
18 Mo	**MLK Jr. Birthday (obs.)**	PSC	7:18	5:03	10:50p̄	4:41p	7:06	5:15	10:53p̄	4:43p
19 Tu	Edgar Allen Poe born, 1809	CET	7:18	5:04	11:49p̄	5:22p	7:06	5:16	11:48p̄	5:23p
20 We	Edwin "Buzz" Aldrin born, 1930	PSC	7:17	5:06	None	6:03p	7:05	5:17	None	6:04p
21 Th	Moon at apogee 8:10am	CET	7:17	5:07	12:47â	6:44p	7:05	5:18	12:44â	6:46p
22 Fr	Sir Francis Bacon born, 1561	ARI	7:16	5:08	1:46â	7:28p	7:05	5:19	1:40â	7:30p
23 Sa	Saturn in conjunction	TAU	7:15	5:09	2:46â	8:14p	7:04	5:20	2:37â	8:16p
3. Third Sunday after Epiphany			Day's Length: 9h 56m Astron. Twilight: 1h 25m				Day's Length: 10h 18m Astron. Twilight: 1h 19m			
24 Su	Winston Churchill died, 1965	TAU	7:15	5:10	3:47â	9:04p	7:04	5:21	3:35â	9:06p
25 Mo	Virginia Woolf born, 1882	TAU	7:14	5:11	4:47â	9:56p	7:03	5:22	4:34â	9:58p
26 Tu	Virginia rejoined the Union, 1870	GEM	7:13	5:13	5:44â	10:50p	7:02	5:23	5:30â	10:53p
27 We	David Young born, 1781	GEM	7:12	5:14	6:37â	11:46p	7:02	5:24	6:23â	11:48p
28 Th	Jupiter in conjunction	CAN	7:11	5:15	None	None	7:01	5:25	5:24p̄	None
29 Fr	GMT adopted by Scotland, 1848	LEO	7:11	5:16	6:17p̄	12:40a	7:00	5:26	6:30p̄	12:42a
30 Sa	Mercury retrograde	LEO	7:10	5:17	7:27p̄	1:33a	7:00	5:27	7:38p̄	1:35a
4. Fourth Sunday after Epiphany			Day's Length: 10h 01m Astron. Twilight: 1h 24m				Day's Length: 10h 29m Astron. Twilight: 1h 18m			
31 Su	3M began selling Scotch tape, 1930	LEO	7:09	5:19	8:38p̄	2:24a	6:59	5:28	8:45p̄	2:26a

JANUARY 2021 WEATHER FORECAST

ZONE 1 Northeast & New England

1-3: Fair, cold. Dress warmly for Philly's Mummers Parade. **4-7:** Increasingly cloudy. **8-11:** Mixed clouds and sun. **12-15:** Coastal storm brings heavy snowfall to upstate New York, central/northern New England; wintry mix farther south. Rough seas along the coast. **16-19:** Fair but very cold. **20-23:** Changeable skies. **24-27:** Mixed clouds and sunshine. **28-31:** Partly sunny, blustery.

ZONE 2 Great Lakes, Ohio Valley & Midwest

1-3: Fair, then increasingly cloudy skies. **4-7:** Cloudy with a few snow or rain showers. **8-11:** Clearing skies, turning colder. **12-15:** Storm tracks from Chicago to Mid-Atlantic Coast. Snow north; showers south. **16-19:** Fair but very cold. **20-23:** Some snow or flurries. **24-27:** Changeable skies. **28-31:** Generally fair skies.

ZONE 3 Southeast

1-3: Fair/pleasant. **4-7:** Lowering and thickening clouds. **8-11:** Mixed clouds and sun. **12-15:** Wintry mix parts of West Virginia and Virginia. Farther south, scattered showers. **16-19:** Fair and dry; very cold for Virginias. **20-23:** Snowy for West Virginia and high terrain of western Virginia and North Carolina; sleet, freezing rain Tennessee, parts of South Carolina, Georgia, Alabama, Mississippi. Showers elsewhere. **24-27:** Mixed clouds and sunshine. **28-31:** Gusty winds; intervals of sunshine and clouds.

ZONE 4 North Central States

1-3: Snow Northern Plains. **4-7:** Lots of clouds, widespread snow showers and flurries. **8-11:** Unsettled with blustery winds. **12-15:** Clearing; chilly winds diminish. **16-19:** Fair skies. **20-23:** Snow Missouri and much of Kansas. Changeable skies; very cold elsewhere with scattered flurries. **24-27:** Unsettled, blustery weather. **28-31:** Clouds/wind/snow.

ZONE 5 South Central States

1-3: Snow Southern Plains. **4-7:** Lots of clouds; widespread rain showers, possible wet snow. **8-11:** Unsettled, blustery winds; brief, hard showers for Southern Plains. **12-15:** Clearing, chilly winds diminish. **16-19:** Fair skies. **20-23:** Snow Oklahoma, northern Texas; freezing rain, sleet central Texas; showers south Texas. **24-27:** Unsettled, blustery. **28-31:** Cloudy, windy, mixed precipitation changes to rain.

ZONE 6 Northwest

1-3: Changeable skies Idaho, Oregon, Washington. Stormy with gales along Pacific Coast. **4-7:** Clearing skies sweep inland from Pacific Coast. **8-11:** Changeable skies Pacific Northwest, becoming unsettled with rain and snow over high elevations of Cascades. **12-15:** Clear skies, chilly along Pacific Coast. **16-19:** Becoming very unsettled. **20-23:** Clearing skies and chilly. **24-27:** Showers along Pacific Coast, spreading inland. **28-31:** Unsettled, stormy.

ZONE 7 Southwest

1-3: Stormy Pacific Coast. Showers in California and at the Tournament of Roses Parade. **4-7:** Clearing skies sweep inland from the Pacific Coast. **8-11:** Showers in California spread east. **12-15:** Clear skies and chilly Pacific Coast. Frosts South Plateau. **16-19:** Stormy conditions develop. **20-23:** Clearing skies and cold; frosts for parts of California. **24-27:** Showers Pacific Coast, spreading inland. **28-31:** Unsettled and stormy again as another in a seemingly unending series of Pacific disturbances comes onshore.

2nd Month FEBRUARY 2021 28 Days

AQUARIUS
January 19 to
February 17

PISCES
February 18 to
March 19

ALTHOUGH THE WINTER GREY WITH AGE, YET REIGNS A SOVEREIGN KING;
SOL'S PLASTIC RAYS WILL SOON ASSAUGE, AND USHER IN THE SPRING.

MOON'S PHASES
EASTERN STANDARD TIME

◔ Last Quarter	4th	12:37 pm
● New Moon	11th	2:06 pm
◑ First Quarter	19th	1:47 pm
○ Full Moon	27th	3:17 am

Subtract 1 hour for CST, 2 hours for MST, and 3 hours for PST.

SUN ON MERIDIAN CIVIL TIME

Day	H:MM:SS
1st	12:14:06
8th	12:14:39
15th	12:14:35
22nd	12:13:54

MOON'S PLACE AT 7am ASTRONOMICALLY

DATE		ASTRONOMY, HOLIDAYS, AND EVENTS		CALENDAR FOR NORTHERN STATES (EST) 40°N. Lat. 75°W. Long.				CALENDAR FOR SOUTHERN STATES (CST) 35°N. Lat. 90°W. Long.			
				SUN RISES	SUN SETS	EARLIEST MOONRISE MOONSET	MOON'S MERIDIAN PASSAGE	SUN RISES	SUN SETS	EARLIEST MOONRISE MOONSET	MOON'S MERIDIAN PASSAGE
1	Mo	Mars in eastern quadrature	VIR	7:08	5:20	9:49p̄	3:14a	6:58	5:29	9:52p̄	3:16a
2	Tu	Groundhog Day (Candlemas)	VIR	7:07	5:21	10:59p̄	4:03a	6:57	5:30	10:59p̄	4:05a
3	We	Midpoint of winter; Moon at perigee 2:08pm	VIR	7:06	5:22	None	4:52a	6:57	5:31	None	4:54a
4	Th	Charles Lindbergh born, 1902	LIB	7:05	5:23	12:11ā	5:43a	6:56	5:32	12:07ā	5:45a
5	Fr	Henry "Hank" Aaron born, 1934	LIB	7:04	5:25	1:23ā	6:36a	6:55	5:33	1:16ā	6:38a
6	Sa	Spanish-American War ended, 1899	OPH	7:03	5:26	2:36ā	7:32a	6:54	5:34	2:25ā	7:34a

5. Fifth Sunday after Epiphany Day's Length: 10h 25m Astron. Twilight: 1h 23m — Day's Length: 10h 42m Astron. Twilight: 1h 17m

7	Su	11th Amendment ratified, 1795	OPH	7:02	5:27	3:46ā	8:30a	6:53	5:35	3:33ā	8:32a
8	Mo	Boy Scouts Day; James Dean born, 1931	SAG	7:01	5:28	4:50ā	9:29a	6:52	5:36	4:36ā	9:32a
9	Tu	Volleyball was invented, 1895	SAG	7:00	5:29	5:47ā	10:28a	6:51	5:37	5:33ā	10:30a
10	We	U.S. ratified 25th Amendment, 1967	CAP	6:58	5:31	6:35ā	11:24a	6:50	5:38	6:23ā	11:26a
11	Th	Nelson Mandela freed after 27 years, 1990	CAP	6:57	5:32	5:25p̄	12:17p	6:49	5:39	5:39p̄	12:19p
12	Fr	Lincoln's Birthday	AQU	6:56	5:33	6:31p̄	1:06p	6:48	5:40	6:42p̄	1:08p
13	Sa	Patty Berg born, 1918	AQU	6:55	5:34	7:35p̄	1:51p	6:47	5:41	7:42p̄	1:53p

6. Sixth Sunday after Epiphany Day's Length: 10h 42m Astron. Twilight: 1h 22m — Day's Length: 10h 56m Astron. Twilight: 1h 16m

14	Su	Valentine's Day	PSC	6:53	5:35	8:36p̄	2:35p	6:46	5:42	8:40p̄	2:36p
15	Mo	**Presidents' Day**; Galileo born, 1564	CET	6:52	5:37	9:36p̄	3:16p	6:45	5:43	9:37p̄	3:18p
16	Tu	Shrove Tuesday/Mardi Gras	PSC	6:51	5:38	10:35p̄	3:57p	6:44	5:44	10:33p̄	3:59p
17	We	Ash Wednesday	CET	6:50	5:39	11:34p̄	4:39p	6:43	5:45	11:29p̄	4:40p
18	Th	Moon at apogee 5:24am	ARI	6:48	5:40	None	5:21p	6:42	5:46	None	5:23p
19	Fr	USSR launched *Mir* space station, 1986	TAU	6:47	5:41	12:34ā	6:06p	6:41	5:47	12:26ā	6:08p
20	Sa	Mercury direct; Ansel Adams born, 1902	TAU	6:46	5:42	1:34ā	6:54p	6:40	5:48	1:23ā	6:56p

7. First Sunday of Lent Day's Length: 10h 59m Astron. Twilight: 1h 21m — Day's Length: 11h 10m Astron. Twilight: 1h 15m

21	Su	Sewing machine patented, 1842	TAU	6:44	5:43	2:34ā	7:44p	6:39	5:49	2:21ā	7:46p
22	Mo	Washington's birthday (Traditional)	GEM	6:43	5:45	3:31ā	8:37p	6:37	5:50	3:17ā	8:40p
23	Tu	1st mass polio vaccination began, 1954	GEM	6:41	5:46	4:26ā	9:32p	6:36	5:51	4:12ā	9:34p
24	We	Ember Day	CAN	6:40	5:47	5:15ā	10:27p	6:35	5:52	5:01ā	10:29p
25	Th	Fast of Esther	CAN	6:39	5:48	5:58ā	11:21p	6:34	5:53	5:47ā	11:23p
26	Fr	Ember Day; Purim	LEO	6:37	5:49	6:36ā	None	6:33	5:54	6:27ā	None
27	Sa	Ember Day; John Steinbeck born, 1902	LEO	6:36	5:50	6:20p̄	12:14a	6:31	5:54	6:29p̄	12:16a

8. Second Sunday of Lent Day's Length: 11h 17m Astron. Twilight: 1h 20m — Day's Length: 11h 25m Astron. Twilight: 1h 15m

28	Su	1st vaudeville theater opened, 1883	VIR	6:34	5:51	7:33p̄	1:05a	6:30	5:55	7:38p̄	1:08a

FEBRUARY 2021 WEATHER FORECAST

ZONE 1 Northeast & New England

1-3: Turning unusually mild, with scattered showers, thunderstorms. **4-7:** Turning much colder. Storm moving north along Mid-Atlantic Coast brings significant snowfall. **8-11:** Lingering clouds, flurries. **12-15:** Blizzard conditions Northeast Corridor, 1-2 foot accumulations possible. Scattered flurries farther inland. **16-19:** Mixed sun, clouds. **20-23:** Mostly cloudy. **24-28:** Unsettled, cold.

ZONE 2 Great Lakes, Ohio Valley & Midwest

1-3: Initially mild, then sharply colder with showery weather changing to snow. **4-7:** Significant snowfall possible eastern sections Ohio and Kentucky; otherwise, clearing, much colder. **8-11:** Scattered showers, flurries. **12-15:** Sun, clouds; lingering flurries. **16-19:** Turning fair, colder. **20-23:** Relatively pleasant Ohio River Valley. **24-28:** Clouds; snow showers.

ZONE 3 Southeast

1-3: Unseasonable warmth, scattered showers, thunderstorms. Potential tornadic activity over Florida, parts of southern Alabama, Mississippi, Georgia. **4-7:** Stormy along Carolina coast. Parts of West Virginia, Virginia: possible sleet/freezing rain, snow. Wet Super Bowl LV at Raymond James Stadium in Tampa. **8-11:** Lingering clouds, few showers. **12-15:** Coastal storm revs-up as it moves northeast from western Gulf of Mexico; increasingly windy, rainy; snowy parts of North Carolina, Virginia. **16-19:** Sun, clouds. **20-23:** Showery Florida Panhandle, Alabama, Mississippi, possible wintry mix north of Interstate 20. **24-28:** Unsettled, unseasonably chilly.

ZONE 4 North Central States

1-3: Widespread snow. **4-7:** Fair skies, much colder. **8-11:** Unsettled weather Northern Plains, snow for Dakotas, Minnesota, Iowa, Nebraska; sleet for Kansas/Missouri. **12-15:** Changeable skies. **16-19:** Clearing, colder. **20-23:** Moderate snowfall southern Kansas; wintry mix southern Missouri. Some clouds and sun elsewhere. **24-28:** Unsettled weather.

ZONE 5 South Central States

1-3: Snow showers, flurries, then clearing. **4-7:** Fair, much colder. **8-11:** Unsettled weather Southern Plains, sleet Arkansas, Texas-Oklahoma Panhandle. Rain across central, southern Texas. **12-15:** Changeable skies. **16-19:** Clearing/colder. **20-23:** Heavy snow eastern New Mexico, much of Oklahoma, Texas; wintry mix Arkansas, northern Louisiana. Showery southern Texas, Louisiana. Messy Mardi Gras. **24-28:** Unsettled conditions persist.

ZONE 6 Northwest

1-3: Breezy, showery. **4-7:** Fair skies, then unsettled. **8-11:** Clearing skies along Pacific Coast. **12-15:** Stormy weather moves in. **16-19:** Clearing skies, turning chilly. **20-23:** Snow, rain. **24-28:** Milder temps accompany stormy weather.

ZONE 7 Southwest

1-3: Heavy rains, gusty winds California, western Nevada; scattered showers elsewhere. **4-7:** Fair skies give way to cloudy skies, showers. **8-11:** Clearing skies along Pacific Coast. **12-15:** Stormy weather spreads inland. **16-19:** Skies clear but turning colder. Frosts parts of California. **20-23:** Changeable skies. **24-28:** Gusty winds, unsettled weather.

MARCH 2021

3rd Month   **MARCH 2021**   31 Days

PISCES
February 18 to
March 19

ARIES
March 20 to
April 18

**NOW SPRING HAS COME, THE BIRDS REJOICE, AND CHAUNT THE CHEERFUL LAY;
THE FARMER WITH EXULTING JOYS, PREPARES FOR APRIL'S DAY.**

MOON'S PHASES
EASTERN DAYLIGHT TIME

◐ Last Quarter	5th	8:30 pm	
● New Moon	13th	5:21 am	
◑ First Quarter	21st	10:40 am	
○ Full Moon	28th	2:48 pm	

Subtract 1 hour for CDT, 2 hours for MDT, and 3 hours for PDT.

SUN ON MERIDIAN CIVIL TIME

Day	H:MM:SS
1st	12:12:43
8th	12:11:09
15th	13:09:17
22nd	13:07:14
29th	13:05:07

MOON'S PLACE AT 7am ASTRONOMICALLY

CALENDAR FOR NORTHERN STATES
(EDT)
40°N. Lat.
75°W. Long.

CALENDAR FOR SOUTHERN STATES
(CDT)
35°N. Lat.
90°W. Long.

DATE		ASTRONOMY, HOLIDAYS, AND EVENTS		SUN RISES	SUN SETS	EARLIEST MOONRISE MOONSET	MOON'S MERIDIAN PASSAGE	SUN RISES	SUN SETS	EARLIEST MOONRISE MOONSET	MOON'S MERIDIAN PASSAGE
1	Mo	Peace Corps est., 1961	VIR	6:33	5:52	8:46p̄	1:56a	6:29	5:56	8:47p̄	1:58a
2	Tu	Moon at perigee 12:27am	VIR	6:31	5:54	10:00p̄	2:47a	6:27	5:57	9:57p̄	2:49a
3	We	Alexander Graham Bell born, 1847	LIB	6:30	5:55	11:14p̄	3:38a	6:26	5:58	11:08p̄	3:41a
4	Th	Emile Berliner invented microphone, 1877	LIB	6:28	5:56	None	4:32a	6:25	5:59	None	4:34a
5	Fr	G. Westinghouse patented air brake, 1872	SCO	6:27	5:57	12:28ā	5:27a	6:24	6:00	12:18ā	5:30a
6	Sa	Great Atlantic Coast Storm of 1962	OPH	6:25	5:58	1:39ā	6:25a	6:22	6:01	1:26ā	6:27a

9. Third Sunday of Lent — Day's Length: 11h 35m / Astron. Twilight: 1h 20m — Day's Length: 11h 41m / Astron. Twilight: 1h 15m

7	Su	Monopoly was invented, 1933	SAG	6:23	5:59	2:45ā	7:24a	6:21	6:01	2:31ā	7:26a
8	Mo	Oliver Wendell Holmes born, 1841	SAG	6:22	6:00	3:44ā	8:22a	6:20	6:02	3:29ā	8:24a
9	Tu	Connecticut became 5th state, 1788	CAP	6:20	6:01	4:33ā	9:18a	6:18	6:03	4:20ā	9:20a
10	We	Moon, Jupiter, Saturn visible SE 5:47am	CAP	6:19	6:02	5:14ā	10:11a	6:17	6:04	5:03ā	10:13a
11	Th	Blizzard of '88 began, 1888	AQU	6:17	6:03	5:49ā	11:00a	6:15	6:05	5:40ā	11:02a
12	Fr	Girl Scouts Day; U.S. Post Office est., 1789	AQU	6:16	6:04	6:18ā	11:46a	6:14	6:06	6:12ā	11:48a
13	Sa	Julia Flikke 1st female colonel, 1942	AQU	6:14	6:05	6:24p̄	12:30p	6:13	6:06	6:29p̄	12:31p

10. Fourth Sunday of Lent — Day's Length: 11h 54m / Astron. Twilight: 1h 20m — Day's Length: 11h 56m / Astron. Twilight: 1h 14m

14	Su	Daylight Saving Time begins	CET	7:12	7:06	8:25p̄	2:12p	7:11	7:07	8:27p̄	2:13p
15	Mo	Automatic voting machine invented, 1892	CET	7:11	7:07	9:25p̄	2:53p	7:10	7:08	9:23p̄	2:55p
16	Tu	Delaware enacted 1st fertilizer law, 1871	PSC	7:09	7:08	10:24p̄	3:34p	7:09	7:09	10:20p̄	3:36p
17	We	St. Patrick's Day	ARI	7:08	7:10	11:23p̄	4:16p	7:07	7:10	11:16p̄	4:18p
18	Th	Moon at apogee 1:09am	TAU	7:06	7:11	None	5:00p	7:06	7:11	None	5:02p
19	Fr	Moon, Mars best visible in the W. 10:09pm	TAU	7:04	7:12	12:23ā	5:46p	7:04	7:11	12:13ā	5:48p
20	Sa	Vernal equinox (1st day of spring) 5:37am	TAU	7:03	7:13	1:23ā	6:35p	7:03	7:12	1:11ā	6:37p

11. Fifth Sunday of Lent — Day's Length: 12h 12m / Astron. Twilight: 1h 20m — Day's Length: 12h 11m / Astron. Twilight: 1h 15m

21	Su	Yosemite Valley discovered in CA, 1851	TAU	7:01	7:14	2:21ā	7:26p	7:02	7:13	2:07ā	7:28p
22	Mo	Joseph Priestly invented seltzer, 1733	GEM	7:00	7:15	3:16ā	8:19p	7:00	7:14	3:01ā	8:21p
23	Tu	Wright Brothers airplane patented, 1903	GEM	6:58	7:16	4:06ā	9:13p	6:59	7:15	3:52ā	9:15p
24	We	Harry Houdini born, 1874	CAN	6:56	7:17	4:51ā	10:06p	6:57	7:15	4:38ā	10:09p
25	Th	Annunciation Day	LEO	6:55	7:18	5:30ā	10:59p	6:56	7:16	5:20ā	11:02p
26	Fr	Venus in superior conjunction	LEO	6:53	7:19	6:05ā	11:51p	6:55	7:17	5:58ā	11:54p
27	Sa	Corkscrew was patented, 1860	LEO	6:51	7:20	6:36ā	None	6:53	7:18	6:32ā	None

12. Passion/Palm Sunday — Day's Length: 12h 31m / Astron. Twilight: 1h 20m — Day's Length: 12h 27m / Astron. Twilight: 1h 15m

28	Su	1st Day of Passover	VIR	6:50	7:21	7:23ā	12:43a	6:52	7:19	7:26ā	12:45a
29	Mo	Niagara Falls stopped flowing, ice jam, 1848	VIR	6:48	7:22	8:39p̄	1:35a	6:50	7:19	8:38p̄	1:37a
30	Tu	Moon at perigee 2:23am	VIR	6:47	7:23	9:56p̄	2:27a	6:49	7:20	9:51p̄	2:29a
31	We	Ford Motor Co. debuted V-8 engine, 1932	LIB	6:45	7:24	11:13p̄	3:22a	6:48	7:21	11:04p̄	3:24a

MARCH 2021 WEATHER FORECAST

ZONE 1 Northeast & New England

1-3: Lingering clouds, residual showers. **4-7:** Coastal disturbance brings gusty winds and a healthy dose of precipitation. **8-11:** Another coastal system brings more unsettled weather. **12-15:** A return to sunny skies. **16-19:** Fair weather. **20-23:** Fair weather continues. **24-27:** Storm tracks through upstate NY and central New England. Snow north, showery rains south. **28-31:** Continued unsettled for the Northeast and Mid-Atlantic, then gradual clearing.

ZONE 2 Great Lakes, Ohio Valley & Midwest

1-3: Clearing skies. **4-7:** Sunny skies and warmer, especially for southern Illinois, Indiana, and Ohio. **8-11:** Fair skies. **12-15:** Increasing cloudiness. **16-19:** Generally fair weather from Kentucky and points north to the Great Lakes. **20-23:** Changeable skies. **24-27:** Storm tracks from southern Missouri to northern Ohio, bringing a foot or more of snow for Wisconsin, central and northern Illinois, northern Indiana, and southern Michigan; showers and thunderstorms Ohio, Kentucky, central and southern Indiana, and southern Illinois. **28-31:** Clearing and windy.

ZONE 3 Southeast

1-3: More clouds than sun, possible shower. **4-7:** Windy and rainy. **8-11:** More rain and wind. **12-15:** Clearing skies. **16-19:** Fair and dry. **20-23:** More fair and dry weather conditions. **24-27:** Widespread showers; thundery for parts of Mississippi and western Tennessee. **28-31:** Showery, then fair.

ZONE 4 North Central States

1-3: Sun-filled skies across the Northern Plains. **4-7:** Increasingly cloudy skies. **8-11:** Fair skies. **12-15:** Stormy conditions from the Northern Rockies, spreading east. **16-19:** Fair skies gradually return. **20-23:** Sunshine gives way to increasing, thickening cloudiness. **24-27:** A major storm evolves over the central Rockies and pushes east-north-eastward, bringing a hefty snowfall (10-18") to Nebraska, Iowa, Kansas, and parts of South Dakota, Minnesota, and Missouri. **28-31:** Clear skies most areas. Unseasonably cold temperatures over the Northern Plains.

ZONE 5 South Central States

1-3: Fair skies across the Southern Plains. **4-7:** Increasingly cloudy. **8-11:** Fair skies for most areas. **12-15:** Stormy conditions arrive from the Southern Rockies. **16-19:** Gradual clearing. **20-23:** Sunshine gives way to clouds. **24-27:** Showers and thunderstorms, possibly strong-to-severe, over Texas, Oklahoma, and eastern New Mexico. **28-31:** Mainly sunny.

ZONE 6 Northwest

1-3: Fair for Washington, Oregon, Idaho. **4-7:** Unsettled conditions. **8-11:** Mild along the Pacific Coast. **12-15:** Gales for the Washington and Oregon coasts. **16-19:** Showers along Pacific Coast, spreading east. **20-23:** Clearing skies in Idaho, Oregon, and Washington. **24-27:** Gales again on the Pacific Coast. **28-31:** Clear and cold.

ZONE 7 Southwest

1-3: Pleasant conditions for the Southwest. **4-7:** Unsettled weather evolves and spreads east. **8-11:** Mild along the Pacific Coast. **12-15:** Very unsettled conditions, with gusty winds and copious amounts of precipitation. **16-19:** Showers along Pacific Coast, spreading east. **20-23:** Sun-filled skies and pleasant, especially for California. **24-27:** Gales again on the Pacific Coast. **28-31:** A spell of pleasantly mild weather.

4ᵗʰ Month — APRIL 2021 — 30 Days

ARIES
March 20 to
April 18

TAURUS
April 19 to
May 19

HAIL, APRIL WITH HER SMILING FACE HAS COME TO CHEER THE PLAIN;
THE GRASS IS SEEN TO START APACE, AS DOES THE NEEDFUL GRAIN.

MOON'S PHASES
EASTERN DAYLIGHT TIME

☽ Last Quarter	4ᵗʰ	6:02 am
● New Moon	11ᵗʰ	10:31 pm
☾ First Quarter	20ᵗʰ	2:59 am
○ Full Moon	26ᵗʰ	11:32 pm

Subtract 1 hour for CDT, 2 hours for MDT,
and 3 hours for PDT.

SUN ON MERIDIAN CIVIL TIME

Day	H:MM:SS
1ˢᵗ	13:04:13
8ᵗʰ	13:02:13
15ᵗʰ	13:00:26
22ⁿᵈ	12:58:56
29ᵗʰ	12:57:47

DATE	ASTRONOMY, HOLIDAYS, AND EVENTS	MOON'S PLACE AT 7am ASTRONOMICALLY	CALENDAR FOR NORTHERN STATES (EDT) 40°N. Lat. 75°W. Long.				CALENDAR FOR SOUTHERN STATES (CDT) 35°N. Lat. 90°W. Long.			
			SUN RISES	SUN SETS	EARLIEST MOONRISE MOONSET	MOON'S MERIDIAN PASSAGE	SUN RISES	SUN SETS	EARLIEST MOONRISE MOONSET	MOON'S MERIDIAN PASSAGE
1 Th	April Fools' Day; Holy Thursday	SCO	6:43	7:25	None	4:18a	6:46	7:22	None	4:21a
2 Fr	Good Friday	OPH	6:42	7:26	12:28â	5:17a	6:45	7:23	12:16â	5:20a
3 Sa	Alaska's Mt. McKinley was climbed, 1910	SAG	6:40	7:27	1:38â	6:17a	6:43	7:23	1:24â	6:20a

13. Easter Sunday
Day's Length: 12h 49m · Astron. Twilight: 1h 21m
Day's Length: 12h 42m · Astron. Twilight: 1h 16m

DATE	ASTRONOMY, HOLIDAYS, AND EVENTS		SUN RISES	SUN SETS	EARLIEST MOONRISE MOONSET	MOON'S MERIDIAN PASSAGE	SUN RISES	SUN SETS	EARLIEST MOONRISE MOONSET	MOON'S MERIDIAN PASSAGE
4 Su	Martin Luther King Jr. assassinated, 1968	SAG	6:39	7:28	2:41â	7:17a	6:42	7:24	2:26â	7:19a
5 Mo	Easter Monday	CAP	6:37	7:29	3:33â	8:14a	6:41	7:25	3:19â	8:16a
6 Tu	Moon, Saturn best visible in SE 5:26am	CAP	6:35	7:30	4:16â	9:08a	6:39	7:26	4:04â	9:10a
7 We	Billie Holiday born, 1915	CAP	6:34	7:31	4:52â	9:58a	6:38	7:27	4:42â	10:00a
8 Th	Hank Aaron hit 715ᵗʰ home run, 1974	AQU	6:32	7:32	5:22â	10:44a	6:37	7:27	5:15â	10:46a
9 Fr	NASA named American astronauts, 1959	AQU	6:31	7:33	5:48â	11:28a	6:35	7:28	5:44â	11:30a
10 Sa	Britain issued 1ˢᵗ copyright law, 1710	PSC	6:29	7:34	6:12â	12:10p	6:34	7:29	6:11â	12:11p

14. Second Sunday of Easter
Day's Length: 13h 07m · Astron. Twilight: 1h 23m
Day's Length: 12h 57m · Astron. Twilight: 1h 17m

DATE	ASTRONOMY, HOLIDAYS, AND EVENTS		SUN RISES	SUN SETS	EARLIEST MOONRISE MOONSET	MOON'S MERIDIAN PASSAGE	SUN RISES	SUN SETS	EARLIEST MOONRISE MOONSET	MOON'S MERIDIAN PASSAGE
11 Su	Jane Bolin born, 1908	CET	6:28	7:35	None	12:51p	6:33	7:30	6:37â	12:52p
12 Mo	1ˢᵗ use baseball catcher's mask, 1877	PSC	6:26	7:36	8:15p̃	1:32p	6:31	7:31	8:12p̃	1:33p
13 Tu	Metropolitan Museum of Art founded, 1870	ARI	6:25	7:37	9:15p̃	2:13p	6:30	7:31	9:09p̃	2:15p
14 We	Pan-American Day; Moon at apogee 1:59pm	ARI	6:23	7:38	10:15p̃	2:57p	6:29	7:32	10:06p̃	2:58p
15 Th	"Tax Day" every year since 1955	TAU	6:22	7:39	11:15p̃	3:42p	6:27	7:33	11:03p̃	3:44p
16 Fr	Moon, Mars best visible in the W. 9:57pm	TAU	6:20	7:40	None	4:30p	6:26	7:34	11:59p̃	4:32p
17 Sa	Horses 1ˢᵗ imported into colonies, 1629	TAU	6:19	7:41	12:13â	5:19p	6:25	7:35	None	5:21p

15. Third Sunday of Easter
Day's Length: 13h 25m · Astron. Twilight: 1h 24m
Day's Length: 13h 12m · Astron. Twilight: 1h 18m

DATE	ASTRONOMY, HOLIDAYS, AND EVENTS		SUN RISES	SUN SETS	EARLIEST MOONRISE MOONSET	MOON'S MERIDIAN PASSAGE	SUN RISES	SUN SETS	EARLIEST MOONRISE MOONSET	MOON'S MERIDIAN PASSAGE
18 Su	Mercury in superior conjunction	GEM	6:17	7:42	1:09â	6:11p	6:24	7:35	12:54â	6:13p
19 Mo	Patriot's Day (ME & MA)	GEM	6:16	7:43	2:00â	7:03p	6:22	7:36	1:46â	7:05p
20 Tu	Shirley Temple appeared in 1ˢᵗ movie, 1934	CAN	6:14	7:44	2:46â	7:55p	6:21	7:37	2:33â	7:58p
21 We	Spanish-American War began, 1898	CAN	6:13	7:45	3:26â	8:47p	6:20	7:38	3:15â	8:49p
22 Th	Earth Day	LEO	6:11	7:46	4:02â	9:38p	6:19	7:39	3:53â	9:40p
23 Fr	U.S. Army Reserve was created, 1908	LEO	6:10	7:47	4:33â	10:29p	6:18	7:39	4:28â	10:31p
24 Sa	Library of Congress est., 1800	VIR	6:09	7:48	5:03â	11:19p	6:16	7:40	5:00â	11:21p

16. Fourth Sunday of Easter
Day's Length: 13h 42m · Astron. Twilight: 1h 26m
Day's Length: 13h 26m · Astron. Twilight: 1h 19m

DATE	ASTRONOMY, HOLIDAYS, AND EVENTS		SUN RISES	SUN SETS	EARLIEST MOONRISE MOONSET	MOON'S MERIDIAN PASSAGE	SUN RISES	SUN SETS	EARLIEST MOONRISE MOONSET	MOON'S MERIDIAN PASSAGE
25 Su	Seeing Eye dog first used, 1928	VIR	6:07	7:49	5:31â	None	6:15	7:41	5:33â	None
26 Mo	1ˢᵗ Saturn observations, 1514	VIR	6:06	7:50	6:00â	12:11a	6:14	7:42	6:06â	12:13a
27 Tu	Moon at perigee 11:29am	LIB	6:05	7:51	8:47p̃	1:05a	6:13	7:43	8:40p̃	1:07a
28 We	Addressograph patented, 1896	LIB	6:03	7:52	10:06p̃	2:02a	6:12	7:44	9:55p̃	2:04a
29 Th	Dismantling Berlin Wall began, 1990	OPH	6:02	7:53	11:22p̃	3:02a	6:11	7:44	11:09p̃	3:05a
30 Fr	Lag B'Omer	OPH	6:01	7:54	None	4:04a	6:10	7:45	None	4:07a

APRIL 2021 WEATHER FORECAST

ZONE 1 Northeast & New England

1-3: Sunshine then unsettled weather. **4-7:** Periods of rain for Easter Sunday but becoming sunny. **8-11:** Fair skies, then turning stormy. **12-15:** Thunderstorms move off East Coast; becoming fair. **16-19:** Turning unsettled with showers in New England down to Mid-Atlantic Coast. Soggy Patriot's Day. **20-23:** Fair Northeast, Mid-Atlantic States; unseasonably warm. **24-27:** Potent thunderstorms sweep east through New England, much of the Northeast. **28-30:** Sunny skies return.

ZONE 2 Great Lakes, Ohio Valley & Midwest

1-3: Unstable conditions. **4-7:** Rain sweeps through Great Lakes, points east, then clearing skies. **8-11:** Thundery weather Ohio Valley, Great Lakes area. **12-15:** Clearing along Mississippi River. **16-19:** Turning chilly and unsettled. **20-23:** Heavy-to-severe thunderstorms Wisconsin, Illinois, and parts of western Kentucky. **24-27:** Big thunderstorms march east through Ohio Valley, as well as central and eastern Great Lakes. **28-30:** Unsettled weather sweeps in from the west.

ZONE 3 Southeast

1-3: Dry, pleasant initially, then unsettled. **4-7:** Showers, then clearing. **8-11:** Becoming thundery. Showers could threaten Masters Tournament in Augusta, GA. **12-15:** Thunderstorms move off the coast; becoming fair. Gulf Coast quite chilly. **16-19:** Mix of clouds and sun, small risk of a shower. **20-23:** Fair/very warm, then unsettled. Heavy thunderstorms Tennessee, Mississippi. **24-27:** Another round of thunderstorms marches eastward through Tennessee Valley. **28-30:** Sunshine gives way to increasingly cloudy skies from the west.

ZONE 4 North Central States

1-3: A spell of stormy weather. **4-7:** Clearing skies. **8-11:** Strong, gusty winds spread east from Northern Rockies out over Northern Plains. **12-15:** Fair, dry for most areas. **16-19:** Unsettled/showery. **20-23:** Potentially severe thunderstorms extend from Minnesota south through Iowa and Missouri. Storms capable of frequent lightning, damaging winds, large hail, and even a few tornadoes. **24-27:** Fair skies. **28-30:** Cloudy/showery weather sweeps in from the west.

ZONE 5 South Central States

1-3: Unsettled weather. **4-7:** Sunshine, dry weather. **8-11:** Blustery winds spread east. **12-15:** Fair skies prevail for most areas. **16-19:** Unsettled weather. **20-23:** Potentially severe thunderstorms for Arkansas, down into Louisiana. Storms may be capable of cloud-to-ground lightning, damaging winds, large hail, and tornadoes. **24-27:** Abundant sunshine. **28-30:** Clouds, showers move in from the west.

ZONE 6 Northwest

1-3: Unsettled weather. **4-7:** Fair skies. **8-11:** Gales along Pacific Coast, spreading eastward. **12-15:** Fair, dry. **16-19:** Unsettled conditions, then clearing skies. **20-23:** Partly to mostly sunny skies. **24-27:** Continued fair weather. **28-30:** Clouds, wind, rain move in from the Pacific.

ZONE 7 Southwest

1-3: Threatening skies for the region. **4-7:** Fair skies, abundant sunshine. **8-11:** Gales along the Pacific Coast, spreading eastward. **12-15:** Fair for most areas: sunny days and cold nights. **16-19:** Generally fair weather. **20-23:** Partly to mostly sunny skies. **24-27:** Continued fair. **28-30:** Blustery winds, accompanied by clouds and showers.

MAY 2021

5th Month | 31 Days

TAURUS
April 19 to
May 19

GEMINI
May 20 to
June 19

WITH VERDURE THE WIDE EARTH'S OVERSPREAD, AND TREES ADORNED WITH BLOOMS;
THE PATHS IN MAY BOW SWEET TO TREAD, MID FORESTS OF PERFUME.

MOON'S PHASES
EASTERN DAYLIGHT TIME

◑ Last Quarter 3rd 3:50 pm
● New Moon 11th 3:00 pm
◐ First Quarter 19th 3:13 pm
○ Full Moon 26th 7:14 am

Subtract 1 hour for CDT, 2 hours for MDT,
and 3 hours for PDT.

SUN ON MERIDIAN
CIVIL TIME

Day	H:MM:SS
1st	12:57:32
8th	12:56:58
15th	12:56:51
22nd	12:57:12
29th	12:57:57

MOON'S PLACE AT 7am ASTRONOMICALLY

CALENDAR FOR NORTHERN STATES (EDT) — 40°N. Lat. 75°W. Long.

CALENDAR FOR SOUTHERN STATES (CDT) — 35°N. Lat. 90°W. Long.

DATE	ASTRONOMY, HOLIDAYS, AND EVENTS		SUN RISES	SUN SETS	EARLIEST MOONRISE MOONSET	MOON'S MERIDIAN PASSAGE	SUN RISES	SUN SETS	EARLIEST MOONRISE MOONSET	MOON'S MERIDIAN PASSAGE
1 Sa	Kentucky Derby; Law Day	SAG	5:59	7:55	12:31â	5:07a	6:09	7:46	12:16â	5:09a

17. Fifth Sunday of Easter

Day's Length: 13h 58m — Astron. Twilight: 1h 28m
Day's Length: 13h 39m — Astron. Twilight: 1h 21m

2 Su	Orthodox Easter	SAG	5:58	7:56	1:29â	6:07a	6:08	7:47	1:15â	6:09a
3 Mo	Saturn in western quadrature	CAP	5:57	7:57	2:16â	7:03a	6:07	7:48	2:04â	7:06a
4 Tu	Kent State Students' Memorial Day, 1970	CAP	5:56	7:58	2:55â	7:55a	6:06	7:48	2:44â	7:57a
5 We	13th Amendment passed, 1865	AQU	5:55	7:59	3:27â	8:43a	6:05	7:49	3:19â	8:45a
6 Th	Yankees team traveled by plane, 1946	AQU	5:54	8:00	3:54â	9:27a	6:04	7:50	3:49â	9:29a
7 Fr	Johannes Brahms born, 1833	PSC	5:52	8:01	4:18â	10:10a	6:03	7:51	4:16â	10:11a
8 Sa	V. E. Day; Harry S. Truman born, 1884	CET	5:51	8:02	4:41â	10:50a	6:02	7:52	4:42â	10:52a

18. Sixth Sunday of Easter

Day's Length: 14h 13m — Astron. Twilight: 1h 30m
Day's Length: 13h 52m — Astron. Twilight: 1h 22m

9 Su	Mother's Day; Mike Wallace born, 1918	PSC	5:50	8:03	5:03â	11:31a	6:01	7:52	5:07â	11:33a
10 Mo	Clapton recorded I Shot the Sheriff, 1974	CET	5:49	8:04	5:26â	12:12p	6:00	7:53	5:33â	12:14p
11 Tu	Moon at apogee 6:11pm	ARI	5:48	8:05	5:51â	12:55p	5:59	7:54	6:01â	12:56p
12 We	Moon, Mercury, Venus b. visible NW 8:37pm	TAU	5:47	8:06	9:08p̄	1:39p	5:58	7:55	8:57p̄	1:41p
13 Th	Ascension Day	TAU	5:46	8:07	10:07p̄	2:26p	5:58	7:56	9:54p̄	2:28p
14 Fr	George Lucas born, 1944	TAU	5:45	8:08	11:04p̄	3:15p	5:57	7:56	10:50p̄	3:17p
15 Sa	Armed Forces Day; Spring Astronomy Day	GEM	5:44	8:09	11:57p̄	4:06p	5:56	7:57	11:42p̄	4:08p

19. Seventh Sunday of Easter

Day's Length: 14h 27m — Astron. Twilight: 1h 32m
Day's Length: 14h 03m — Astron. Twilight: 1h 24m

16 Su	Russian spacecraft landed on Venus, 1969	GEM	5:43	8:10	None	4:58p	5:55	7:58	None	5:00p
17 Mo	Shavuot; 1st Kentucky Derby, 1875	CAN	5:43	8:11	12:44â	5:50p	5:55	7:59	12:30â	5:52p
18 Tu	Mt. Saint Helens erupted, 1980	CAN	5:42	8:12	1:26â	6:40p	5:54	8:00	1:13â	6:42p
19 We	Johns Hopkins born, 1795	LEO	5:41	8:13	2:02â	7:30p	5:53	8:00	1:52â	7:32p
20 Th	Fountain pen patented, 1830	LEO	5:40	8:14	2:33â	8:19p	5:53	8:01	2:26â	8:21p
21 Fr	Jupiter in western quadrature	LEO	5:39	8:14	3:02â	9:07p	5:52	8:02	2:58â	9:09p
22 Sa	National Maritime Day	VIR	5:39	8:15	3:30â	9:57p	5:51	8:02	3:29â	9:59p

20. Pentecost Sunday

Day's Length: 14h 38m — Astron. Twilight: 1h 34m
Day's Length: 14h 12m — Astron. Twilight: 1h 26m

23 Su	Saturn retrograde	VIR	5:38	8:16	3:58â	10:48p	5:51	8:03	4:01â	10:51p
24 Mo	1st U.S. passenger train service, 1830	VIR	5:37	8:17	4:27â	11:43p	5:50	8:04	4:34â	11:45p
25 Tu	Moon at perigee 9:57pm	LIB	5:37	8:18	5:00â	None	5:50	8:05	5:11â	None
26 We	Ember Day; John Wayne born, 1907	SCO	5:36	8:19	5:40â	12:42a	5:49	8:05	5:55â	12:44a
27 Th	Bubonic Plague, San Francisco, 1907	OPH	5:35	8:20	10:10p̄	1:44a	5:49	8:06	9:56p̄	1:46a
28 Fr	Ember Day	SAG	5:35	8:20	11:15p̄	2:48a	5:48	8:07	11:01p̄	2:51a
29 Sa	Ember Day; Mercury retrograde	SAG	5:34	8:21	None	3:52a	5:48	8:07	11:56p̄	3:54a

21. Trinity Sunday

Day's Length: 14h 48m — Astron. Twilight: 1h 36m
Day's Length: 14h 20m — Astron. Twilight: 1h 27m

30 Su	Brassiere was invented, 1889	CAP	5:34	8:22	12:10â	4:52a	5:48	8:08	None	4:55a
31 Mo	**Memorial Day**	CAP	5:33	8:23	12:53â	5:48a	5:47	8:09	12:42â	5:50a

MAY 2021 WEATHER FORECAST

ZONE 1 Northeast & New England

1-3: Scattered showers, then clearing and pleasant weather. **4-7:** Pleasant spring weather continues. **8-11:** Showers and thunderstorms from the west sweep east; New England is particularly affected. **12-15:** Fair skies, then becoming unsettled. **16-19:** Fair and pleasant weather. **20-23:** Thunderstorms sweep across the Atlantic Coast, then clear. Residual showers could threaten the Preakness Stakes. **24-27:** Fair skies; gusty winds for New England. **28-31:** Hot over Mid-Atlantic States. Showers sweep up through New England.

ZONE 2 Great Lakes, Ohio Valley & Midwest

1-3: Clearing skies. **4-7:** Pleasant spring weather across the Great Lakes and all points south. Great weather for Derby Day in Louisville. **8-11:** Scattered thunderstorms. **12-15:** Mixed clouds and sun. **16-19:** Pleasant for the Ohio Valley and Great Lakes area. **20-23:** Mixed sun and clouds. **24-27:** Warm temperatures. **28-31:** Showers rapidly sweep east from the Great Lakes. Showers could make for a wet track for the Indy-500.

ZONE 3 Southeast

1-3: Warm and more humid, with mixed clouds and sun. Risk of a shower or thunderstorm. **4-7:** Continued warm; very pleasant spring weather. **8-11:** Mixed clouds and sun, chance of a thunderstorm or two. **12-15:** Sun and clouds. **16-19:** Fair/pleasant weather; becoming unsettled by the 19th. **20-23:** Thunderstorms sweep in; quite windy along coastal areas. Clearing by the 23rd. **24-27:** Mainly dry with warm temperatures. **28-31:** Hot and humid with developing showers, especially along the Gulf Coast.

ZONE 4 North Central States

1-3: A spell of dry and pleasant weather. **4-7:** Widespread showery and thundery weather. **8-11:** Skies slowly clear over the North Central States. **12-15:** Changeable skies; breezy under a mix of sun and clouds. **16-19:** Fair initially, then becoming very unsettled. **20-23:** Skies slowly clear. **24-27:** Hot weather for the Northern Plains. Thunderstorms developing over the Northern Rockies. **28-31:** Becoming mostly pleasant.

ZONE 5 South Central States

1-3: Fair and dry. **4-7:** Showers and thunderstorms. **8-11:** Gradual clearing. **12-15:** Mix of sun and clouds. Gusty winds for Texas west into New Mexico. **16-19:** Starting off fair, then unsettled. **20-23:** Skies clear. **24-27:** Hot weather for the Southern Plains. Thunderstorms develop over the Southern Rockies. **28-31:** Mostly fair skies.

ZONE 6 Northwest

1-3: Pleasant weather. **4-7:** Heavy showers. **8-11:** Fair skies. **12-15:** Local showers for Washington, Oregon, and Idaho. **16-19:** Fair initially for the Pacific Coast, then becoming very unsettled. **20-23:** Skies slowly clear. **24-27:** Mixed clouds and sun. **28-31:** Mostly pleasant weather.

ZONE 7 Southwest

1-3: Pleasant weather. **4-7:** Changeable skies. **8-11:** Fair for the West Coast. **12-15:** Gusty winds for the South Plateau. **16-19:** Fair initially for the Pacific Coast, then becoming very unsettled. **20-23:** Skies slowly clear. Pleasant weather for California. **24-27:** Mixed clouds and sun. **28-31:** Mostly pleasant weather returns.

JUNE 2021

6th Month   **JUNE 2021**   **30 Days**

GEMINI
May 20 to
June 19

CANCER
June 20 to
July 21

**SOL'S HEATING RAYS EACH MIST RETRACTS, THAT HOVERS OVER THE PLAIN;
THE CLOUDS OVERHEAD GROW THICK AND BLACK, IN TORRENTS POURS THE RAIN.**

MOON'S PHASES
EASTERN DAYLIGHT TIME

◐ Last Quarter	2nd	3:24 am
● New Moon	10th	6:53 am
◑ First Quarter	17th	11:54 pm
○ Full Moon	24th	2:40 pm

Subtract 1 hour for CDT, 2 hours for MDT,
and 3 hours for PDT.

SUN ON MERIDIAN
CIVIL TIME

Day	H:MM:SS
1st	12:58:24
8th	12:59:38
15th	13:01:05
22nd	13:02:36
29th	13:04:04

DATE	ASTRONOMY, HOLIDAYS, AND EVENTS	MOON'S PLACE AT 7am ASTRONOMICALLY	SUN RISES	SUN SETS	EARLIEST MOONRISE MOONSET	MOON'S MERIDIAN PASSAGE	SUN RISES	SUN SETS	EARLIEST MOONRISE MOONSET	MOON'S MERIDIAN PASSAGE
			CALENDAR FOR NORTHERN STATES (EDT) 40°N. Lat. 75°W. Long.				**CALENDAR FOR SOUTHERN STATES** (CDT) 35°N. Lat. 90°W. Long.			
1 Tu	Hurricane season begins	AQU	5:33	8:23	1:28ã	6:39a	5:47	8:09	1:20ã	6:41a
2 We	Maine 1st state to prohibit alcohol, 1851	AQU	5:32	8:24	1:58ã	7:25a	5:47	8:10	1:52ã	7:27a
3 Th	Corpus Christi; Jefferson Davis born, 1808	AQU	5:32	8:25	2:23ã	8:08a	5:46	8:10	2:20ã	8:10a
4 Fr	Women's Suffrage bill passed, 1919	CET	5:32	8:25	2:46ã	8:50a	5:46	8:11	2:46ã	8:51a
5 Sa	WWI draft began for American men, 1917	PSC	5:32	8:26	3:08ã	9:30a	5:46	8:11	3:11ã	9:32a

22. Corpus Christi Sunday — Day's Length: 14h 55m — Astron. Twilight: 1h 38m — Day's Length: 14h 26m — Astron. Twilight: 1h 28m

6 Su	Children's Day; Electric iron patented, 1882	CET	5:31	8:27	3:31ã	10:11a	5:46	8:12	3:37ã	10:13a
7 Mo	Moon at apogee 10:40pm	ARI	5:31	8:27	3:55ã	10:53a	5:46	8:13	4:04ã	10:55a
8 Tu	Commercial ice cream manufactured, 1786	TAU	5:31	8:28	4:22ã	11:37a	5:45	8:13	4:34ã	11:39a
9 We	Withholding tax on payrolls authorized, 1943	TAU	5:31	8:28	4:54ã	12:23p	5:45	8:13	5:08ã	12:25p
10 Th	Orthodox Ascension Day	TAU	5:31	8:29	5:30ã	1:12p	5:45	8:14	5:47ã	1:14p
11 Fr	Moon, Venus best visible in the NW 9:11pm	GEM	5:30	8:29	9:53p̃	2:03p	5:45	8:14	9:39p̃	2:05p
12 Sa	Abner Doubleday created baseball, 1839	GEM	5:30	8:30	10:43p̃	2:54p	5:45	8:15	10:28p̃	2:57p

23. Third Sunday after Pentecost — Day's Length: 15h 00m — Astron. Twilight: 1h 39m — Day's Length: 14h 30m — Astron. Twilight: 1h 29m

13 Su	Moon, Mars best visible in the W. 9:48pm	GEM	5:30	8:30	11:26p̃	3:46p	5:45	8:15	11:13p̃	3:48p
14 Mo	Flag Day; Earliest sunrise of 2021	CAN	5:30	8:31	None	4:37p	5:45	8:16	11:53p̃	4:39p
15 Tu	Arkansas became 25th state, 1836	LEO	5:30	8:31	12:03ã	5:27p	5:45	8:16	None	5:29p
16 We	Anne Frank: Diary of a Young Girl, 1952	LEO	5:30	8:31	12:36ã	6:15p	5:45	8:16	12:28ã	6:17p
17 Th	Statue of Liberty arrived in NYC, 1885	LEO	5:30	8:32	1:05ã	7:02p	5:46	8:17	1:00ã	7:04p
18 Fr	Atlantic City, NJ opened Steel Pier, 1898	VIR	5:31	8:32	1:32ã	7:49p	5:46	8:17	1:30ã	7:51p
19 Sa	Guy Lombardo born, 1902	VIR	5:31	8:32	1:58ã	8:38p	5:46	8:17	2:00ã	8:40p

24. Fourth Sunday after Pentecost — Day's Length: 15h 01m — Astron. Twilight: 1h 39m — Day's Length: 14h 31m — Astron. Twilight: 1h 29m

20 Su	Father's Day; Summer solstice 11:32pm	VIR	5:31	8:32	2:26ã	9:29p	5:46	8:17	2:31ã	9:31p
21 Mo	Vinyl Records began mass production, 1948	LIB	5:31	8:33	2:56ã	10:24p	5:46	8:18	3:05ã	10:26p
22 Tu	Mercury direct; V-Mail	LIB	5:31	8:33	3:31ã	11:23p	5:47	8:18	3:44ã	11:26p
23 We	Moon at perigee 6:02am	OPH	5:32	8:33	4:14ã	None	5:47	8:18	4:30ã	None
24 Th	St. John the Baptist (Midsummer Day)	SAG	5:32	8:33	5:05ã	12:26a	5:47	8:18	5:24ã	12:29a
25 Fr	1st barbed wire patented, 1867	SAG	5:32	8:33	9:56p̃	1:31a	5:47	8:18	9:41p̃	1:33a
26 Sa	Bicycle patented, 1819	SAG	5:33	8:33	10:45p̃	2:34a	5:48	8:18	10:33p̃	2:37a

25. Fifth Sunday after Pentecost — Day's Length: 15h 00m — Astron. Twilight: 1h 39m — Day's Length: 14h 30m — Astron. Twilight: 1h 29m

27 Su	Fast of Tammuz; Latest sunset of 2021	CAP	5:33	8:33	11:25p̃	3:34a	5:48	8:18	11:15p̃	3:36a
28 Mo	Federal Housing Administration, 1938	CAP	5:33	8:33	11:58p̃	4:28a	5:48	8:18	11:50p̃	4:31a
29 Tu	Apple iPhone went on sale, 2007	AQU	5:34	8:33	None	5:18a	5:49	8:18	None	5:20a
30 We	Meteor exploded in Siberia, 1908	AQU	5:34	8:33	12:25ã	6:04a	5:49	8:18	12:21ã	6:06a

JUNE 2021 WEATHER FORECAST

ZONE 1 Northeast & New England

1-3: Fair skies. **4-7:** Big thunderstorms for the Mid-Atlantic region. Thunderstorms also continue over the Northeast States. **8-11:** Showers spreading east to the Atlantic Coast. "Mudders Day" for Belmont Stakes? Clouds could eclipse the solar eclipse at dawn on the 10th. **12-15:** Pleasant weather. **16-19:** Severe thunderstorms, especially over New England. **20-23:** Fair, warm. **24-27:** Showers initially, then clearing skies. **28-30:** Fair skies.

ZONE 2 Great Lakes, Ohio Valley & Midwest

1-3: Scattered heavy thunderstorms. **4-7:** Thunderstorms continue over the Great Lakes, then clearing. **8-11:** Variable cloudiness with a few showers possible. Clouds might frustrate prospective skywatchers of the solar eclipse on the 10th. **12-15:** Dry and tranquil. **16-19:** Thundery weather over the Great Lakes. **20-23:** Increasingly cloudy skies and warm. **24-27:** Fair skies. **28-30:** Fair weather continues.

ZONE 3 Southeast

1-3: Severe thunderstorms spreading into Mississippi Valley. Some of these storms are capable of large hail, damaging winds, and even tornadic activity. **4-7:** Big thunderstorms sweep across much of Southeast, down to Gulf Coast States. **8-11:** Becoming unsettled in Mississippi Valley with showers. Dry elsewhere. **12-15:** Hazy skies. **16-19:** Severe thunderstorms from Mississippi Valley, spreading east. **20-23:** Sunny to partly cloudy, hazy and warm. **24-27:** Showers initially, then clearing. **28-30:** Hazy sunshine.

ZONE 4 North Central States

1-3: Severe thunderstorm threat for Northern Rockies. Thunderstorms also for the Northern Plains; possible large hail, damaging winds, and even tornadic activity. **4-7:** Clearing skies. **8-11:** Scattered thunderstorms and warmer. **12-15:** Hot and dry. **16-19:** Strong storms initially, then clearing skies. **20-23:** Scattered thunderstorms for the Northern Rockies and Northern Plains. **24-27:** Fair skies. **28-30:** Violent thunderstorms spread in from the Northern Rockies and move east.

ZONE 5 South Central States

1-3: Severe thunderstorm threat; some storms are capable of large hail, damaging winds, and even tornadic activity. **4-7:** Clearing skies. **8-11:** Scattered thunderstorms and warmer. **12-15:** Hot, dry conditions. **16-19:** Strong thunderstorms and then clearing skies. **20-23:** Scattered thunderstorms. **24-27:** Sunny skies. **28-30:** Some hefty thunderstorms develop over the Southern Rockies and then migrate eastward.

ZONE 6 Northwest

1-3: Clearing skies. **4-7:** Fair skies. **8-11:** Fair skies continue. **12-15:** Showery weather developing. **16-19:** Cooler over the West under a mix of clouds and sun. **20-23:** Changeable skies. **24-27:** Fair weather. **28-30:** Mixed clouds and sun.

ZONE 7 Southwest

1-3: Clearing skies. **4-7:** Fair weather. **8-11:** Fair skies for most areas. Pleasant weather for California. **12-15:** Hot and dry for most areas. **16-19:** Cooler conditions under a mix of clouds and sun. **20-23:** Changeable skies. **24-27:** Fair weather. **28-30:** Mixed clouds and sun.

JULY 2021

7th Month — **31 Days**

CANCER
June 20 to
July 21

LEO
July 22 to
August 21

THE MOWER WALKS WITH SCYTHE IN HAND, TO YONDER FIELD AWAY;
THE GRASS HE PROSTRATES OVER THE LAND; HOW SWEET THE NEW MADE HAY.

MOON'S PHASES
EASTERN DAYLIGHT TIME

☽ Last Quarter	1st	5:11 pm
● New Moon	9th	9:17 pm
☾ First Quarter	17th	6:11 am
○ Full Moon	23rd	10:37 pm
☽ Last Quarter	31st	9:16 am

Subtract 1 hour for CDT, 2 hours for MDT, and 3 hours for PDT.

SUN ON MERIDIAN CIVIL TIME

Day	H:MM:SS
1st	13:04:27
8th	13:05:39
15th	13:06:32
22nd	13:06:59
29th	13:06:57

MOON'S PLACE AT 7am ASTRONOMICALLY

CALENDAR FOR NORTHERN STATES
(EDT)
40°N. Lat.
75°W. Long.

CALENDAR FOR SOUTHERN STATES
(CDT)
35°N. Lat.
90°W. Long.

DATE		ASTRONOMY, HOLIDAYS, AND EVENTS		SUN RISES	SUN SETS	EARLIEST MOONRISE MOONSET	MOON'S MERIDIAN PASSAGE	SUN RISES	SUN SETS	EARLIEST MOONRISE MOONSET	MOON'S MERIDIAN PASSAGE
1	Th	1st zoo opened in U.S., 1874	PSC	5:35	8:33	12:49â	6:47a	5:50	8:18	12:48â	6:48a
2	Fr	Midpoint of 2021	CET	5:35	8:33	1:12â	7:28a	5:50	8:18	1:14â	7:30a
3	Sa	Dog Days begin	PSC	5:36	8:33	1:35â	8:09a	5:51	8:18	1:40â	8:11a

26. Sixth Sunday after Pentecost
Day's Length: 14h 56m — Astron. Twilight: 1h 38m
Day's Length: 14h 27m — Astron. Twilight: 1h 28m

4	Su	**Independence Day**	ARI	5:36	8:32	1:59â	8:51a	5:51	8:18	2:07â	8:52a
5	Mo	Moon at apogee 10:54am	TAU	5:37	8:32	2:25â	9:34a	5:52	8:18	2:36â	9:36a
6	Tu	Merv Griffin born, 1925	TAU	5:38	8:32	2:54â	10:19a	5:52	8:17	3:08â	10:21a
7	We	1st American saint canonized, 1946	TAU	5:38	8:32	3:29â	11:07a	5:53	8:17	3:45â	11:09a
8	Th	John D. Rockefeller born, 1839	TAU	5:39	8:31	4:10â	11:57a	5:53	8:17	4:28â	12:00m
9	Fr	Doughnut cutter patented, 1872	GEM	5:39	8:31	4:58â	12:49p	5:54	8:17	5:17â	12:52p
10	Sa	Highest temp., Death Valley, CA, 1913	GEM	5:40	8:30	9:25p̂	1:42p	5:54	8:16	9:11p̂	1:44p

27. Seventh Sunday after Pentecost
Day's Length: 14h 49m — Astron. Twilight: 1h 36m
Day's Length: 14h 21m — Astron. Twilight: 1h 27m

11	Su	John Quincy Adams born, 1767	CAN	5:41	8:30	10:05p̂	2:34p	5:55	8:16	9:53p̂	2:36p
12	Mo	Congress authorized Medal of Honor, 1862	LEO	5:42	8:30	10:39p̂	3:24p	5:55	8:16	10:30p̂	3:26p
13	Tu	NYC experienced electrical blackout, 1977	LEO	5:42	8:29	11:09p̂	4:13p	5:56	8:15	11:03p̂	4:15p
14	We	U.S. space probe sent Mars images, 1965	LEO	5:43	8:28	11:36p̂	5:00p	5:57	8:15	11:33p̂	5:02p
15	Th	St. Swithin's Day	VIR	5:44	8:28	None	5:47p	5:57	8:14	None	5:49p
16	Fr	Oklahoma City used parking meters, 1935	VIR	5:45	8:27	12:02â	6:34p	5:58	8:14	12:03â	6:36p
17	Sa	Art Linkletter born, 1912	VIR	5:45	8:27	12:28â	7:23p	5:59	8:13	12:32â	7:25p

28. Eighth Sunday after Pentecost
Day's Length: 14h 40m — Astron. Twilight: 1h 35m
Day's Length: 14h 13m — Astron. Twilight: 1h 26m

18	Su	Fast of Av	LIB	5:46	8:26	12:56â	8:14p	5:59	8:13	1:04â	8:17p
19	Mo	Insulin introduced, 1923	LIB	5:47	8:25	1:28â	9:10p	6:00	8:12	1:40â	9:12p
20	Tu	*Apollo 11* astronauts walk on Moon, 1969	OPH	5:48	8:25	2:06â	10:09p	6:01	8:12	2:21â	10:12p
21	We	Moon at perigee 6:33am	OPH	5:49	8:24	2:52â	11:12p	6:01	8:11	3:10â	11:15p
22	Th	Gregor Mendel born, 1822	SAG	5:49	8:23	3:48â	None	6:02	8:10	4:08â	None
23	Fr	Ice cream cone invented, 1904	SAG	5:50	8:22	4:53â	12:15a	6:03	8:10	5:13â	12:18a
24	Sa	Amelia Earhart born, 1898	CAP	5:51	8:21	9:18p̂	1:17a	6:04	8:09	9:07p̂	1:19a

29. Ninth Sunday after Pentecost
Day's Length: 14h 28m — Astron. Twilight: 1h 33m
Day's Length: 14h 04m — Astron. Twilight: 1h 24m

25	Su	Wyoming became U.S. territory, 1868	CAP	5:52	8:20	9:54p̂	2:14a	6:04	8:08	9:46p̂	2:16a
26	Mo	Moon, Jupiter best visible in S. 1:54am	AQU	5:53	8:20	10:24p̂	3:07a	6:05	8:08	10:19p̂	3:09a
27	Tu	Norman Lear born, 1922	AQU	5:54	8:19	10:50p̂	3:55a	6:06	8:07	10:48p̂	3:57a
28	We	World War I officially began, 1914	PSC	5:55	8:18	11:14p̂	4:40a	6:06	8:06	11:15p̂	4:42a
29	Th	NASA authorized by Congress, 1958	CET	5:56	8:17	11:37p̂	5:23a	6:07	8:05	11:41p̂	5:25a
30	Fr	Elvis Presley made professional debut, 1954	PSC	5:57	8:16	None	6:05a	6:08	8:04	None	6:06a
31	Sa	1st time men rode in vehicle on moon, 1971	ARI	5:57	8:15	12:01â	6:46a	6:09	8:04	12:08â	6:48a

JULY 2021 WEATHER FORECAST

ZONE 1 Northeast & New England

1-3: Strong-to-severe thunderstorms. **4-7:** Mostly fair. **8-11:** Some thunderstorms New England. Clearing Mid-Atlantic States. **12-15:** Hefty thunderstorms push to Atlantic Coast. **16-19:** More thunderstorms, then clearing. **20-23:** Another round of scattered thunderstorms, strong/gusty winds. **24-27:** Pleasant initially, then becoming unsettled. **28-31:** Thunderstorms at first for New England, then clearing skies. Gales along coastal plain.

ZONE 2 Great Lakes, Ohio Valley & Midwest

1-3: Thundery from Great Lakes to Kentucky, then clearing. **4-7:** Mostly fair. **8-11:** Scattered thunderstorms. **12-15:** Hefty thunderstorms roll through the Ohio Valley and Great Lakes area. **16-19:** Fair, cooler weather. **20-23:** Scattered gusty thunderstorms. **24-27:** A few showers, thunderstorms Great Lakes down through Ohio Valley to Kentucky. **28-31:** Thunderstorms at first for Ohio River Valley, points east, then clearing skies.

ZONE 3 Southeast

1-3: Severe thunderstorms sweep east, then clearing. **4-7:** Mostly fair skies. **8-11:** Continued mainly fair. **12-15:** Severe thunderstorms, some capable of spawning tornadoes for Tennessee and Mississippi valleys, sweep eastward. **16-19:** More thunderstorms, then clearing skies, cooler. **20-23:** More scattered thunderstorms and strong and gusty winds. **24-27:** Pleasant at first, then becoming unsettled. Dangerous thunderstorms sweep east into Mississippi Valley. **28-31:** Gales along coastal plain.

ZONE 4 North Central States

1-3: Fair across Northern Plains, points westward. **4-7:** Becoming unsettled. **8-11:** Continued unsettled most areas. **12-15:** Dangerous storms Northern Rockies, Northern Plains, then slowly clearing. **16-19:** Fair, turning cooler. **20-23:** Scattered thunderstorms, especially over Minnesota, Iowa, Missouri; strong, gusty winds. **24-27:** Showery conditions persist. **28-31:** Fair skies.

ZONE 5 South Central States

1-3: Fair across Southern Plains, points west. **4-7:** Becoming unsettled. **8-11:** Continued unsettled. Monsoonal thunderstorms New Mexico. **12-15:** Severe thunderstorms, tornadoes, from Texas and points east through Arkansas, Louisiana. Potent thunderstorm threat over parts of Southern Rockies, Southern Plains, as well as points eastward; then slowly clearing. **16-19:** Fair, cooler. **20-23:** Scattered thunderstorms, especially Arkansas and Louisiana; strong/gusty winds. **24-27:** Showers persist. Monsoonal showers New Mexico. **28-31:** Fair weather.

ZONE 6 Northwest

1-3: Fair skies from Pacific Coast spreading inland. **4-7:** Pleasant weather continues. **8-11:** Fair, then becoming unsettled. **12-15:** Fair skies. **16-19:** Fair, cooler. **20-23:** Showers clear Washington, Oregon, Idaho. **24-27:** Showery weather returns. **28-31:** Fair skies.

ZONE 7 Southwest

1-3: Fair skies from Pacific Coast spreading inland. **4-7:** Pleasant weather continues. **8-11:** Fair weather, then turning unsettled. Monsoonal thunderstorms Arizona. **12-15:** Fair skies continue. **16-19:** Fair, cooler. **20-23:** Partly cloudy skies. **24-27:** Sun and clouds. Monsoonal shower activity Arizona. **28-31:** Fair weather.

AUGUST 2021

8ᵗʰ Month — 31 Days

LEO
July 22 to
August 21

VIRGO
August 22 to
September 21

THE GATHERING CLOUDS BESPREAD THE SKY, AND GENTLE SHOWERS DESCEND;
THE RIPENING FRUITS WE JUST DESCRY, AS SUMMER IS AT END.

MOON'S PHASES
EASTERN DAYLIGHT TIME

● New Moon	8ᵗʰ	9:50 am
◑ First Quarter	15ᵗʰ	11:20 am
○ Full Moon	22ⁿᵈ	8:02 am
◐ Last Quarter	30ᵗʰ	3:13 am

Subtract 1 hour for CDT, 2 hours for MDT, and 3 hours for PDT.

SUN ON MERIDIAN
CIVIL TIME

Day	H:MM:SS
1ˢᵗ	13:06:48
8ᵗʰ	13:06:05
15ᵗʰ	13:04:54
22ⁿᵈ	13:03:16
29ᵗʰ	13:01:17

CALENDAR FOR NORTHERN STATES (EDT) — 40°N. Lat. 75°W. Long.

CALENDAR FOR SOUTHERN STATES (CDT) — 35°N. Lat. 90°W. Long.

DATE	ASTRONOMY, HOLIDAYS, AND EVENTS	MOON'S PLACE AT 7am ASTRONOMICALLY	SUN RISES	SUN SETS	EARLIEST MOONRISE MOONSET	MOON'S MERIDIAN PASSAGE	SUN RISES	SUN SETS	EARLIEST MOONRISE MOONSET	MOON'S MERIDIAN PASSAGE
30. Tenth Sunday after Pentecost					Day's Length: 14h 15m / Astron. Twilight: 1h 30m				Day's Length: 13h 53m / Astron. Twilight: 1h 23m	
1 Su	Mercury in superior conjunction	ARI	5:58	8:14	12:26ã	7:29a	6:09	8:03	12:36ã	7:31a
2 Mo	Moon at apogee 3:38am	TAU	5:59	8:13	12:54ã	8:14a	6:10	8:02	1:07ã	8:16a
3 Tu	Calvin Coolidge sworn in as president, 1923	TAU	6:00	8:11	1:27ã	9:01a	6:11	8:01	1:42ã	9:03a
4 We	Department of Energy est., 1977	TAU	6:01	8:10	2:05ã	9:50a	6:12	8:00	2:23ã	9:52a
5 Th	Neil A. Armstrong born, 1930	GEM	6:02	8:09	2:51ã	10:42a	6:12	7:59	3:10ã	10:44a
6 Fr	Andy Warhol born, 1928	GEM	6:03	8:08	3:44ã	11:34a	6:13	7:58	4:03ã	11:37a
7 Sa	Midpoint of summer; US Dept. War est., 1789	CAN	6:04	8:07	4:44ã	12:27p	6:14	7:57	5:02ã	12:29p
31. Eleventh Sunday after Pentecost					Day's Length: 14h 01m / Astron. Twilight: 1h 28m				Day's Length: 13h 41m / Astron. Twilight: 1h 21m	
8 Su	Refrigerator patented, 1899	CAN	6:05	8:06	5:48ã	1:19p	6:15	7:56	6:04ã	1:21p
9 Mo	*Walden* published, 1854	LEO	6:06	8:04	9:11p̄	2:09p	6:16	7:55	9:04p̄	2:11p
10 Tu	FDR was stricken with polio, 1921	LEO	6:07	8:03	9:39p̄	2:57p	6:16	7:54	9:35p̄	2:59p
11 We	Dog Days end	VIR	6:08	8:02	10:06p̄	3:45p	6:17	7:53	10:05p̄	3:47p
12 Th	1ˢᵗ communications satellite launched, 1960	VIR	6:09	8:00	10:32p̄	4:32p	6:18	7:52	10:35p̄	4:34p
13 Fr	The Beatles' "Help!" released (U.S.), 1965	VIR	6:10	7:59	10:59p̄	5:20p	6:19	7:50	11:06p̄	5:22p
14 Sa	V. J. Day; Social Security Act enacted, 1935	VIR	6:11	7:58	11:30p̄	6:10p	6:19	7:49	11:40p̄	6:13p
32. Twelfth Sunday after Pentecost					Day's Length: 13h 45m / Astron. Twilight: 1h 26m				Day's Length: 13h 28m / Astron. Twilight: 1h 20m	
15 Su	Assumption B.V.M.; Sir Walter Scott born, 1771	LIB	6:12	7:56	None	7:04p	6:20	7:48	None	7:06p
16 Mo	Otto Messmer born, 1892	SCO	6:13	7:55	12:05ã	8:01p	6:21	7:47	12:18ã	8:03p
17 Tu	Moon at perigee 5:23am	OPH	6:14	7:54	12:47ã	9:01p	6:22	7:46	1:04ã	9:03p
18 We	Anti-Cigarette League est., 1919	SAG	6:15	7:52	1:38ã	10:02p	6:22	7:45	1:57ã	10:05p
19 Th	Jupiter in opposition	SAG	6:15	7:51	2:38ã	11:03p	6:23	7:43	2:58ã	11:06p
20 Fr	*Voyager 2* was launched, 1977	CAP	6:16	7:49	3:45ã	None	6:24	7:42	4:04ã	None
21 Sa	Moon, Saturn best visible in S. 12:16am	CAP	6:17	7:48	4:56ã	12:01a	6:25	7:41	5:13ã	12:04a
33. Thirteenth Sunday after Pentecost					Day's Length: 13h 28m / Astron. Twilight: 1h 24m				Day's Length: 13h 14m / Astron. Twilight: 1h 18m	
22 Su	Moon, Jupiter best visible in S. 12:58am	AQU	6:18	7:47	6:08ã	12:55a	6:25	7:40	6:21ã	12:58a
23 Mo	Gene Kelly born, 1912	AQU	6:19	7:45	8:50p̄	1:45a	6:26	7:38	8:47p̄	1:47a
24 Tu	Hurricane Andrew made landfall, 1992	AQU	6:20	7:44	9:15p̄	2:32a	6:27	7:37	9:15p̄	2:34a
25 We	National Park Service est., 1916	CET	6:21	7:42	9:38p̄	3:16a	6:28	7:36	9:41p̄	3:18a
26 Th	1ˢᵗ Edsel manufactured, 1957	PSC	6:22	7:41	10:02p̄	3:58a	6:28	7:34	10:08p̄	4:00a
27 Fr	1ˢᵗ oil well successfully drilled, 1859	PSC	6:23	7:39	10:26p̄	4:41a	6:29	7:33	10:35p̄	4:42a
28 Sa	MLK Jr. gave "I Have a Dream" speech, 1963	ARI	6:24	7:37	10:53p̄	5:23a	6:30	7:32	11:05p̄	5:25a
34. Fourteenth Sunday after Pentecost					Day's Length: 13h 11m / Astron. Twilight: 1h 23m				Day's Length: 13h 00m / Astron. Twilight: 1h 17m	
29 Su	Moon at apogee 10:22pm	TAU	6:25	7:36	11:24p̄	6:07a	6:31	7:30	11:39p̄	6:09a
30 Mo	*David Letterman Show* premiered, 1993	TAU	6:26	7:34	11:59p̄	6:53a	6:31	7:29	None	6:55a
31 Tu	California most populated state, 1964	TAU	6:27	7:33	None	7:42a	6:32	7:28	12:17ã	7:44a

AUGUST 2021 WEATHER FORECAST

ZONE 1 Northeast & New England

1-3: Hot and sultry for the East, turning unsettled. **4-7:** Clearing skies, cooler then turning unsettled. **8-11:** Tropical cyclone threat along coastal plain. Otherwise, scattered showers. **12-15:** Clearing skies. **16-19:** Unsettled; gusty winds. **20-23:** Pleasant, then turning unsettled. **24-27:** Thunderstorms throughout Mid-Atlantic States; gales New England coast. **28-31:** Hot, small shower risk.

ZONE 2 Great Lakes, Ohio Valley & Midwest

1-3: Showery, thundery weather. **4-7:** Unsettled, but cooler Great Lakes, Ohio Valley. **8-11:** Scattered showers. **12-15:** Sunny to partly cloudy skies, pleasant for Great Lakes, Ohio Valley. **16-19:** Unsettled; gusty winds Great Lakes, Ohio Valley. **20-23:** Continued unsettled. **24-27:** Variable cloudiness. **28-31:** Scattered showers, very warm, muggy.

ZONE 3 Southeast

1-3: Hot, sultry weather, then turning unsettled with showery/thundery weather. **4-7:** Hurricane threat Florida, points north, through Georgia, Carolinas, Virginia coast. Remaining hot, sticky elsewhere, with widely scattered showers, thunderstorms. **8-11:** Scattered thunderstorms, muggy. Gusty winds Mississippi Valley. **12-15:** Continued humid, scattered showers, thunderstorms. **16-19:** Scattered thunderstorms. **20-23:** Pleasant, then turning unsettled. **24-27:** Hazy, humid, thunderstorms. **28-31:** Hot, steamy temperatures.

ZONE 4 North Central States

1-3: Hot across Northern Plains, with a few thunderstorms. **4-7:** Fair skies, hot over Northern Plains; possible thunderstorm. **8-11:** Thunderstorms over Northern Rockies, spreading east. **12-15:** Mostly sunny skies. **16-19:** Clear skies, pleasant. **20-23:** Stormy Northern Rockies, on east through Northern Plains, points east. **24-27:** Mostly fair, cooler. **28-31:** Scattered showers, then fair. Thunderstorms Northern Plains.

ZONE 5 South Central States

1-3: Hot across Plains, isolated thunderstorms. **4-7:** Fair skies, hot, with a thunderstorm or two. Monsoonal thunderstorms for New Mexico. **8-11:** Scattered thunderstorms. **12-15:** Fair skies. **16-19:** Abundant sunshine. **20-23:** Stormy weather spreads in from the west. **24-27:** Clearing, cooler. **28-31:** Hurricane threat Texas/Louisiana Gulf Coast. Elsewhere, a few showers/thunderstorms, then clearing. More monsoonal showers for New Mexico.

ZONE 6 Northwest

1-3: Becoming unsettled. **4-7:** Scattered showers, few thunderstorms. **8-11:** Clearing skies elsewhere. **12-15:** Becoming unsettled Washington, Oregon, Idaho. **16-19:** Pleasant weather. **20-23:** Gales along Pacific Coast. **24-27:** Mostly fair, cooler. **28-31:** Unsettled West Coast.

ZONE 7 Southwest

1-3: Becoming unsettled across Pacific States, along South Plateau. **4-7:** Scattered showers, few thunderstorms. Monsoonal thunderstorms Arizona. **8-11:** Clearing skies. **12-15:** Mostly sunny skies. **16-19:** Pleasant weather for most of the region. **20-23:** Gales along West Coast. **24-27:** Mostly fair, cooler. **28-31:** Unsettled West Coast. Monsoonal showers Arizona.

SEPTEMBER 2021

9th Month · **30 Days**

VIRGO
August 22 to
September 21

LIBRA
September 22 to
October 22

NOW AUTUMN'S GOLDEN STORES BEHOLD, WITH FRUIT EACH TREE IS CROWNED;
PEACHES IN SUITS OF RED OR GOLD, EACH TWIG BOWS TOWARD THE GROUND.

MOON'S PHASES — EASTERN DAYLIGHT TIME

 New Moon 6th 8:52 pm
◑ First Quarter 13th 4:39 pm
○ Full Moon 20th 7:55 pm
◐ Last Quarter 28th 9:57 pm

Subtract 1 hour for CDT, 2 hours for MDT, and 3 hours for PDT.

SUN ON MERIDIAN CIVIL TIME

Day	H:MM:SS
1st	13:00:21
8th	12:58:01
15th	12:55:33
22nd	12:53:03
29th	12:50:39

				NORTHERN STATES (EDT) 40°N. Lat. 75°W. Long.				SOUTHERN STATES (CDT) 35°N. Lat. 90°W. Long.			
DATE	ASTRONOMY, HOLIDAYS, AND EVENTS	MOON'S PLACE AT 7am ASTRONOMICALLY		SUN RISES	SUN SETS	EARLIEST MOONRISE MOONSET	MOON'S MERIDIAN PASSAGE	SUN RISES	SUN SETS	EARLIEST MOONRISE MOONSET	MOON'S MERIDIAN PASSAGE
1 We	Lily Tomlin born, 1939	GEM		6:28	7:31	12:42â	8:32a	6:33	7:26	1:01â	8:34a
2 Th	Terry Bradshaw born, 1948	GEM		6:29	7:30	1:32â	9:24a	6:33	7:25	1:52â	9:26a
3 Fr	Sinatra started solo singing career, 1942	CAN		6:30	7:28	2:29â	10:17a	6:34	7:24	2:48â	10:19a
4 Sa	Paul Harvey born, 1918	CAN		6:31	7:26	3:32â	11:09a	6:35	7:22	3:49â	11:11a

35. Fifteenth Sunday after Pentecost — Day's Length: 12h 53m / Astron. Twilight: 1h 22m — Day's Length: 12h 45m / Astron. Twilight: 1h 16m

5 Su	1st Labor Day parade, NYC, 1882	LEO		6:32	7:25	4:39â	12:00p	6:36	7:21	4:54â	12:02p
6 Mo	**Labor Day**	LEO		6:33	7:23	5:48â	12:50p	6:36	7:19	6:00â	12:52p
7 Tu	Rosh Hashanah (New Year 5782)	LEO		6:33	7:22	8:08p̄	1:39p	6:37	7:18	8:06p̄	1:41p
8 We	ESPN made its debut, 1979	VIR		6:34	7:20	8:34p̄	2:27p	6:38	7:17	8:36p̄	2:29p
9 Th	Fast of Gedaliah; Moon, Venus visible in W.	VIR		6:35	7:18	9:02p̄	3:16p	6:39	7:15	9:07p̄	3:18p
10 Fr	Traditional peak of hurricane season	VIR		6:36	7:17	9:31p̄	4:07p	6:39	7:14	9:41p̄	4:09p
11 Sa	Moon at perigee 5:54am	LIB		6:37	7:15	10:05p̄	5:00p	6:40	7:12	10:18p̄	5:02p

36. Sixteenth Sunday after Pentecost — Day's Length: 12h 35m / Astron. Twilight: 1h 21m — Day's Length: 12h 30m / Astron. Twilight: 1h 15m

12 Su	1st practical typewriter sold, 1873	SCO		6:38	7:13	10:45p̄	5:56p	6:41	7:11	11:01p̄	5:58p
13 Mo	1st diesel automobile introduced, 1977	OPH		6:39	7:12	11:33p̄	6:55p	6:41	7:09	11:51p̄	6:57p
14 Tu	Holy Cross Day	SAG		6:40	7:10	None	7:55p	6:42	7:08	None	7:58p
15 We	Ember Day; William H. Taft born, 1857	SAG		6:41	7:08	12:29â	8:56p	6:43	7:07	12:49â	8:58p
16 Th	Yom Kippur	SAG		6:42	7:07	1:34â	9:53p	6:44	7:05	1:53â	9:56p
17 Fr	Ember Day; Citizenship Day	CAP		6:43	7:05	2:43â	10:48p	6:44	7:04	3:00â	10:50p
18 Sa	Ember Day; Frankie Avalon born, 1939	CAP		6:44	7:03	3:53â	11:38p	6:45	7:02	4:07â	11:40p

37. Seventeenth Sunday after Pentecost — Day's Length: 12h 17m / Astron. Twilight: 1h 20m — Day's Length: 12h 15m / Astron. Twilight: 1h 15m

19 Su	1st underground nuclear test, 1957	AQU		6:45	7:02	5:01â	None	6:46	7:01	5:12â	None
20 Mo	*The Captain & Tennille* show premiered, 1976	AQU		6:46	7:00	6:08â	12:25a	6:47	6:59	6:15â	12:27a
21 Tu	Succot; *The Hobbit* published, 1937	PSC		6:47	6:58	7:40p̄	1:10a	6:47	6:58	7:42p̄	1:12a
22 We	Autumnal equinox (1st day of fall) 3:21pm	CET		6:48	6:57	8:03p̄	1:53a	6:48	6:57	8:08p̄	1:54a
23 Th	Flashbulbs were patented, 1930	PSC		6:49	6:55	8:27p̄	2:35a	6:49	6:55	8:35p̄	2:37a
24 Fr	*The Love Boat* debuted on ABC, 1977	ARI		6:50	6:54	8:53p̄	3:18a	6:49	6:54	9:04p̄	3:19a
25 Sa	William Faulkner born, 1897	ARI		6:50	6:52	9:22p̄	4:01a	6:50	6:52	9:36p̄	4:03a

38. Eighteenth Sunday after Pentecost — Day's Length: 11h 59m / Astron. Twilight: 1h 20m — Day's Length: 12h 00m / Astron. Twilight: 1h 14m

26 Su	Gold Star Mother's Day; Moon apogee 5:40pm	TAU		6:51	6:50	9:56p̄	4:47a	6:51	6:51	10:12p̄	4:48a
27 Mo	Mercury retrograde; Thomas Nast born, 1840	TAU		6:52	6:49	10:35p̄	5:34a	6:52	6:49	10:53p̄	5:36a
28 Tu	Ed Sullivan born, 1902	TAU		6:53	6:47	11:21p̄	6:23a	6:52	6:48	11:41p̄	6:25a
29 We	Simchat Torah; Michaelmas Day	GEM		6:54	6:45	None	7:14a	6:53	6:47	None	7:16a
30 Th	Japan's nuclear accident, 1999	GEM		6:55	6:44	12:15â	8:06a	6:54	6:45	12:34â	8:08a

SEPTEMBER 2021 WEATHER FORECAST

ZONE 1 Northeast & New England
1-3: Continued hot. **4-7:** Dangerous thunderstorms. **8-11:** Pleasant weather into New England. Humid, with hit-or-miss showers for the Mid-Atlantic States. **12-15:** Thunderstorms, then turning fair. **16-19:** Pleasant initially, then thunderstorms developing. **20-23:** Severe thunderstorms, accompanied by "drownpours" and potentially damaging winds. **24-27:** Fair skies into New England, then becoming unsettled. **28-30:** Fair weather.

ZONE 2 Great Lakes, Ohio Valley & Midwest
1-3: Pleasant weather. **4-7:** Violent thunderstorms from Kentucky north through the Great Lakes area. **8-11:** Pleasant along the Ohio River Valley and points north. **12-15:** Clearing skies for most of the sections. **16-19:** Damaging thunderstorms for the Midwest—especially potent for Kentucky. **20-23:** Rainy weather from the Great Lakes and points south tapers off and ends by the 23rd. **24-27:** Fair skies in the Ohio Valley, then becoming unsettled. **28-30:** Fair and dry with pleasant temperatures.

ZONE 3 Southeast
1-3: Continued hot. **4-7:** Violent thunderstorms throughout the Mississippi Valley. **8-11:** Hot and humid, with hit-or-miss showers, especially for the Carolinas, Georgia, and into Florida. **12-15:** Thunderstorms, then turning fair. **16-19:** Pleasant initially, then big thunderstorms develop. **20-23:** Gales along the Gulf and Atlantic coasts; scattered thunderstorms. **24-27:** More thunderstorms. Showery and breezy for the Mississippi Valley. **28-30:** Sultry, with a continued risk of showers and thunderstorms.

ZONE 4 North Central States
1-3: Pleasant weather. **4-7:** Scattered thunderstorms. **8-11:** Clear skies. **12-15:** Mainly fair. **16-19:** Violent thunderstorms. **20-23:** Rain, then clearing skies and cooler temperatures. **24-27:** Changeable skies, some sun/some clouds, risk of passing showers. **28-30:** Turning fair and pleasant.

ZONE 5 South Central States
1-3: Tranquil weather. **4-7:** Scattered thunderstorms. **8-11:** Fair skies. **12-15:** Mostly sunny. **16-19:** Heavy thunderstorms. **20-23:** Rainy skies, then decreasing cloudiness. **24-27:** Variable cloudiness with an ongoing risk of a shower. **28-30:** Sunshine and comfortably warm.

ZONE 6 Northwest
1-3: Fair, then turning unsettled. **4-7:** Clearing skies. **8-11:** Clear skies. **12-15:** Fair weather continues. **16-19:** Gales along the Pacific Coast. **20-23:** Fair skies and turning cooler. **24-27:** Unsettled for Idaho, Oregon, and Washington. **28-30:** More unsettled weather.

ZONE 7 Southwest
1-3: Sunny on the West Coast, then turning unsettled. **4-7:** Mixed sun and clouds with just a slight risk of a passing shower. **8-11:** Clear skies and dry weather over the Southwest. **12-15:** Fair skies. **16-19:** Gales along the Pacific Coast. **20-23:** Fair skies and turning cooler from the West Coast to points eastward. **24-27:** Sunny to partly cloudy. **28-30:** Becoming unsettled.

OCTOBER 2021

10th Month — **10th Month** 31 Days

LIBRA
September 22 to
October 22

SCORPIO
October 23 to
November 20

AND NOW THE FROST IS SEEN IN MORN, OVERSPREADING FIELDS WITH WHITE; THE FARMER GATHERS IN HIS CORN, WITH PLEASURE AND DELIGHT.

MOON'S PHASES
EASTERN DAYLIGHT TIME

- ● New Moon 6th 7:05 am
- ◐ First Quarter 12th 11:25 pm
- ○ Full Moon 20th 10:57 am
- ◑ Last Quarter 28th 4:05 pm

Subtract 1 hour for CDT, 2 hours for MDT, and 3 hours for PDT.

SUN ON MERIDIAN CIVIL TIME

Day	H:MM:SS
1st	12:50:00
8th	12:47:54
15th	12:46:10
22nd	12:44:53
29th	12:44:10

CALENDAR FOR NORTHERN STATES (EDT) 40°N. Lat. 75°W. Long.

CALENDAR FOR SOUTHERN STATES (CDT) 35°N. Lat. 90°W. Long.

DATE		ASTRONOMY, HOLIDAYS, AND EVENTS	MOON'S PLACE AT 7am ASTRONOMICALLY	SUN RISES	SUN SETS	EARLIEST MOONRISE MOONSET	MOON'S MERIDIAN PASSAGE	SUN RISES	SUN SETS	EARLIEST MOONRISE MOONSET	MOON'S MERIDIAN PASSAGE
1	Fr	1st "Model T" Ford built, 1908	CAN	6:56	6:42	1:15â	8:58a	6:55	6:44	1:33â	9:00a
2	Sa	Rome became capital of Italy, 1870	LEO	6:57	6:40	2:20â	9:49a	6:56	6:42	2:35â	9:51a

39. Nineteenth Sunday after Pentecost
Day's Length: 11h 41m / Astron. Twilight: 1h 20m
Day's Length: 11h 45m / Astron. Twilight: 1h 15m

3	Su	Motor-driven vacuum cleaner patented, 1893	LEO	6:58	6:39	3:27â	10:39a	6:56	6:41	3:40â	10:41a
4	Mo	1st carving began on Mt. Rushmore, 1927	LEO	6:59	6:37	4:37â	11:28a	6:57	6:40	4:46â	11:30a
5	Tu	1st televised White House Address, 1947	VIR	7:00	6:36	5:48â	12:17p	6:58	6:38	5:54â	12:19p
6	We	George Westinghouse born, 1846	VIR	7:01	6:34	7:00â	1:06p	6:59	6:37	7:02â	1:08p
7	Th	*The Frank Sinatra Show* debuted, 1950	VIR	7:02	6:32	7:30p̄	1:57p	6:59	6:35	7:38p̄	1:59p
8	Fr	Moon at perigee 1:20pm	LIB	7:03	6:31	8:03p̄	2:51p	7:00	6:34	8:15p̄	2:53p
9	Sa	Fire Prevention Day; Fall Astronomy Day	LIB	7:04	6:29	8:41p̄	3:48p	7:01	6:33	8:57p̄	3:50p

40. Twentieth Sunday after Pentecost
Day's Length: 11h 22m / Astron. Twilight: 1h 20m
Day's Length: 11h 30m / Astron. Twilight: 1h 15m

10	Su	Saturn direct	OPH	7:05	6:28	9:28p̄	4:48p	7:02	6:31	9:46p̄	4:50p
11	Mo	**Columbus Day**; Eleanor Roosevelt born, 1884	SAG	7:06	6:26	10:23p̄	5:49p	7:03	6:30	10:43p̄	5:52p
12	Tu	Columbus Day (traditional)	SAG	7:07	6:25	11:25p̄	6:50p	7:03	6:29	11:46p̄	6:53p
13	We	Messier discovered Whirlpool Galaxy, 1773	SAG	7:08	6:23	None	7:49p	7:04	6:27	None	7:52p
14	Th	E.E. Cummings born, 1894	CAP	7:09	6:22	12:33â	8:44p	7:05	6:26	12:52â	8:46p
15	Fr	*I Love Lucy* premiered, 1951	CAP	7:11	6:20	1:43â	9:35p	7:06	6:25	1:58â	9:37p
16	Sa	Noah Webster born, 1758	AQU	7:12	6:19	2:51â	10:22p	7:07	6:24	3:04â	10:24p

41. Twenty-first Sunday after Pentecost
Day's Length: 11h 05m / Astron. Twilight: 1h 21m
Day's Length: 11h 15m / Astron. Twilight: 1h 15m

17	Su	Albert Einstein moved to Princeton, NJ, 1933	AQU	7:13	6:17	3:58â	11:07p	7:08	6:22	4:06â	11:09p
18	Mo	Mercury direct; Jupiter direct	PSC	7:14	6:16	5:02â	11:49p	7:09	6:21	5:07â	11:51p
19	Tu	Basketball introduced to Olympics, 1933	CET	7:15	6:14	6:04â	None	7:09	6:20	6:06â	None
20	We	George Nader born, 1921	PSC	7:16	6:13	7:06â	12:31a	7:10	6:19	7:04â	12:33a
21	Th	Daniel Boone born, 1734	ARI	7:17	6:12	6:55p̄	1:13a	7:11	6:18	7:04p̄	1:15a
22	Fr	College of NJ (Princeton) chartered, 1879	ARI	7:18	6:10	7:22p̄	1:57a	7:12	6:16	7:35p̄	1:58a
23	Sa	1st U.S. horseshoe champ. tourney, 1915	TAU	7:19	6:09	7:54p̄	2:41a	7:13	6:15	8:09p̄	2:43a

42. Twenty-second Sunday after Pentecost
Day's Length: 10h 47m / Astron. Twilight: 1h 21m
Day's Length: 11h 00m / Astron. Twilight: 1h 16m

24	Su	United Nations Day; Moon apogee 11:19am	TAU	7:20	6:08	8:31p̄	3:28a	7:14	6:14	8:49p̄	3:30a
25	Mo	John Steinbeck awarded Nobel Prize, 1962	TAU	7:21	6:06	9:14p̄	4:17a	7:15	6:13	9:33p̄	4:19a
26	Tu	Pat Sajak born, 1946	GEM	7:22	6:05	10:04p̄	5:07a	7:16	6:12	10:24p̄	5:09a
27	We	1st newsreel featuring sound released, 1927	GEM	7:24	6:04	11:01p̄	5:58a	7:16	6:11	11:20p̄	6:00a
28	Th	Jonas Salk born, 1914	CAN	7:25	6:02	None	6:49a	7:17	6:10	None	6:51a
29	Fr	NYSE crash, Great Depression began, 1929	CAN	7:26	6:01	12:03â	7:39a	7:18	6:09	12:20â	7:41a
30	Sa	Saturn in eastern quadrature	LEO	7:27	6:00	1:08â	8:28a	7:19	6:08	1:22â	8:30a

43. Twenty-third Sunday after Pentecost
Day's Length: 10h 31m / Astron. Twilight: 1h 22m
Day's Length: 10h 46m / Astron. Twilight: 1h 17m

31	Su	Halloween	LEO	7:28	5:59	2:15â	9:16a	7:20	6:07	2:26â	9:18a

OCTOBER 2021 WEATHER FORECAST

ZONE 1 Northeast & New England

1-3: Thunderstorms sweep east into New England. **4-7:** Clear skies and unseasonably chilly. **8-11:** Unsettled with rain. **12-15:** Pleasantly dry weather. **16-19:** Gusty winds/heavy downpours. **20-23:** Fair skies and windy. **24-27:** Scattered showers, then becoming fair. **28-31:** Turning stormy over the Atlantic Seaboard with heavy rains and widespread flooding; some flakes of wet snow could mix in over higher elevations of New England.

ZONE 2 Great Lakes, Ohio Valley & Midwest

1-3: Thunderstorms across Great Lakes. **4-7:** Fair skies. **8-11:** Breezy and showery conditions. **12-15:** Fair, then increasingly cloudy skies. **16-19:** Mixed sun and clouds. **20-23:** Very unsettled conditions. **24-27:** Fair skies. **28-31:** Stormy for the Ohio Valley and Great Lakes where some wet snow could mix in.

ZONE 3 Southeast

1-3: Thunderstorms spread east to the Mississippi Valley. **4-7:** Fair skies. **8-11:** Unsettled with rain. Gusty winds for the Mississippi Valley. **12-15:** Pleasant weather. Fair, then increasingly cloudy skies. Hurricane threat for South Florida. **16-19:** Stormy weather, especially over the Gulf Coastal States. **20-23:** Very unsettled over the Mississippi Valley. Increasingly cloudy elsewhere and windy. **24-27:** Scattered showers, then becoming fair. **28-31:** Turning stormy.

ZONE 4 North Central States

1-3: Thunderstorms across the Northern Plains. **4-7:** Fair, colder weather. **8-11:** Gusty winds into the Northern Plains States. **12-15:** Fair initially, then turning very unsettled. **16-19:** Clearing skies across the Northern Plains States. **20-23:** Very unsettled over the Northern Plains and points east. **24-27:** Pleasant conditions. **28-31:** Fair, turning colder in the Rocky Mountains. Farther to the east, stormy for Minnesota, Iowa, and Missouri.

ZONE 5 South Central States

1-3: Scattered thunderstorms. **4-7:** A colder surge of air moves in; dry. **8-11:** Breezy and dry. **12-15:** Increasingly cloudy with some heavy rains. **16-19:** Skies clear. **20-23:** Clouds, rains return. **24-27:** Pleasantly dry. **28-31:** Turning colder with increasingly cloudy skies and stormy conditions for Arkansas and Louisiana.

ZONE 6 Northwest

1-3: Clearing in Washington, Oregon, and Idaho. **4-7:** Fair, chillier. **8-11:** Gusty winds for the Pacific Coast. **12-15:** Fair initially, then turning very unsettled. **16-19:** Clearing skies. **20-23:** Fine and dry weather. **24-27:** Fair skies, then becoming stormy. **28-31:** Fair skies, turning chillier.

ZONE 7 Southwest

1-3: Rain showers along the South Plateau. **4-7:** Fair, colder weather. **8-11:** Gusty winds for the Pacific Coast. **12-15:** Fair initially for the West Coast and points east, then turning very unsettled. Dust storms over the Southwest. **16-19:** Clearing skies for the West Coast. **20-23:** Fine weather for the West Coast. **24-27:** Fair skies for the West Coast, then becoming stormy. **28-31:** Fair skies, turning colder.

NOVEMBER 2021

11th Month · 30 Days

SCORPIO
October 23 to November 20

SAGITTARIUS
November 21 to December 20

TIME ON HIS WING FAST HASTES AWAY, AND CHILLS EACH WARM SUCCEED;
TO CAPRICORN SOL HASTES EACH DAY, SO NIGHTS THE DAY EXCEED.

MOON'S PHASES
EASTERN STANDARD TIME

● New Moon	4th	5:15 pm
☽ First Quarter	11th	7:46 am
○ Full Moon	19th	3:57 am
☾ Last Quarter	27th	7:28 am

Subtract 1 hour for CST, 2 hours for MST, and 3 hours for PST.

SUN ON MERIDIAN
CIVIL TIME

Day	H:MM:SS
1st	12:44:03
8th	11:44:16
15th	11:45:09
22nd	11:46:42
29th	11:48:55

CALENDAR FOR NORTHERN STATES
(EST)
40°N. Lat. 75°W. Long.

CALENDAR FOR SOUTHERN STATES
(CST)
35°N. Lat. 90°W. Long.

DATE		ASTRONOMY, HOLIDAYS, AND EVENTS	MOON'S PLACE AT 7am ASTRONOMICALLY	SUN RISES	SUN SETS	EARLIEST MOONRISE MOONSET	MOON'S MERIDIAN PASSAGE	SUN RISES	SUN SETS	EARLIEST MOONRISE MOONSET	MOON'S MERIDIAN PASSAGE
1	Mo	All Saints' Day; *Harpers Bazaar* published, 1867	VIR	7:29	5:57	3:24ă	10:04a	7:21	6:06	3:31ă	10:06a
2	Tu	**Election Day**; All Souls' Day	VIR	7:30	5:56	4:34ă	10:52a	7:22	6:05	4:38ă	10:54a
3	We	Moon, Mercury best visible in E. 6:52am	VIR	7:31	5:55	5:47ă	11:42a	7:23	6:04	5:47ă	11:45a
4	Th	1st air-conditioned car displayed, 1939	LIB	7:33	5:54	7:03ă	12:35p	7:24	6:03	6:59ă	12:38p
5	Fr	Moon at perigee 6:10pm	LIB	7:34	5:53	6:34p̄	1:32p	7:25	6:02	6:48p̄	1:35p
6	Sa	John Philip Sousa born, 1854	SCO	7:35	5:52	7:18p̄	2:33p	7:26	6:01	7:35p̄	2:35p

44. Twenty-fourth Sunday after Pentecost
Day's Length: 10h 15m · Astron. Twilight: 1h 24m
Day's Length: 10h 33m · Astron. Twilight: 1h 18m

7	Su	Daylight Saving Time ends	OPH	6:36	4:51	7:11p̄	2:36p	6:27	5:00	7:31p̄	2:39p
8	Mo	Edmond Halley born, 1656	SAG	6:37	4:50	8:13p̄	3:40p	6:28	4:59	8:34p̄	3:43p
9	Tu	Spiro T. Agnew born, 1918	SAG	6:38	4:49	9:22p̄	4:42p	6:29	4:59	9:42p̄	4:45p
10	We	*Sesame Street* made its debut, 1969	CAP	6:39	4:48	10:33p̄	5:40p	6:30	4:58	10:50p̄	5:42p
11	Th	**Veterans Day**	CAP	6:41	4:47	11:43p̄	6:33p	6:31	4:57	11:56p̄	6:35p
12	Fr	1st drive-up bank opened, 1946	AQU	6:42	4:46	None	7:21p	6:32	4:56	None	7:23p
13	Sa	Holland Tunnel opened, 1927	AQU	6:43	4:45	12:50ă	8:06p	6:33	4:56	1:00ă	8:08p

45. Twenty-fifth Sunday after Pentecost
Day's Length: 10h 00m · Astron. Twilight: 1h 25m
Day's Length: 10h 22m · Astron. Twilight: 1h 19m

14	Su	Sadie Hawkins Day	PSC	6:44	4:44	1:55ă	8:49p	6:34	4:55	2:01ă	8:50p
15	Mo	Jupiter in eastern quadrature	CET	6:45	4:44	2:57ă	9:30p	6:35	4:54	3:00ă	9:32p
16	Tu	Burgess Meredith born, 1908	PSC	6:46	4:43	3:58ă	10:12p	6:36	4:54	3:57ă	10:13p
17	We	Gordon Lightfoot born, 1938	CET	6:47	4:42	4:59ă	10:54p	6:36	4:53	4:55ă	10:56p
18	Th	Nintendo released the GameCube, 2001	ARI	6:49	4:41	6:00ă	11:38p	6:37	4:53	5:53ă	11:40p
19	Fr	Lunar eclipse 4:03am	TAU	6:50	4:41	4:55p̄	None	6:38	4:52	5:09p̄	None
20	Sa	Moon at apogee 8:57pm	TAU	6:51	4:40	5:29p̄	12:24a	6:39	4:52	5:47p̄	12:26a

46. Christ the King Sunday
Day's Length: 9h 48m · Astron. Twilight: 1h 26m
Day's Length: 10h 11m · Astron. Twilight: 1h 20m

21	Su	Rebecca Felton 1st female senator, 1922	TAU	6:52	4:40	6:41p̄	1:12a	6:40	4:51	6:29p̄	1:14a
22	Mo	Rodney Dangerfield born, 1921	GEM	6:53	4:39	6:58p̄	2:02a	6:41	4:51	7:18p̄	2:04a
23	Tu	Franklin Pierce born, 1804	GEM	6:54	4:38	7:52p̄	2:52a	6:42	4:50	8:12p̄	2:54a
24	We	Dale Carnegie born, 1888	CAN	6:55	4:38	8:52p̄	3:43a	6:43	4:50	9:09p̄	3:45a
25	Th	**Thanksgiving Day**	CAN	6:56	4:38	9:54p̄	4:33a	6:44	4:50	10:10p̄	4:35a
26	Fr	Great Appalachian Storm dumped 57", 1950	LEO	6:57	4:37	10:59p̄	5:21a	6:45	4:50	11:11p̄	5:23a
27	Sa	NYC's Pennsylvania Station opened, 1910	LEO	6:58	4:37	None	6:08a	6:46	4:49	None	6:10a

47. First Sunday of Advent
Day's Length: 9h 37m · Astron. Twilight: 1h 27m
Day's Length: 10h 02m · Astron. Twilight: 1h 21m

28	Su	Mercury in superior conjunction	LEO	7:00	4:36	12:05ă	6:54a	6:47	4:49	12:14ă	6:56a
29	Mo	Chanukah; Louisa May Alcott born, 1832	VIR	7:01	4:36	1:12ă	7:41a	6:48	4:49	1:18ă	7:43a
30	Tu	Hurricane season ends; M. Twain born, 1835	VIR	7:02	4:36	2:22ă	8:28a	6:49	4:49	2:24ă	8:30a

NOVEMBER 2021 WEATHER FORECAST

ZONE 1 Northeast & New England
1-3: Clearing skies, colder. **4-7:** Unsettled conditions. Runners in NYC Marathon may get wet. **8-11:** Pleasant weather. **12-15:** Heavy showers, a few thunderstorms; gale-force winds Mid-Atlantic Coast. Squally across Northeast States; some snow possible New England. **16-19:** Windy, cold. **20-23:** Unsettled, with some wet snow and/or rain in the north. **24-27:** Fair, then turning very unsettled with gusty winds, showers; hopefully the adverse weather holds off until after the Thanksgiving Parade. **28-30:** Clearing skies, turning progressively colder.

ZONE 2 Great Lakes, Ohio Valley & Midwest
1-3: Fair skies, unseasonably cold. **4-7:** Unsettled conditions. **8-11:** Sunshine, then increasing cloudiness. **12-15:** Squalls Ohio Valley, points eastward. **16-19:** Considerable cloudiness, blustery with rain, snow showers. **20-23:** More clouds than sun. Possible shower or flurry. **24-27:** Fair at first, then turning very unsettled with squalls from the Ohio Valley and points east. **28-30:** Considerable cloudiness, increasingly windy, scattered rain and snow showers.

ZONE 3 Southeast
1-3: Clearing skies, colder temperatures. Frosts penetrate into Southland. **4-7:** Unsettled, milder. **8-11:** Pleasant weather. **12-15:** Heavy showers, few thunderstorms; gale-force winds reach over 40 MPH **16-19:** Gusty winds, unseasonably cold. Mostly fair Mississippi River Valley, then becoming overcast, blustery. **20-23:** Fair Mississippi Valley, points westward. Farther east, unsettled with rain. **24-27:** Gusty winds, showery. **28-30:** Gradually clearing skies, turning progressively colder.

ZONE 4 North Central States
1-3: Chilly across Northern Plains. **4-7:** Unsettled. **8-11:** Fair at first, then becoming stormy with some snow possible. **12-15:** Unsettled for Northern Plains, all points west. **16-19:** Mostly fair, then becoming overcast, blustery. **20-23:** Fair skies. **24-27:** Very unsettled, with squally weather over Northern Rockies, Northern Plains, as well as points east; then slowly clearing. **28-30:** Turning very cold.

ZONE 5 South Central States
1-3: Unseasonably cool across Southern Plains, southward to Mexican Border. **4-7:** Cloudy, showery. **8-11:** Fair, then becoming stormy, with some rain or mixed rain, wet snow. **12-15:** More unsettled weather. **16-19:** Tranquil, then becoming cloudy/windy. **20-23:** Dry, clear skies. **24-27:** Squally conditions, then gradual clearing. **28-30:** Temperatures fall precipitously.

ZONE 6 Northwest
1-3: Chilly, dry. **4-7:** Showery, then clearing. **8-11:** Fair, then becoming stormy with some rain and snow possible. **12-15:** Continued unsettled near and along Pacific Coast. **16-19:** Mostly fair. **20-23:** Becoming stormy in Washington, Oregon, Idaho. **24-27:** Still very unsettled, then slowly clearing. **28-30:** Turning much chillier.

ZONE 7 Southwest
1-3: Chilly along the West Coast. **4-7:** Mixed clouds and sun, with a few showers. **8-11:** Fair, then becoming stormy with rain and (over Sierra Nevadas) some snow possible. **12-15:** Unsettled Pacific Coast. Light snow on South Plateau. **16-19:** Mostly fair. **20-23:** Fair skies. **24-27:** Very unsettled in the West, then slowly clearing. **28-30:** Turning much colder.

12th Month   # DECEMBER 2021   **31 Days**

SAGITTARIUS
November 21 to
December 20

CAPRICORN
December 21 to
January 18

COLD BLOWS THE WIND, THE FROZEN RAIN AND FLEECY SNOW DESCEND;
FOR, FREEZING WINTER'S COME AGAIN, AND SO THE YEAR DOES END.

MOON'S PHASES EASTERN STANDARD TIME		SUN ON MERIDIAN CIVIL TIME		
● New Moon	4th 2:43 am	Day	H:MM:SS	
◗ First Quarter	10th 8:36 pm	1st	11:49:39	
○ Full Moon	18th 11:35 pm	8th	11:52:33	
◖ Last Quarter	26th 9:24 pm	15th	11:55:48	
		22nd	11:59:15	
Subtract 1 hour for CST, 2 hours for MST, and 3 hours for PST.		29th	12:02:42	

			CALENDAR FOR NORTHERN STATES (EST) 40°N. Lat. 75°W. Long.				CALENDAR FOR SOUTHERN STATES (CST) 35°N. Lat. 90°W. Long.			
DATE	ASTRONOMY, HOLIDAYS, AND EVENTS	MOON'S PLACE AT 7am ASTRONOMICALLY	SUN RISES	SUN SETS	EARLIEST MOONRISE MOONSET	MOON'S MERIDIAN PASSAGE	SUN RISES	SUN SETS	EARLIEST MOONRISE MOONSET	MOON'S MERIDIAN PASSAGE
1	We	U.S. gas rationing went into effect, 1942	VIR	7:03	4:35	3:44ă	9:18a	6:50	4:49	3:32ă	9:20a
2	Th	1st U.S. savings bank opened, 1816	LIB	7:04	4:35	4:50a	10:12a	6:50	4:48	4:45ă	10:15a
3	Fr	Paul Harvey's 1st national broadcast, 1950	SCO	7:05	4:35	6:10ă	11:11a	6:51	4:48	6:00a	11:13a
4	Sa	Total central solar eclipse 2:33am (not in U.S.)	OPH	7:06	4:35	4:54p̄	12:14p	6:52	4:48	5:12p̄	12:17p

48. Second Sunday of Advent — Day's Length: 9h 28m / Astron. Twilight: 1h 28m — Day's Length: 9h 55m / Astron. Twilight: 1h 22m

5	Su	Prohibition came to an end, 1933	SAG	7:06	4:35	5:53p̄	1:20p	6:53	4:48	6:14p̄	1:23p
6	Mo	Moon, Venus best visible in the SW 5:48pm	SAG	7:07	4:35	7:02p̄	2:26p	6:54	4:48	7:22p̄	2:28p
7	Tu	Pearl Harbor Day; Moon, earliest sunset of yr.	CAP	7:08	4:35	8:16p̄	3:28p	6:55	4:48	8:34p̄	3:31p
8	We	Conception B.V.M	CAP	7:09	4:35	9:29p̄	4:25p	6:55	4:49	9:44p̄	4:27p
9	Th	Clarence Birdseye born, 1886	AQU	7:10	4:35	10:39p̄	5:17p	6:56	4:49	10:50p̄	5:19p
10	Fr	1st Nobel prizes awarded, 1901	AQU	7:11	4:35	11:46p̄	6:04p	6:57	4:49	11:53p̄	6:06p
11	Sa	Betsy Blair born, 1923	AQU	7:12	4:35	None	6:48p	6:58	4:49	None	6:49p

49. Third Sunday of Advent — Day's Length: 9h 23m / Astron. Twilight: 1h 29m — Day's Length: 9h 51m / Astron. Twilight: 1h 22m

12	Su	Frank Sinatra born, 1915	CET	7:12	4:35	12:50ă	7:30p	6:58	4:49	12:53ă	7:31p
13	Mo	Dick Van Dyke born, 1925	PSC	7:13	4:35	1:51ă	8:11p	6:59	4:49	1:52ă	8:13p
14	Tu	Howard Cosell retired, 1984	PSC	7:14	4:36	2:52ă	8:53p	7:00	4:50	2:49ă	8:54p
15	We	Ember Day	ARI	7:15	4:36	3:52ă	9:36p	7:01	4:50	3:46ă	9:38p
16	Th	Jane Austen born, 1775	TAU	7:15	4:36	4:53ă	10:21p	7:01	4:50	4:44ă	10:23p
17	Fr	Ember Day; Moon at apogee 8:57pm	TAU	7:16	4:37	5:54ă	11:08p	7:02	4:51	5:42ă	11:10p
18	Sa	Ember Day; Ty Cobb born 1886	TAU	7:16	4:37	6:53ă	11:58p	7:02	4:51	6:40ă	11:59p

50. Fourth Sunday of Advent — Day's Length: 9h 20m / Astron. Twilight: 1h 29m — Day's Length: 9h 49m / Astron. Twilight: 1h 23m

19	Su	Venus retrograde	GEM	7:17	4:37	4:55p̄	None	7:03	4:52	5:14p̄	None
20	Mo	Sacagawea death anniversary, 1812	GEM	7:18	4:38	5:47p̄	12:48a	7:03	4:52	6:07p̄	12:50a
21	Tu	Winter solstice (1st day of winter) 10:59am	GEM	7:18	4:38	6:45p̄	1:39a	7:04	4:53	7:03p̄	1:41a
22	We	U.S. Golf Association formed, 1894	CAN	7:19	4:39	7:47p̄	2:29a	7:04	4:53	8:03p̄	2:31a
23	Th	James Gregory born, 1911	LEO	7:19	4:39	8:50p̄	3:18a	7:05	4:54	9:04p̄	3:20a
24	Fr	Ava Gardner born, 1922	LEO	7:19	4:40	9:55p̄	4:05a	7:05	4:54	10:05p̄	4:07a
25	Sa	**Christmas Day**	LEO	7:20	4:41	11:00p̄	4:50a	7:06	4:55	11:06p̄	4:52a

51. First Sunday after Christmas — Day's Length: 9h 21m / Astron. Twilight: 1h 29m — Day's Length: 9h 49m / Astron. Twilight: 1h 22m

26	Su	Coffee percolator patented, 1865	VIR	7:20	4:41	None	5:35a	7:06	4:55	None	5:37a
27	Mo	Radio City Music Hall opened its doors, 1932	VIR	7:21	4:42	12:06ă	6:20a	7:06	4:56	12:09ă	6:22a
28	Tu	Iowa became 29th state, 1846	VIR	7:21	4:43	1:14ă	7:04a	7:07	4:57	1:14ă	7:09a
29	We	1st American YMCA, Boston, 1851	LIB	7:21	4:43	2:25ă	7:57a	7:07	4:57	2:21ă	7:59a
30	Th	California's 1st freeway opened, 1940	LIB	7:21	4:44	3:41ă	8:51a	7:08	4:58	3:33ă	8:54a
31	Fr	New Year's Eve	OPH	7:21	4:45	4:59ă	9:51a	7:08	4:59	4:48ă	9:53a

DECEMBER 2021 WEATHER FORECAST

ZONE 1 Northeast & New England

1-3: Partly cloudy New England; showers Mid-Atlantic. **4-7:** Storm sweeps off Mid-Atlantic Coast bringing a widespread snowfall. **8-11:** Turning colder. **12-15:** Cold; a few showers, flurries. **16-19:** Unsettled initially; possibly icy, then clearing. **20-23:** Increasingly cloudy, with rain showers. **24-27:** Frigidly cold weather arrives in time for the Christmas holiday; scattered snow showers, flurries. **28-31:** Fair, cold initially, then becoming milder as we ring in 2022.

ZONE 2 Great Lakes, Ohio Valley & Midwest

1-3: Clouds, cold winds, a few flurries. **4-7:** Snowy for the LP of Michigan, Ohio, Kentucky, Indiana, eastern Illinois. **8-11:** Scattered flurries, cold. **12-15:** Cold, dry. **16-19:** Unsettled weather. **20-23:** Skies cloud up. **24-27:** Brutally cold Christmas season. **28-31:** Fair with moderating temperatures for New Year.

ZONE 3 Southeast

1-3: Squalls Mississippi Valley. Showers from Mid-Atlantic region down into Gulf Coast States, including Florida. **4-7:** Snow West Virginia, northern Virginia. Elsewhere, showers and strong-to-severe thunderstorms, possibly a few tornadoes. **8-11:** Clear, cold. Widespread frosts. **12-15:** Cold, dry initially, then scattered showers. **16-19:** Showers, then clearing. **20-23:** Increasingly cloudy skies. **24-27:** Dry, cold for Christmas. **28-31:** Fair, cold, then becoming milder in time for 2022.

ZONE 4 North Central States

1-3: Gusty winds, widespread rains, heavy snow Montana, Wyoming, Colorado, all spreading east into parts of Dakotas, Nebraska, Kansas. **4-7:** Pleasant conditions. **8-11:** Some light snow or flurries. **12-15:** Fair, then turning unsettled. **16-19:** Clouds gradually give way to clearing. **20-23:** A blast of Arctic frigidity with -20 to -40° temps; scattered snow showers. **24-27:** Fair skies and not so frigid for Christmas. **28-31:** Scattered snow showers blow in for 2022.

ZONE 5 South Central States

1-3: Gusty winds, widespread rains, snow for New Mexico, east into Texas/Oklahoma panhandle. **4-7:** Dry, tranquil. **8-11:** Light rain showers. **12-15:** Cold, with fair skies, then becoming unsettled. **16-19:** Clouds gradually give way to sun. **20-23:** Very cold with a passing snow shower, flurry. **24-27:** Clearing skies; still quite cold. **28-31:** New year arrives on a flaky note with a few scattered flurries.

ZONE 6 Northwest

1-3: Gusty winds, widespread rains, and (over Cascades) snow. **4-7:** Fair skies, chilly, then turning stormy with strong winds, heavy precipitation. **8-11:** Windy, partial clearing. **12-15:** Fair, then turning unsettled. **16-19:** Clearing on West Coast, points east. **20-23:** Very unsettled. **24-27:** Fair, chilly. **28-31:** 2022 arrives on a wet note.

ZONE 7 Southwest

1-3: Gusty winds, widespread rain, and (over high elevations) snow. **4-7:** Fair skies, cold initially, then turning stormy, with strong winds, copious amounts of precipitation. **8-11:** Big storm evolves: gusty winds, then clearing skies. **12-15:** Fair in California, then turning unsettled. **16-19:** Clearing on West Coast and points east. **20-23:** Windy, showery weather. **24-27:** Fair skies; colder along the Pacific Coast. **28-31:** Clearing in time for New Year's.

AVERAGE FROST DATES

*The dates listed below are normal averages for a light frost in selected towns.
The definition of a light frost is when the temperatures are between 29°–32°F. During a
light frost, tender plants may be killed, with little destructive effect on more hardy vegetation.*

*There is a 50% probability that a frost may occur after the spring date and before the fall date listed
(as well as a 50% chance one could happen earlier in the spring or later in the fall). Dates are courtesy
of the National Climatic Data Center and the National Oceanic and Atmospheric Administration.*

ALABAMA	FIRST	LAST		CONNECTICUT	FIRST	LAST
Birmingham	Nov 9	Apr 2		Danbury	Oct 9	May 1
Huntsville	Nov 4	Mar 30		Hartford	Oct 9	Apr 26
Mobile	Nov 29	Feb 28		Stamford	Oct 17	Apr 29
Montgomery	Nov 12	Mar 11		**DELAWARE**	**FIRST**	**LAST**
ALASKA	**FIRST**	**LAST**		Dover	Oct 30	Apr 8
Anchorage	Sep 23	May 8		Lewes	Nov 5	Apr 6
Fairbanks	Sep 8	May 15		Wilmington	Nov 15	Apr 10
Juneau	Oct 4	May 8		**WASHINGTON, DC**	**FIRST**	**LAST**
Nome	Aug 31	Jun 11			Nov 15	
ARIZONA	**FIRST**	**LAST**				Mar 29
Flagstaff	Sep 22	Jun 9		**FLORIDA**	**FIRST**	**LAST**
Phoenix	Dec 16	Jan 30		Jacksonville	Dec 3	Feb 26
Tucson	Nov 29	Feb 16		Orlando	Jan 8	Jan 30
Yuma	Dec 20	Jan 24		Tallahassee	Nov 17	Mar 22
ARKANSAS	**FIRST**	**LAST**		Tampa	Jan 19	Jan 21
Fort Smith	Oct 31	Mar 31		**GEORGIA**	**FIRST**	**LAST**
Jonesboro	Nov 4	Mar 29		Atlanta	Nov 16	Mar 24
Little Rock	Nov 12	Mar 22		Augusta	Nov 7	Mar 30
Texarkana	Nov 16	Mar 13		Columbus	Nov 19	Mar 11
CALIFORNIA	**FIRST**	**LAST**		Savannah	Nov 25	Mar 1
Fresno	Dec 3	Feb 4		**IDAHO**	**FIRST**	**LAST**
Red Bluff	Dec 1	Feb 22		Boise	Oct 8	May 5
Sacramento	Dec 4	Feb 10		Idaho Falls	Sep 20	May 27
San Bernardino	Dec 24	Jan 21		Moscow	Sep 20	May 25
Tahoe City	Sep 19	Jun 18		Salmon	Sep 20	May 25
COLORADO	**FIRST**	**LAST**		**ILLINOIS**	**FIRST**	**LAST**
Denver	Oct 4	Apr 30		Chicago	Oct 24	Apr 20
Grand Junction	Oct 16	May 1		Mt. Vernon	Oct 14	Apr 14
Julesburg	Sep 24	May 7		Quincy	Oct 22	Apr 10
Pueblo	Oct 5	Apr 30		Springfield	Oct 13	Apr 13

NOTE: Higher elevations in HAWAII do occasionally see at-or-near freezing temperatures but definitive frost dates are not available.

AVERAGE FROST DATES

INDIANA	FIRST	LAST
Evansville	Nov 3	Apr 3
Indianapolis	Oct 18	Apr 18
South Bend	Oct 19	Apr 26
Terre Haute	Oct 15	Apr 20

IOWA	FIRST	LAST
Cedar Rapids	Oct 6	Apr 25
Des Moines	Oct 12	Apr 20
Fort Dodge	Oct 4	Apr 29
Sioux City	Oct 3	Apr 26

KANSAS	FIRST	LAST
Garden City	Oct 11	Apr 27
Great Bend	Oct 19	Apr 13
Independence	Oct 25	Apr 8
Topeka	Oct 11	Apr 19

KENTUCKY	FIRST	LAST
Ashland	Oct 13	May 4
Lexington	Oct 25	Apr 15
Mayfield	Oct 21	Apr 17
Murray	Oct 28	Apr 5

LOUISIANA	FIRST	LAST
Alexandria	Nov 19	Mar 6
Baton Rouge	Nov 29	Feb 26
Monroe	Nov 15	Mar 3
Shreveport	Nov 18	Mar 10

MAINE	FIRST	LAST
Augusta	Oct 8	Apr 27
Bangor	Oct 7	May 7
Portland	Oct 6	May 2
Presque Isle	Sep 20	May 21

MARYLAND	FIRST	LAST
Baltimore	Oct 29	Apr 11
Frederick	Oct 30	Apr 9
Salisbury	Oct 30	Apr 5

MASSACHUSETTS	FIRST	LAST
Amherst	Oct 29	Apr 17

MASSACHUSETTS (CONT.)	FIRST	LAST
Boston	Nov 7	Apr 7
New Bedford	Nov 2	Apr 13
Worcester	Nov 14	Apr 26

MICHIGAN	FIRST	LAST
Cheboygan	Oct 10	May 18
Detroit	Oct 17	Apr 26
Grand Rapids	Oct 8	May 5
Marquette	Oct 13	May 11

MINNESOTA	FIRST	LAST
Baudette	Sep 21	May 16
Duluth	Oct 17	May 15
Minneapolis	Oct 5	Apr 30
Willmar	Oct 1	Apr 30

MISSISSIPPI	FIRST	LAST
Greenville	Nov 17	Mar 9
Hattiesburg	Nov 19	Mar 12
Jackson	Nov 9	Mar 23
Tupelo	Oct 28	Apr 5

MISSOURI	FIRST	LAST
Jefferson City	Oct 18	Apr 13
Kansas City	Oct 28	Apr 7
Poplar Bluff	Oct 28	Apr 4
St. Louis	Oct 29	Apr 7

MONTANA	FIRST	LAST
Billings	Sep 27	May 8
Bozeman	Sep 19	May 26
Glendive	Sep 29	May 2
Great Falls	Sep 22	May 17
Helena	Sep 18	May 19

NEBRASKA	FIRST	LAST
Grand Island	Oct 8	Apr 26
North Platte	Oct 4	May 5
Omaha	Oct 12	Apr 21
Scottsbluff	Sep 27	May 3

AVERAGE FROST DATES

NEVADA	FIRST	LAST	OHIO	FIRST	LAST
Elko	Oct 10	Jun 9	Cincinnati	Oct 23	Apr 13
Ely	Sep 6	Jun 18	Cleveland	Oct 23	Apr 30
Las Vegas	Nov 27	Feb 16	Columbus	Oct 13	Apr 26
Reno	Oct 3	May 21	Toledo	Oct 8	May 1
NEW HAMPSHIRE	**FIRST**	**LAST**	**OKLAHOMA**	**FIRST**	**LAST**
Berlin	Sep 21	May 20	Beaver	Oct 14	Apr 18
Concord	Sep 21	May 20	Enid	Nov 3	Apr 4
Keene	Sep 26	May 13	Lawton	Nov 7	Mar 29
Nashua	Oct 3	May 7	Tulsa	Nov 7	Mar 27
NEW JERSEY	**FIRST**	**LAST**	**OREGON**	**FIRST**	**LAST**
Atlantic City	Nov 11	Mar 31	Baker	Sep 13	Jun 3
Cape May	Nov 6	Apr 6	Eugene	Oct 19	Apr 22
New Brunswick	Oct 20	Apr 20	Klamath Falls	Sep 18	Jun 7
Newark	Nov 7	Apr 3	Portland	Nov 15	Mar 23
NEW MEXICO	**FIRST**	**LAST**	**PENNSYLVANIA**	**FIRST**	**LAST**
Albuquerque	Oct 28	Apr 16	Erie	Oct 29	Apr 29
Carlsbad	Nov 3	Apr 3	Lebanon	Oct 13	Apr 27
Santa Rosa	Oct 22	Apr 19	Philadelphia	Nov 4	Apr 6
NEW YORK	**FIRST**	**LAST**	Pittsburgh	Oct 17	Apr 29
Albany	Oct 3	May 2	Wilkes Barre	Oct 16	Apr 26
Buffalo	Oct 19	Apr 24	**RHODE ISLAND**	**FIRST**	**LAST**
Elmira	Oct 3	May 9	Kingston	Oct 3	May 8
Lake Placid	Sep 11	Jun 7	Newport	Nov 7	Apr 15
New York City	Nov 15	Apr 1	Providence	Oct 22	Apr 16
Syracuse	Oct 13	Apr 28			
NORTH CAROLINA	**FIRST**	**LAST**	**SOUTH CAROLINA**	**FIRST**	**LAST**
Asheville	Oct 25	Apr 12	Charleston	Nov 25	Mar 9
Charlotte	Nov 9	Apr 11	Columbia	Nov 1	Apr 1
Fayetteville	Nov 5	Mar 28	Florence	Nov 7	Mar 26
Raleigh-Durham	Oct 28	Apr 10	Greenville	Nov 4	Apr 4
NORTH DAKOTA	**FIRST**	**LAST**	**SOUTH DAKOTA**	**FIRST**	**LAST**
Bismarck	Sep 21	May 14	Hot Springs	Sep 20	May 16
Fargo	Sep 27	May 10	Pierre	Oct 3	May 2
Grand Forks	Sep 27	May 10	Sioux Falls	Sep 28	May 3
Minot	Sep 28	May 9	Watertown	Sep 25	May 10

AVERAGE FROST DATES

TENNESSEE	FIRST	LAST	VIRGINIA *(CONT.)*	FIRST	LAST
Chattanooga	Nov 4	Apr 1	Richmond	Oct 30	Apr 6
Knoxville	Oct 22	Apr 16	Roanoke	Oct 22	Apr 13
Memphis	Nov 13	Mar 22	**WASHINGTON**	**FIRST**	**LAST**
Nashville	Oct 28	Apr 6	Olympia	Oct 6	May 5
TEXAS	**FIRST**	**LAST**	Seattle	Nov 17	Mar 10
Amarillo	Oct 20	Apr 18	Spokane	Oct 3	May 2
Dallas	Nov 25	Mar 3	Vancouver	Oct 15	Apr 20
Houston	Dec 20	Feb 8	**WEST VIRGINIA**	**FIRST**	**LAST**
San Antonio	Nov 25	Feb 28	Charleston	Oct 21	Apr 22
UTAH	**FIRST**	**LAST**	Martinsburg	Oct 19	Apr 19
Cedar City	Oct 1	May 21	Morgantown	Oct 18	Apr 30
Logan	Sep 29	May 14	**WISCONSIN**	**FIRST**	**LAST**
Salt Lake City	Oct 25	Apr 19	Appleton	Oct 7	May 4
VERMONT	**FIRST**	**LAST**	Eau Claire	Sep 29	May 7
Burlington	Oct 3	May 8	Madison	Oct 2	May 10
Montpelier	Oct 1	May 11	Milwaukee	Oct 14	Apr 27
Rutland	Sep 28	May 13	**WYOMING**	**FIRST**	**LAST**
VIRGINIA	**FIRST**	**LAST**	Casper	Sep 19	May 22
Charlottesville	Oct 31	Apr 7	Cheyenne	Sep 26	May 12
Norfolk	Nov 23	Mar 20	Gillette	Sep 4	May 18

United States Department of Agriculture (USDA) Plant Hardiness Zone Map

Helps gardeners and growers determine which plants are most likely to thrive in a specific area

Download a detailed, full-color map here:
http://planthardiness.ars.usda.gov

Cold- & Frost-Tolerant ANNUALS: Pot Marigold, Bachelor's Button, Larkpsur, Sweet Pea, Sweet Alyssum, Bells of Ireland, Forget-Me-Not, Black-Eyed Susan, Pansy, Viola, Johnny Jump-Up, Snapdragon, Dusty Miller & Phlox.

Cold- & Frost-Tolerant VEGETABLES: Beets, Broccoli, Brussels Sprouts, Cabbage, Carrots, Cauliflower, Chard, Collards, Garlic, Kale, Lettuce, Mustard, Onions, Parsley, Spinach & Turnips.

- -

 GREEN THUMB?
More gardening tips and how-tos can be found online at **FarmersAlmanac.com**.

GARDENING ACCORDING TO THE MOON

QUICK VIEW TABLE FOR 2021

	Plant Aboveground Crops	Plant Root Crops	Transplant	Plant Seedbeds	Plant Flowers	Kill Plant Pests
JANUARY	4, 5, 9, 26-28, 31	10, 15-18, 21-23	10, 17, 18	9, 10, 17, 18	9, 10, 15, 16	1-3, 6-8, 11-14, 19, 20, 24, 25, 29, 30
FEBRUARY	1, 2, 5, 6, 23, 24, 28, 29	11-14, 18, 19	13, 14	5, 6, 13, 14	5, 6, 11, 12	3, 4, 7-10, 15-17, 20-22, 25-27
MARCH	3-5, 26, 27, 31	10-13, 16, 17, 21, 22	12, 13, 21, 22	3-5, 12, 13, 31	3-5, 10, 11, 31	1, 2, 6-9, 14, 15, 18-20, 23-25, 28-30
APRIL	1, 6, 22-24, 27, 28	7-9, 12-14, 17-19	8, 9, 17-19	1, 8, 9, 27, 28	1, 6, 7, 27, 28	2-5, 10, 11, 15, 16, 20, 21, 25, 26, 29, 30
MAY	4-6, 24-26, 31	7, 10, 11, 14-16, 19-21	7, 14-16, 19-21	6, 7, 24-26	4, 5, 24-26, 31	1-3, 8, 9, 12, 13, 17, 18, 22, 23, 27-30
JUNE	1-3, 21, 22, 27-30	6, 7, 11, 12, 16, 17	11, 12, 16, 17	2, 3, 21, 22, 29, 30	1, 21, 22, 27, 28	4, 5, 8-10, 13-15, 18-20, 23-26
JULY	4, 24-28, 31	5, 8-10, 13-15, 18, 19	8-10, 13-15, 18, 19	18, 19, 27, 28	18, 19, 24-26	1-3, 6, 7, 11, 12, 16, 17, 20-23, 29, 30
AUGUST	1, 21-24, 27, 28	4-6, 9-11, 14-16	4-6, 9-11, 14-16	14-16, 23, 24	14-16, 21, 22	2, 3, 7, 8, 12, 13, 17-20, 25, 26, 29-31
SEPTEMBER	1, 17-20, 23-25, 28, 29	2, 6, 7, 11, 12	2, 6, 7, 11, 12	11, 12, 19, 20	11, 12, 17, 18	3-5, 8-10, 13-16, 21, 22, 26, 27, 30
OCTOBER	16-18, 21, 22, 25-27, 30	3-5, 8, 9, 15, 31	3-5, 8, 9, 31	8, 9, 17, 18	8, 9, 15, 16	1, 2, 6, 7, 10-14, 19, 20, 23, 24, 28, 29
NOVEMBER	17, 18, 21-23, 26-28	1, 4-6, 11-14	1, 4-6, 13, 14	4-6, 13, 14	4-6, 11, 12	2, 3, 7-10, 15, 16, 19, 20, 24, 25, 29, 30
DECEMBER	14-16, 19, 20, 24, 25	1-3, 8-11, 29, 30	1-3, 10, 11, 29, 30	1-3, 10, 11, 29, 30	1-3, 8, 9, 29, 30	4-7, 12, 13, 17, 18, 21-23, 26-28, 31

2021 GARDENING ACCORDING TO THE MOON

The most favorable days for planting aboveground vegetables, root and forage crops, and for doing other gardening tasks as determined by the phases of the Moon.

HELPFUL GARDENING DEFINITIONS

Aboveground Crops	Crops that produce their yield above the soil, such as corn, peppers, squash, etc.
Root Crops	Crops that produce their yield below the soil, such as potatoes, radishes, carrots, etc.
Vine Crops	These are plants that grow on a vine such as beans, cucumbers, pumpkins, etc.
Forage Crops	These are crops that are grown for livestock to graze on.
Seedbeds	A bed of soil cultivated for planting seeds or seedlings before being transplanted.
Seedlings	A young plant, especially one that grows from a seed rather than from a cutting.
Transplanting	To uproot and replant a growing plant or an already well-established plant.
Favorable, Good, and Best	These terms are all considered beneficial days for planting seeds. "Good" and "Favorable" both pretty much mean the same. However, "Best" is considered the prime, optimal days for planting seeds.

(continued)

2021 GARDENING ACCORDING TO THE MOON

The most favorable days for planting aboveground vegetables, root and forage crops, and for doing other gardening tasks as determined by the phases of the Moon in 2021.

JANUARY 1-4: A barren time. Best for killing weeds, briars, poison ivy, and other plant pests. Clear wood lots and fencerows. **5, 6:** A favorable time for sowing grains, hay, and forage crops. Plant flowers. Favorable days for planting root crops. **7, 8:** Start seedbeds. Good days for transplanting. Plant carrots, turnips, onions, beets, Irish potatoes, other root crops in the South. Also good for leafy vegetables. **9, 10:** Do no planting. **11, 12:** Good planting days for root crops where climate permits. **13, 14:** A good time to kill plant pests or do plowing. Poor for planting. **15-17:** Extra good for peppers, tomatoes, peas and other vine crops. Fine for planting any aboveground crop where the climate permits. **18, 19:** Barren days, do no planting. **20-22:** Fine for planting beans, peppers, cucumbers, melons, and other aboveground crops where climate is suitable. **23, 24:** Poor days for planting, seeds tend to rot in ground. **25, 26:** Plant seedbeds and flower gardens. Best planting days for aboveground crops, especially peas, beans, cucumbers, and squash where climate is suitable. **27-31:** A barren time. Best for killing weeds, briars, poison ivy, and other plant pests. Clear wood lots and fencerows.

FEBRUARY 1, 2: Fine for sowing grains, hay, and forage crops. Plant flowers. Favorable days for planting root crops. **3, 4:** Start seedbeds. Good days for transplanting. Plant carrots, turnips, onions, beets, Irish potatoes, and other root crops in the South. Lettuce and other leafy vegetables will do well. **5, 6:** Poor planting days. **7, 8:** Any root crops that can be planted now will do well. **9-11:** Barren days. Fine for clearing, plowing, fertilizing, and killing plant pests. **12, 13:** Extra good for cucumbers, peas, cantaloupes, and other vine crops. Set strawberry plants. Plant peppers, sweet corn, tomatoes, and other aboveground crops in southern Florida, California, and Texas. **14, 15:** Seeds planted now will

2021 GARDENING ACCORDING TO THE MOON

grow poorly and yield little. **16-18:** Fine for planting beans, peppers, cucumbers, melons, and other aboveground crops where climate is suitable. **19, 20:** Any seed planted now will tend to rot. **21-23:** Plant seedbeds and flower gardens. Fine for planting beans, tomatoes, corn, cotton, cucumbers, peppers, melons, and other aboveground crops where climate allows. **24-27:** Clear ground, turn sod, kill plant pests. **28:** Fine for sowing grains, hay, and forage crops. Plant flowers. Favorable day for planting root crops.

MARCH 1: Fine for sowing grains, hay, and forage crops. Plant flowers. Favorable day for planting root crops. **2, 3:** Start seedbeds. Good days for transplanting. Excellent time for planting root crops that can be planted now. Also good for leafy vegetables. **4, 5:** Barren days, do no planting. **6-8:** Any root crops that can be planted now will do well. **9, 10:** A barren period, best suited for killing plant pests. Do plowing and cultivating. **11, 12:** Good for planting cucumbers, melons, pumpkins, and other vine crops. Set strawberry plants. Good days for transplanting. Favorable days for planting beets, carrots, radishes, salsify, turnips, peanuts, and other root crops. **13-15:** Cultivate and spray, do general farm work, but no planting. **16, 17:** Favorable for planting crops bearing yield above the ground. **18-20:** Seeds planted now tend to rot in ground. **21, 22:** Excellent for sowing seedbeds and flower gardens. Best planting days for aboveground crops, especially peas, beans, cucumbers, and squash where climate permits. **23-27:** A most barren period, best for killing plant pests or doing chores around the farm. **28, 29:** Fine for sowing grains, hay, and forage crops. Plant flowers. Favorable days for planting root crops. **30, 31:** Start seedbeds. Good days for transplanting. Excellent time for

planting root crops that can be planted now. Also good for leafy vegetables.

APRIL 1, 2: Neither plant nor sow on these barren days. **3, 4:** Favorable days for planting beets, carrots, turnips, radishes, onions, and other root crops. **5, 6:** Excellent time to kill weeds, briars, poison ivy, and other plant pests. **7-9:** Set strawberry plants. Excellent for any vine crops, such as beans, peas, and cucumbers. Good days for transplanting. Favorable days for planting root crops. **10, 11:** Poor planting days. Break ground or cultivate. **12-14:** Favorable for planting beans, corn, cotton, tomatoes, peppers, and other aboveground crops. **15, 16:** Poor days for planting, seeds tend to rot in ground. **17-19:** Plant seedbeds and start flower gardens. Plant tomatoes, beans, peppers, corn, cotton, and other aboveground crops on these most fruitful days. **20-23:** Grub out weeds, briars, and other plant pests. **24, 25:** A favorable time for sowing grains, hay, and fodder crops. Plant flowers. Plant corn, melons, squash, tomatoes, and other aboveground crops. **26, 27:** Start seedbeds. Good days for transplanting. Good days for planting beets, carrots, radishes, turnips, peanuts, and other root crops. Also good for leafy vegetables. **28, 29:** Neither plant nor sow on these barren days. **30:** Favorable day for planting beets, carrots, turnips, radishes, onions, and other root crops.

MAY 1: Plant late beets, potatoes, onions, carrots, and other root crops. **2, 3:** Kill plant pests on these barren days. **4-6:** Fine for vine crops. Set strawberry plants. Good days for transplanting. Favorable time for planting late root crops. **7, 8:** Poor planting. Fine for cultivating or spraying. **9-11:** First two days are good days for transplanting. First two days are also when planted root crops will yield well. Last day is favorable for planting beans, corn, cotton, tomatoes, peppers,

(continued)

2021 GARDENING ACCORDING TO THE MOON

and other aboveground crops. **12, 13:** Any seed planted now will tend to rot. **14-16:** Plant seedbeds and flower gardens. Most favorable for corn, cotton, okra, beans, peppers, eggplant, and other aboveground crops. **17-20:** A barren period. Favorable for killing plant pests, cultivating, or taking a short vacation. **21, 22:** Favorable time for sowing hay, fodder crops, and grains. Plant flowers. Excellent time for planting corn, beans, peppers, and other aboveground crops. **23, 24:** Plant seedbeds. Excellent for planting aboveground crops, and planting leafy vegetables. **25, 26:** Seeds planted now will do poorly and yield little. **27-29:** Plant late beets, potatoes, onions, carrots, and other root crops. **30, 31:** Kill plant pests on these barren days.

JUNE 1, 2: Set strawberry plants. Excellent for any vine crops such as beans, peas, and cucumbers. Good days for transplanting. Favorable time for planting late root crops. **3-5:** Cut hay or do plowing on these barren days. **6, 7:** Good days for transplanting. Good days for planting root crops. **8-10:** Seeds planted now tend to rot in ground. **11, 12:** Excellent for sowing seedbeds and flower gardens. Plant tomatoes, beans, peppers, corn, cotton, and other aboveground crops on these most fruitful days. **13-17:** Poor period for planting. Kill plant pests, clear fencerows, or clear land. **18, 19:** Sow grains and forage crops. Plant flowers. Favorable for planting peas, beans, tomatoes, and other fall crops bearing aboveground. **20, 21:** Plant seedbeds. Extra good for planting fall lettuce, cabbage, cauliflower, collards, and other leafy vegetables. All aboveground crops planted now will do well. **22, 23:** Poor planting days, cut hay or do general farm work. **24, 25:** Plant late beets, potatoes, onions, carrots, and other root crops. **26, 27:** Poor days for

planting. Kill plant pests, spray, fertilize, do general farm work. **28, 29:** Set strawberry plants. Excellent for any vine crops such as beans, peas, and cucumbers. Good days for transplanting. Favorable time for planting late root crops. **30:** Cut hay or do plowing on this barren day.

JULY 1, 2: A barren period. **3, 4:** Good days for transplanting. Root crops that can be planted now will yield well. **5-7:** Poor days for planting, seeds tend to rot in ground. **8, 9:** Plant seedbeds and flower gardens. First day is a good day for transplanting. First day is also most fruitful day for planting root crops. Second day is most favorable for corn, cotton, okra, beans, peppers, eggplant, and other aboveground crops. **10-14:** A most barren period. Kill plant pests and do general farm work. **15, 16:** Sow grains and forage crops. Plant flowers. Favorable for planting peas, beans, tomatoes, and other fall crops bearing aboveground. **17, 18:** Start seedbeds. Extra good for fall cabbage, lettuce, cauliflower, mustard greens, and other leafy vegetables. Good for any aboveground crop that can be planted now. **19, 20:** Barren days, neither plant nor sow. **21, 22:** Any aboveground crops that can be planted now will do well. **23, 24:** Good days for killing weeds, briars, and other plant pests. Poor for planting. **25-27:** Set strawberry plants. Good days for transplanting. Good days for planting beets, carrots, radishes, salsify, turnips, peanuts, and other root crops. Also good for vine crops. **28, 29:** A barren period. **30, 31:** Good days for transplanting. Root crops that can be planted now will yield well.

AUGUST 1: Good day for transplanting. Root crops that can be planted now will yield well. **2, 3:** Any seed planted now will tend to rot. **4-6:** Plant seedbeds and flower gardens. Good days for transplanting. Most favorable days for planting beets, onions, turnips, and other root

2021 GARDENING ACCORDING TO THE MOON

crops. **7-10:** Best for killing weeds, briars, poison ivy, and other plant pests. Clear wood lots and fencerows. **11, 12:** Excellent for sowing grains, winter wheat, oats, and rye. Plant flowers. Good days for planting aboveground crops. **13, 14:** Plant seedbeds. Plant peas, beans, tomatoes, peppers, and other aboveground crops in southern Florida, California, and Texas. Extra good for leafy vegetables. **15-17:** Cut winter wood, do clearing and plowing, but no planting. **18, 19:** A good time to plant aboveground crops. **20, 21:** Barren days, fine for killing plant pests. **22, 23:** Excellent for any vine crops such as beans, peas, and cucumbers. Good days for transplanting. Favorable days for planting root crops. **24-26:** Neither plant nor sow on these barren days. **27, 28:** Good days for transplanting. Root crops that can be planted now will yield well. **29-31:** Any seed planted now will tend to rot.

SEPTEMBER 1, 2: Plant seedbeds and flower gardens. Good days for transplanting. Fine planting days for fall potatoes, turnips, onions, carrots, beets, and other root crops. **3-6:** Clear ground, turn sod, or kill plant pests. **7-9:** Excellent for sowing grains, hay, and forage crops. Plant flowers. Good days for planting peas, beans, tomatoes, peppers, and other aboveground crops in southern Florida, Texas, and California. **10, 11:** Start seedbeds. Excellent time for planting aboveground crops that can be planted now, including leafy vegetables which will do well. **12, 13:** Clear fencerows, wood lots, and fields, but do no planting. **14, 15:** Any aboveground crops that can be planted now will do well. **16, 17:** Poor planting days. Kill plant pests. **18, 19:** Extra good for vine crops. Favorable days for planting aboveground crops. **20-22:** A poor time to plant. **23, 24:** Good days for transplanting. Good days for planting root crops.

25-27: Seeds planted now tend to rot in ground. **28, 29:** Plant seedbeds and flower gardens. Good days for transplanting. Fine planting days for fall potatoes, turnips, onions, carrots, beets, and other root crops. **30:** Clear ground, turn sod, or kill plant pests.

OCTOBER 1-4: A most barren period, best for killing plant pests or doing chores around the farm. **5, 6:** Fine for sowing grains, hay, and forage crops. Plant flowers. First day is a favorable day for planting root crops. Second day is a favorable day for planting beans, peas, squash, sweet corn, tomatoes, and other aboveground crops in southern Florida, Texas, and California. **7, 8:** Start seedbeds. Favorable days for planting aboveground crops, and leafy vegetables such as lettuce, cabbage, kale, and celery where climate is suitable. **9, 10:** Do clearing and plowing, but no planting. **11, 12:** Plant tomatoes, peas, beans, and other aboveground crops, indoors in the North and outdoors in lower South. **13, 14:** Poor planting days. Kill poison ivy, weeds, clear land, but no planting. **15-17:** Extra good for vine crops. Favorable days for planting aboveground crops where climate is suitable. **18, 19:** Barren days, do no planting. **20-22:** Good days for transplanting. Good days for planting beets, carrots, onions, turnips, and other hardy root crops where climate is suitable. **23, 24:** Poor days for planting, seeds tend to rot in ground. **25-27:** Start seedbeds and flower gardens. Good days for transplanting. Best planting days for fall potatoes, turnips, onions, carrots, beets, and other root crops where climate is suitable. **28-31:** A most barren period, best for killing plant pests or doing chores around the farm.

NOVEMBER 1, 2: Favorable time for sowing grains, hay, and fodder crops. Plant flowers. Favorable days for planting root

(continued)

crops. **3, 4:** Start seedbeds. First day is a good day for transplanting. First day is also when to plant carrots, beets, onions, turnips, Irish potatoes, and other root crops in the South. Second day is good for planting cabbage, celery, cauliflower, Brussels sprouts, collards, and other leafy vegetables in southern Florida, Texas, and California. **5, 6:** Poor planting days. **7, 8:** Good days for planting peas, squash, corn, tomatoes, and other aboveground crops in southern Florida, Texas, and California. **9-11:** A good time to kill plant pests or do plowing. Poor for planting. **12, 13:** Extra good for vine crops. Favorable days for planting aboveground crops where climate allows. **14, 15:** Seeds planted now will grow poorly and yield little. **16-18:** Fine for planting beans, peppers, cucumbers, melons, and other aboveground crops where climate is suitable. **19, 20:** Any seed planted now will tend to rot. **21-23:** Start seedbeds and flower gardens. Good days for transplanting. Best planting days for fall potatoes, turnips, onions, carrots, beets, and other root crops where climate is suitable. **24-28:** Grub out weeds, briars, and other plant pests. **29, 30:** Favorable time for sowing grains, hay, and fodder crops. Plant flowers. Favorable days for planting root crops.

DECEMBER 1, 2: Start seedbeds. Good days for transplanting. Plant carrots, beets, onions, turnips, Irish potatoes, and other root crops in the South. **3, 4:** Do no planting. **5, 6:** Plant sweet corn, beans, peppers, and other aboveground crops where climate is suitable. **7, 8:** Barren days. Fine for clearing, plowing, fertilizing, and killing plant pests. **9, 10:** Extra good for cucumbers, peas, cantaloupes, and other vine crops. Plant peppers, sweet corn, tomatoes, and other aboveground crops in southern Florida, California, and Texas. **11-13:** A barren period. **14, 15:** Fine for planting beans, peppers, cucumbers, melons, and other

aboveground crops where climate is suitable. **16-18:** Seeds planted now tend to rot in ground. **19, 20:** Start seedbeds and flower gardens. Good days for transplanting. Most favorable days for planting beets, onions, turnips, and other root crops where climate allows. **21-25:** A barren period. Favorable for killing plant pests, cultivating, or taking a short vacation. **26, 27:** Plant flowers. Fine for sowing hay, fodder crops, and grains. Favorable days for planting root crops. **28, 29:** Start seedbeds. Good days for transplanting. Plant carrots, beets, onions, turnips, Irish potatoes, and other root crops in the South. **30, 31:** Do no planting.

STOP FOOT & LEG PAIN FAST!

Smooth Gator's Foot and Leg Rub is a topical cream made with all natural ingredients like CAMPHOR, ROSEMARY and PEPPERMINT.

This safe, non-greasy formula relieves pain associated with neuropathy, nerve conditions and/or poor circulation in your foot and legs below the knee.

> With all natural oils, relieve night-time sensations of numbness, tingling, and burning!

Perfect for increased circulation for your feet and lower legs, to soothe hot/cold and burning sensations, and to desensitize nerve endings.

It's easy! Just apply liberally to feet and lower legs before bedtime, or before and after any long periods of standing. Don't rub in, just rub on, and it will absorb on its own. Experience the dramatic results!

Call Smooth Gator today at **727-278-3137** for your pain relief needs or visit **smoothgator.com**

FREE NATURAL LIP BALM WITH EVERY ORDER!

Smooth Gator | 727-278-3137 | smoothgator.com

$**44**^{95} per bottle

173

By Cynthia McMurray

FINDING THE WAY HOME:
ANIMALS' AMAZING SENSE OF DIRECTION

Advances in technology aimed at improving our lives are often welcomed inventions. For example, GPS has allowed many of us, especially those with no sense of direction, to feel more confident when driving or walking to a new location. But have you ever thought about how animals—some domesticated and others wild— find not only their way home but places to migrate to each year?

Thanks to Mother Nature, certain animals have a built-in location-finding capability that relies on everything from sight and smell to more intricate magnetic methods of geolocation. Some animals even have innate map-based orientation systems. Here are a few examples of some impressive navigators who don't need help from any AI device.

PIGEONS

Historically, pigeons played an important role in relaying messages. Since they have an innate homing ability, pigeons were routinely used for such things as announcing the winner of the ancient Olympics and sending covert messages during numerous wars.

The way it worked was that pigeons were first transported to a specific destination. Once there, a message would be attached to the bird, which would then naturally fly back to its home with the message for the recipient accompanying it.

Charles Darwin determined that all pigeons ultimately descend from one species—the wild rock dove. Historians claim that early on, humans began breeding pigeons that excelled in specific traits, ultimately creating different varieties such as homing and carrier pigeons. But how could these pigeons find their way home?

Scientists surmise the pigeon's ability to hone in on various locations with such precision is a result of a "map-and-compass" type of navigation system. In other words, they orient themselves relative to a goal site, using a combination of the Sun and other celestial light patterns, sight and smell, various gravity anomalies, and the Earth's magnetic field. Scientists believe special neurons within their inner ears may help them process such things as minute changes in direction and the strength and polarity of the magnetic fields around them.

While the science and technology behind today's navigational systems is quite sophisticated, the fact that these animals can navigate just as well undoubtedly puts them ahead of humans when it comes to finding their way around.

BUTTERFLIES

For humans, heading south for the winter is as easy as hopping on a plane, but for millions of monarch butterflies that make the yearly 3,000-mile trek from Canada to Mexico, they must rely on a built-in, genetically encoded GPS system. According to a new University of Washington study, butterflies use an internal "compass" that integrates two specific pieces of information—the time of day and the Sun's position on the horizon. To configure this information, they monitor the Sun's position using their extremely complex compound eyes, and an natural clock-like system within their antennae. They send this information through specific neurons to their brains and determine which direction is southwest. If they are blown off course, they simply recalculate, much like our car's GPS system.

SALMON

Every year, thousands of juvenile salmon, with no prior migratory experience, make their way downstream to specific oceanic feeding grounds hundreds of miles from the riverbed where they were born. Several years later, with pinpoint accuracy, they return to that same river to breed. While the actual process is much more in-depth, scientists have determined that young salmon use a navigation system similar to pigeons (although it's more developed since fish must continuously account for drifting caused by currents without the stationary visual land to use as reference).

Ultimately, salmon use a combination of environmental cues, including length of the day, the Sun's position and angle in the sky, water salinity and temperature gradients, and the Earth's magnetic field. They may also rely on smells, which they start remembering when they first make their way downstream. While some humans can follow their noses to the nearest bakery, it's unlikely they can make their way hundreds of miles away by smell alone!

WHAT ABOUT YOUR PETS?

To help animals survive in the wild, Mother Nature has equipped them with some impressive navigational systems, but what about domesticated animals like our much-loved fur babies? Can they fend for themselves if lost, or has domestication made them less adept than their wild counterparts? How do they measure up to humans?

CATS

According to the Genome Institute, cats, unlike dogs, are really only "semi-domesticated." In fact, scientists go as far as to say there is little difference between the average house cat and wild cats. They commonly even breed with their wild counterparts, thus explaining the number of feral cats.

In general, cats have very powerful senses. In fact, they have more than 19-million scent receptors. They tend to bond strongly to a home location, even marking their territory by spraying urine or rubbing their scent glands (under their chin) onto various items in their home area, which also makes it easier to find their way back.

Cats have incredible eyesight and hearing, and they use their fur, whiskers, and paws to gather information to help them navigate. Scientists have determined that cats can detect the Earth's magnetic fields through iron in their ears and skin, which acts like a natural compass.

(continued)

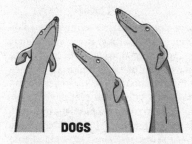

DOGS

Anyone with a dog knows it's all about smells. Dogs are constantly sniffing everything they come in contact with, so it should come as no surprise that they also use their incredible sniffers to navigate.

Dogs' noses contain hundreds of millions of sensory neurons—up to 300 million compared to the 6 million in the human nose—making their sense of smell 10,000 to 100,000 times better than ours. They also have a second olfactory capability humans don't have—the Jacobson's organ, found at the bottom of their nasal passages, which allows them to smell pheromones.

New studies also show dogs can rely on their sense of smell to pick up familiar scents over a 10-mile distance. Add to that the fact dogs see much better at night than humans because they have larger pupils, and dogs are definitely better at navigating than humans. Some researchers suggest if your dog gets lost, you can leave a familiar piece of your clothing or their bed outside to help them find their way home.

Any way you look at it, animals have us beat when it comes to navigating. While some of us may be better than others at finding our way, it's a good thing we can rely on GPS!

Make sure your emergency kit is stocked with the items on the checklist below. Most of the items are inexpensive and easy to find, and any one of them could save your life. Once you take a look at the basic items, consider what unique needs your family might have, such as supplies for pets or seniors.

After an emergency, you may need to survive on your own for several days. Being prepared means having your own food, water and other supplies to last for at least 72 hours. A disaster supplies kit is a collection of basic items your household may need in the event of an emergency.

BASIC DISASTER SUPPLIES KIT

To assemble your kit, store items in airtight plastic bags and put your entire disaster supplies kit in one or two easy-to-carry containers such as plastic bins or a duffel bag.

A basic emergency supply kit could include the following recommended items:

 water—one gallon of water per person per day for at least three days, for drinking and sanitation

 food—at least a three-day supply of non-perishable food

 battery-powered or **hand-crank radio** and a NOAA Weather Radio with tone alert

 flashlight

 first aid kit

 manual can opener—for food

wrench or **pliers**—to turn off utilities

 extra batteries

 whistle—to signal for help

 local maps

 moist towelettes, garbage bags and **plastic ties**—for personal sanitation

 cell phone with **chargers** and a **backup battery**

 dust mask—to help filter contaminated air and plastic sheeting and duct tape to shelter in place

ADDITIONAL EMERGENCY SUPPLIES

Consider adding the following items to your emergency supply kit based on your needs:

- ❏ **prescription medicines**
- ❏ **non-prescription medications**—such as pain relievers, anti-diarrhea medication, antacids or laxatives
- ❏ **glasses** and **contact lens solution**
- ❏ **infant needs**—formula, bottles, diapers, wipes, diaper rash cream
- ❏ **pet food** and **extra water**—for your pet
- ❏ **cash** or **traveler's checks**

- ❏ **important family documents**—such as copies of insurance policies, identification and bank account records saved electronically or in a waterproof, portable container
- ❏ **sleeping bag** or **warm blanket** for each person
- ❏ Complete **change of clothing**—appropriate for your climate and sturdy shoes
- ❏ **fire extinguisher**

- ❏ Household **chlorine bleach** and **medicine dropper**—to disinfect water
- ❏ **matches**—in a waterproof container
- ❏ **feminine supplies** and **personal hygiene items**
- ❏ **mess kits**—paper cups, plates, paper towels and plastic utensils
- ❏ **paper** and **pencil**
- ❏ **activities for children**—books, games, puzzles or other

MAINTAINING YOUR KIT

After assembling your kit remember to maintain it so it's ready when needed:

- Keep canned food in a cool, dry place
- Store boxed food in tightly closed plastic or metal containers
- Replace expired items as needed
- Re-think your needs every year and update your kit as your family's needs change.

Article courtesy of FEMA, and Ready.gov

KIT STORAGE LOCATIONS

Since you do not know where you will be when an emergency occurs, prepare supplies for home, work and vehicles.

Home: Keep this kit in a designated place and have it ready in case you have to leave your home quickly. Make sure all family members know where the kit is kept.

Work: Be prepared to shelter at work for at least 24 hours. Your work kit should include food, water and other necessities like medicines, as well as comfortable walking shoes, stored in a "grab and go" case.

Vehicle: In case you are stranded, keep a kit of emergency supplies in your car.

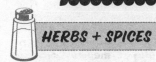

• Baking Substitutes •

HERBS + SPICES

ALLSPICE
for *1 tsp*, **substitute** 1/2 tsp cinnamon + 1/2 tsp ground cloves

APPLE PIE SPICE
for *1 tsp*, **substitute** 1/2 tsp cinnamon + 1/4 tsp nutmeg + 1/8 tsp cardamom

CHIVES, finely chopped
for *2 tsp*, **substitute** 2 tsp green onion tops, finely chopped

GARLIC
for *1 small clove*, **substitute** 1/8 tsp garlic powder OR 1/2 to 1 tsp garlic salt (reduce amount of salt called for in recipe)

GARLIC SALT
for *1 tsp*, **substitute** 1/8 tsp garlic powder + 7/8 tsp salt

PEPPERMINT, dried
for *1 Tbsp*, **substitute** 1/4 cup fresh mint, chopped

PUMPKIN PIE SPICE
for *1 tsp*, **substitute** 1/2 tsp cinnamon + 1/4 tsp ginger + 1/8 tsp allspice + 1/8 tsp nutmeg

SPEARMINT, dried
for *1 Tbsp*, **substitute** 1/4 cup fresh mint, chopped

- - - - - - - - - - - - - - - - -

CHOCOLATE

CHOCOLATE CHIPS, semi-sweet
for *6 oz package*, **substitute** 2 squares unsweetened chocolate + 2 Tbsp shortening + 1/2 cup sugar

CHOCOLATE, unsweetened
for *1 oz or 1 square*, **substitute** 3 Tbsp cocoa + 1 Tbsp butter or margarine

PANTRY

BAKING POWDER
for *1 tsp*, **substitute** 1/3 tsp baking soda + 1/2 tsp cream of tartar OR 1/4 tsp baking soda and 1/4 cup molasses (Decrease liquid amount in recipe by 1-2 Tbsp.)

BROTH (beef or chicken)
for *1 cup*, **substitute** 1 bouillon cube dissolved in 1 cup boiling water OR 1 envelope powdered broth base dissolved in 1 cup boiling water

COCONUT CREAM
for *1 cup*, **substitute** 1 cup heavy or whipping cream

COCONUT MILK
for *1 cup*, **substitute** 1 cup whole or 2% milk

CORNSTARCH (for thickening)
for *1 Tbsp*, **substitute** 2 Tbsp all-purpose flour OR 4 tsp instant tapioca

CORN SYRUP
for *1 cup*, **substitute** 1 cup honey OR 1 cup maple-flavored syrup

HONEY
for *1 cup*, **substitute** 1 1/4 cup sugar + 1/4 cup water

KETCHUP
for *1 cup*, **substitute** 1 cup tomato sauce + 1/4 cup brown sugar + 2 Tbsp vinegar (for use in cooking)

SHORTENING, melted
for *1 cup*, **substitute** 1 cup cooking oil (Substitute only if a recipe calls for melted shortening.)

SHORTENING, solid (used in baking)
for *1 cup*, **substitute** 1 cup butter OR 1 cup margarine

TAPIOCA, granular
for *1 Tbsp*, **substitute** 2 Tbsp pearl tapioca

WORCESTERSHIRE SAUCE
for *1 tsp*, **substitute** 1 tsp bottled steak sauce

BUTTER
for *1 cup*, **substitute**
7/8 to 1 cup hydrogenated fat + 1/2 tsp salt
OR 7/8 cup lard + 1/2 tsp salt
OR 1 cup margarine OR 1 cup
applesauce OR 1 cup avocado

BUTTERMILK
for *1 cup*, **substitute** 1 cup plain yogurt
OR 1 cup whole or skim milk + 1 Tbsp
lemon juice or white vinegar OR 1 cup
milk + 1 3/4 tsp cream of tartar

CREAM, LIGHT (18-20% fat)
for *1 cup*, **substitute** 3/4 cup milk and 3 Tbsp
butter or margarine (for use in cooking or baking) OR 1 cup evaporated milk, undiluted

CREAM, HEAVY (36-40% fat)
for *1 cup*, **substitute** 3/4 cup milk and 1/3 cup
butter or margarine (for use in cooking or
baking) OR 1 cup evaporated skim milk

EGG, WHOLE (uncooked)
for *1 large (3 Tbsp)*, **substitute** 2 Tbsp arrowroot + 3 Tbsp of water OR 2 1/2 Tbsp sifted, dry
whole egg powder + 2 1/2 Tbsp lukewarm water
OR 2 yolks + 1 Tbsp water (in cookies) OR 2
yolks (in custards, cream fillings, or similar mixture)

MILK, EVAPORATED (whole or skim)
for *1 cup*, **substitute** 1 cup whole milk
OR 1 cup regular whipping or heavy cream

MILK, SWEETENED CONDENSED
for *1 can (1 1/3 cup)*, **substitute** 1/3 cup + 2
Tbsp evaporated milk + 1 cup sugar + 3
Tbsp butter or margarine. Heat until sugar
and butter are dissolved.

MILK, WHOLE
for *1 cup*, **substitute** 1 cup reconstituted
non-fat dry milk (optional: add 2 Tbsp butter
or margarine) OR 1/2 cup evaporated milk +
1/2 cup water OR 1 cup almond, hemp, or
soy milk OR 1 cup fruit juice or 1 cup potato
water (for use in baking)

SOUR CREAM, cultured
for *1 cup*, **substitute** 3/4 cup sour milk or
buttermilk + 1/3 cup butter or margarine OR
1 cup plain yogurt OR 3/4 cup milk + 3/4 tsp
lemon juice + 1/3 cup butter or margarine

YOGURT, plain
for *1 cup*, **substitute** 1 cup buttermilk
OR 1 cup cottage cheese, blended
until smooth OR 1 cup sour cream

SUGAR

FLOUR

SUGAR, brown
for *1 cup firmly packed*, **substitute** 1 cup
granulated sugar OR 1 cup granulated
sugar + 1 Tbsp pure maple syrup

SUGAR, granulated
for *1 cup*, **substitute** 1 cup honey
(Decrease liquid called for in recipe by 1/4
cup.) OR 1 1/3 cups molasses (Decrease
liquid in recipe by 1/3 cup.) OR 1 1/2 cups
corn syrup (Decrease liquid called for in
the recipe by 1/4 cup.)

SUGAR, powdered
for *1 cup*, **substitute** Blend 1 cup granulated sugar + 1 tsp cornstarch until a
fine powder

FLOUR, ALL-PURPOSE (for thickening)
for *1 Tbsp*, **substitute** 1 1/2 tsp cornstarch, arrowroot
starch, potato starch, or rice starch OR 1 Tbsp
granular tapioca OR 1 Tbsp waxy rice flour OR 2
Tbsp brown flour OR 1 1/2 Tbsp whole wheat flour

FLOUR, ALL-PURPOSE
for *1 cup sifted*, **substitute** 1 cup + 2 Tbsp cake flour
OR 1 cup rolled oats, crushed OR 1/2 cup cornmeal
OR 1 1/2 cups breadcrumbs OR 3/4 cup whole wheat
flour or bran flour + 1/4 cup all-purpose flour

FLOUR, SELF-RISING
for *1 cup*, **substitute** 1 cup, minus 2 tsp all-purpose
flour + 1 1/2 tsp baking powder + 1/2 tsp salt

Astrologers - Readers

ANGEL PSYCHIC
Clairvoyant Medium Spiritual Astrology,
Positive Energy
1-323-466-3684

ANGELINA Solves All Health, Love, Money & Luck Problems No False Promises 512-470-9147

ANSWERS ALL QUESTIONS Solves life's problems. One call will convince you. Rev. Evette does what others claim. Need help desperately? Call immediately, 100% money back guarantee. 423-894-6699, PO Box 80322, Chattanooga, TN 37414

APRILINA ADVISES Her Powers Bring You Peace Happiness Health and Love 336-210-8507

DO YOU WANT LOVE, LUCK, MONEY? VWith spiritual cleansing you can achieve your goals. Call for your free Tarot card reading. 803-371-7711 811 Saluda St. Rock Hill, SC 29730

MISS RUBY REMOVES HEvil, Bad Luck & Spells. Restores Love & Health 615-584-9881

MOTHER BLACK – Powerful Root Worker, Removes Bad Luck, Immediate Results 912-996-1438

MOTHER ROOT Spiritual Healer, Remove Evil Spirits, Returns Lovers, Cleansing Serious Calls Pls 515-865-4356; 515-244-1322

PROPHET R works with spirits, roots, herbs, candles, lucky hands, and can remove unnatural conditions. Lucky mojo's 919-813-8787

PSYCHIC GUIDANCE Helping All Problems, Removes Negativity, Reunites Lovers, Get Fast Results 832-872-5727

PSYCHIC MIRACLES Love Specialist, Life Coach, Spiritual Protection, Crystal Healing 713-870-5109

PSYCHIC VISION by JULIA Removes Negativity, Creates Energy in Health, Love & Money 402-972-0696

SPIRITUAL HEALER & ADVISOR Helps all matters of life. Health, money & Reunites Lovers 817-613-0509

Books

FREE BIBLE STUDY GUIDE "What is This World Coming To?" Associated Bible Students, PO Box 1783F, Wilmington, DE 19899 info@godspromises.org 888-949-PRAY

FREE BOOK: Divine Plan of the Ages, Why Does a Loving God Permit Calamities? Bible Standard (FAJ), 1156 St. Matthews Road, Chester Springs, PA 19425 www.biblestandard.com

FREE BOOKLETS: Life, Immortality, Soul, Pollution Crisis, Judgement Day, Restitution, sample magazine. Bible Standard (FA), 1156 St. Matthews Road, Chester Springs, PA 19425 www.biblestandard.com

WHY WE LIVE AFTER DEATH and other free booklets available from www.GrailForum.com, 888-205-7307, 786 Jones Road, Vestal NY 13850

Business Opportunities

$800 Weekly Potential! Process HUD/FAH refunds from home. Free information available. Call 860-357-1599

Garden/Farm Supplies

CATTLE AND HOG EQUIPMENT Continuous Fencing, Gates, Hog Haven Farrowing, Nursery and Feeding Floors. See us at http://www.lucoinc.com for other livestock supplies or call 888-816-6707. LUCO Mfg. PO Box 385 Strong City KS 66869

GREEN HAVEN OPEN POLLINATED CORN SEED. Silage, Grain, Wildlife, Available Certified Organic. Early Varieties. Visit us online at www.openpollinated.com 607-566-9253

Miscellaneous

www.azuregreen.net Amulets, Oils, Herbs, Candles, Incense, Statuary, Gemstones, 8,000 items.

Music/Records/Tapes/CDs

ACCORDIONS, CONCERTINAS, Button Boxes, Rolands. Buy, sell, trade, repair, tune. Catalogues $5. Castiglione, PO Box 40, Warren, MI 48090. www.castiglioneaccordions.com 586-755-6050

Interested in Placing a Classified? EMAIL US AT: Advertising@FarmersAlmanac.com

ADVERTISER INDEX

Please contact our advertisers to learn more or order products directly from them.

AgriBilt Building Systems®............................ 33
agribilt.com • 412-593-6043 • gary@agribilt.com

Agrica LLC... 107
https://www.seedgro.com

AgriSupply.. 13
agrisupply.com • 919-772-9722 • pdaniels@ncddi.com

AmeriHerb.. 29
ameriherb.com • 515-232-8614 • herbal@ameriherb.com

Biffy Bag... 49
BiffyBag.com • 651-206-3078 • info@BiffyBag.com

CopperZap LLC.. 90-91
CopperZap.com • 888-411-6114 • info@copperzap.com

Davison Inventing... 29
Inventing.Davison.Fa • 1-800-332-7192

Doggles Protective Eyewear for Dogs.......... 107
Doggles.com • 866-DOGGLES • info@doggles.com

DR Power Equipment 3,15,25,47,67,75,97,101
DRPower.com • 800-687-6575 • info@drpower.com

Dripping Springs Ollas..................................... 21
DrippingSpringsOllas.com • 804-695-7978 •
mk@DrippingSpringsOllas.com

Fields of Dreams Soaps.................................. 107
Mainemadesoap.com • 207-331-5359 •
fieldsofdreamssoaps@gmail.com

firstSTREET
    Perfect Sleep Chair.. 45
    Perfect Walker 55
    WOW Computer.. 103
    Zinger Chair... 87

Franmar Intl/Original Garden Broom 11
TheOriginalGardenBroom.com • 604 -724 -0872 •
gardenbroom@gmail.com

Geiger Promotional Products 77
Geiger.com • 1-888-953-9340 • Geigerorders@Geiger.com

Gravity Defyer 35
gravitydefyer.com • 800-429-0039 •
customercare@gdefy.com

LeafCat LLC 7
leafcat.com • 978-505-1569 • aesadler@leafcat.com

MagniLife... 95
magnilife.com • 800-645-9199 • support@magnilife.com

MICRON Corporation... 71
MicronCorp.com/products • 800-456-0734 •
info@micorncorp.com

Mohican Wind Harps 29
Mohicanwindharps.com • 419-368-3415 •
dan@mohicanwindharps.com

Morris Press Cookbooks.................................. 43
morriscookbooks.com/FA821 • 800-445-6621 x FA821

Morris Publishing... 13
morrispublishing.com/FA821 • 800-650-7888xFA821

Murray McMurray Hatchery 33
McMurrayHatchery.com • 800-456-3280 •
sales@mmhatch.com

Nature's Rite 5
MyNaturesRite.com • 800-991-7088 •
info@mynaturesrite.com

North Country Wind Bells 17
northcountrywindbells.com • 877-930-5435 •
ncbells@tidewater.net

Pipeline Operators for Ag Safety 81-83,
                               Inside back cover
PipelineAgSafety.org

Rataway.com 59
Rataway.com • 805-646-2177 • Ratawayman@aol.com

Red Lake Nation Foods 107
redlakenationfoods.com • 218-679-2611 •
customerservice@redlakenationfoods.com

Rogue Industries 43
rogue-industries.com • 207-642-5400 x 11 •
roguewallet@gmail.com

SeptiCleanse... 21
www.septicleanse.com • 888-899-8345

Smooth Gator, LLC 53, 173
SmoothGator.com • 727-278-3137 •
JeraldKlukow@gmail.com

Summit Responsible Solutions ....
                     Inside front cover, 105
summitresponsiblesolutions.com • 800-227-8664 •
info@summitchemical.com

The Super Salve Co... 17
supersalve.com • 575-539-2768 •
denise@supersalve.com

U.S. Career Institute 9
uscareerinstitute.edu • 866-250-6851 •
admissions@uscareerinstitute.edu

Victory Seed Company 49
VictorySeeds.com • info@victoryseeds.com

Interested in Advertising With Us?

Email Us At: *Advertising@FarmersAlmanac.com*

RIDDLES, PUZZLES & BRAINTEASERS

1. What common 9-letter English word allows you to keep removing its letters one by one, leaving 8 words that are still valid?

2. What ancient invention still used today allows people to see through walls. What is it?

3. What makes this number unique: 8,549,176,320?

4. Which tire doesn't move when a car turns right?

5. If a *can* can jump 5 feet high, then why can't it jump through a window that is 3 feet high?

6. What tree do we all carry in our hands?

7. What can you fill a room with that takes up no space?

8. What type of cheese is made backwards?

9. What nut has a hole and is squishy?

10. This five-letter word becomes shorter when you add two letters to it. What is it?

11. A clerk at the butcher shop is six feet tall and wears size 10 shoes. What does he weigh?

12. A farmer has 19 sheep on his land. One day, a big storm hits and all but seven run away. How many sheep does the farmer have left?

answers

[1] Startling - starting - staring - string - sting - sting - sing - sin - in - I [2] Window
[3] When spelled out, the numbers are listed in alphabetical order. [4] Spare Tire [5] It's closed
[6] Palm [7] Light or noise [8] Edam [9] DoughNUT [10] Short [11] Meat [12] Seven